CARLOS ESTÉVEZ

AF605899

SUNY series in Latin American and Iberian Thought and Culture
Jorge J. E. Gracia and Rosemary Geisdorfer Feal, editors

CARLOS ESTÉVEZ

bottles to the sea

edited by

Jorge J. E. Gracia

translations by

David E. Johnson and Paula Cucurella

state university of new york press

Photographs by Carlos Estévez and Gary Mercer.
Gary Mercer photographs are used by permission.

Published by
STATE UNIVERSITY OF NEW YORK PRESS,
ALBANY

© 2015 State University of New York
Artworks and texts by Carlos Estévez are © Carlos Estévez
Text by Jorge J. E. Gracia is © Jorge J. E. Gracia

All rights reserved
Printed in the United States of America

No part of this book may be used or reproduced in any manner whatsoever without written permission. No part of this book may be stored in a retrieval system or transmitted in any form or by any means including electronic, electrostatic, magnetic tape, mechanical, photocopying, recording, or otherwise without the prior permission in writing of the publisher.

For information, contact
State University of New York Press, Albany, NY
www.sunypress.edu

Production, Laurie Searl
Marketing, Michael Campochiaro

Library of Congress Cataloging-in-Publication Data

Carlos Estévez : Bottles to the sea / Edited by Jorge J. E. Gracia ;
Translated by David E. Johnson and Paula Cucurella.
pages cm. — (SUNY series in Latin American and Iberian thought and culture)
Artist's statement in Spanish and English.
Includes bibliographical references.
ISBN 978-1-4384-5798-7 (pbk. : alk. paper) — ISBN 978-1-4384-5800-7 (e-book)
1. Estévez, Carlos, 1969– Bottles to the sea. 2. Estévez, Carlos, 1969— Criticism and interpretation. 3. Installations (Art)— Cuba. 4. Ocean bottles in art.
I. Gracia, Jorge J. E., editor. II. Johnson, David E., 1959– translator.
N6605.E86A62 2015
709.2—dc23 2015021928

10 9 8 7 6 5 4 3 2 1

CONTENTS

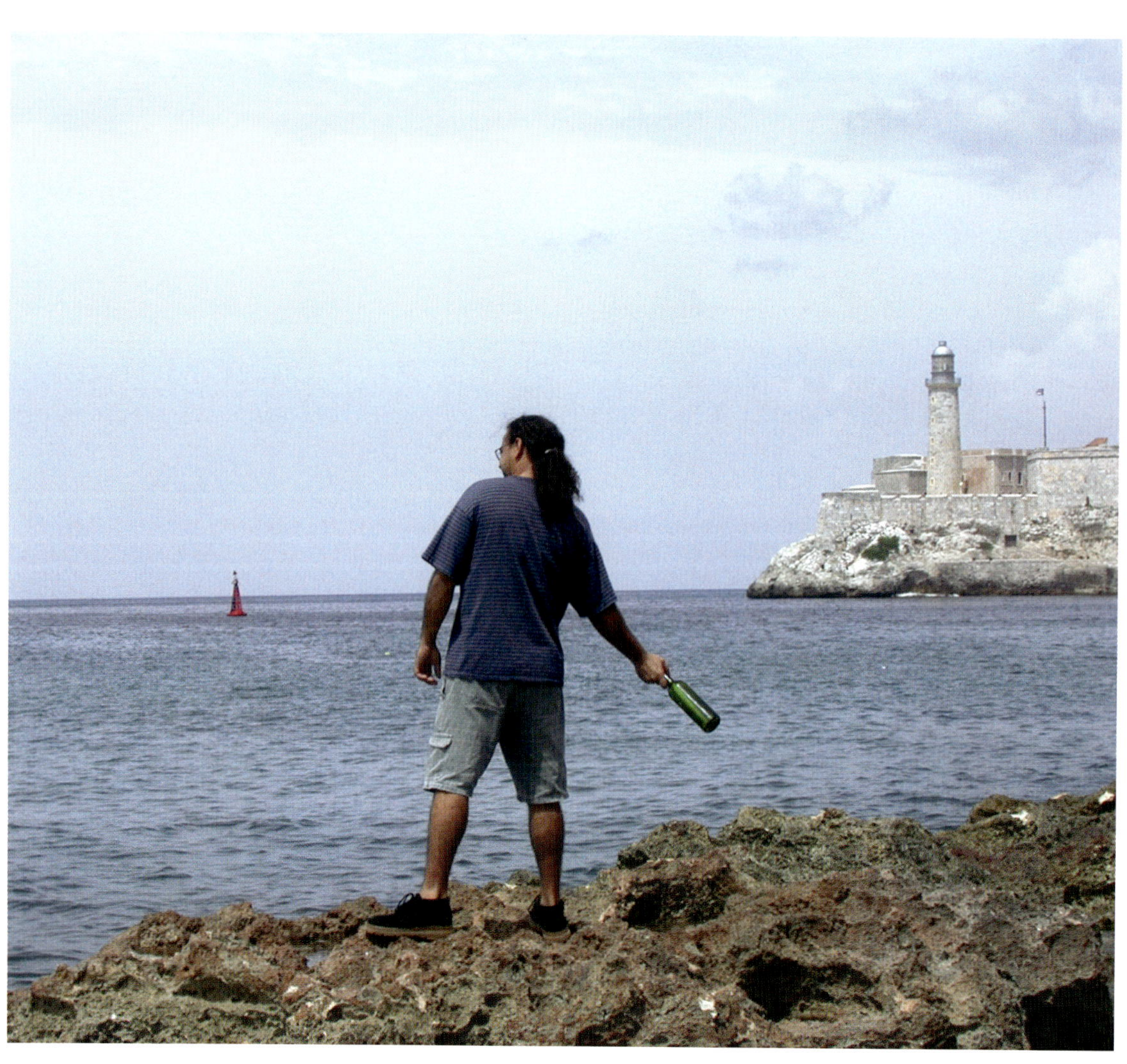

PREFACE

A few years ago, while I was discussing with Carlos Estévez the art pieces to include in a retrospective of his work we were planning to hold at the gallery of the University at Buffalo, he mentioned the possibility of including his installation *Botellas al mar* (*Bottles to the Sea*). This prompted me to carefully look at the work and, from the moment I saw it, I became convinced that this was the kind of art that not only merited inclusion in the retrospective, but also should be the subject of an entire publication. I then formed the idea of publishing a book with the images so that others could also share my enthusiasm. I was impressed by the general notion of a bottle thrown into the sea with a work of art in it, and I was particularly taken by the number, originality, and complexity of the drawings that constituted the core of the installation. This was the kind of art that could serve not only to pose many aesthetic questions, but also to raise issues pertaining to the human condition in general.

At the time I was occupied with other matters that prevented me from devoting to the project the time it merited, so I shelved it for a while without saying anything to Estévez. But the idea kept gnawing at me until I had to take it down from the shelf where I had put it and begin working on it. This is how the present book took shape. My hope is that its readers will be as interested and challenged by the work as I have been since I first encountered it.

The theme of launching bottles to the sea has been used as a metaphor by many writers and artists, but Estévez's installation is one of the most elaborate uses of this metaphor ever created. The work uses a variety of media, including one-hundred drawings enclosed in bottles that are launched to the sea from different parts of the world, at different times and on different occasions. The image opposite speaks for itself. It is a powerful image of the artist in the act of throwing one of the bottles from the promenade known as El Malecón, in Havana. In the distance one sees the image of El Morro, the fortress that guards the port and that is an icon for Cubans.

The book begins with a general essay that introduces readers to some of the many possible interpretive avenues that may be used to delve into the symbolism of the installation. In addition, it provides a characterization of Estévez's work by comparing it to the art of some well-known artists, and explores some examples of the philosophical themes on which the drawings focus. One of the main characteristics of Estévez's work is its philosophical dimension, and so the essay explores the thorny question of the relation between philosophy and art. Among the prominent themes that the drawings take up are the following: love, freewill, spirituality, time, destiny, words, the human soul, communication, male-female relationships, masculinity, femininity, the world of the individual, life's journey, self-knowledge and knowledge in general, truth, the self, the one and the many, predestination, destiny, knowledge of woman, the creator, the battle of life, appearance and reality, God, and God's relation to humans.

A statement by the artist explaining the circumstances under which the idea of the installation was hatched follows the introductory essay. Then color reproductions of the images are provided, accompanied by English translations of the Spanish texts that many of them include as well as transcriptions of the original texts. Each page is devoted to one drawing. The book closes with a biographical note about the artist, a list of the messages, and a pertinent bibliography.

At the very center of Estévez's art is the human being, and particularly the human male. He is depicted realistically in outline or stylized as a puppet (see Pinos-Santos 1995). Women appear less often in the works, and when they do, they often are combined with members of some other categories of beings, such as a man, animal, plant, or inanimate object. Indeed, Estévez frequently combines different kinds of entities, creating an imaginary world of fantasy whose significance is derived from these categories, their immediacy and combination. Particularly frequent and effective is the blending of humans with other entities as machines, buildings, mammals, building blueprints, insects, birds, mollusks, maps, horses, crabs, and plants.

Estévez often uses certain human roles, such as that of the juggler or the king, to explore humanity. Frequently depicted are generic human parts, such as heads, hands, brains, feet, hearts, eyes, digestive tracks, and lungs. Animals, such as horses, centipedes, shells, fish, butterflies, bugs, insects, scorpions, and birds, also are frequently depicted. Plants and their parts, such as leafs, trunks, trees, and flowers, also have a place. Buildings are favorites: windmills, amphitheaters, Gothic churches, lighthouses, bridges, and building blueprints, as well as conglomerates of buildings such as cities. Machines seem to be everywhere: flying contraptions, planes, balloons, and sewing machines, among many others. Monsters of various kinds, usually strange composites of other naturally or humanly created beings, also populate the imaginary world Estévez creates. Apart from all these, Estévez sometimes includes boats and ships. The images of humans, animals, plants, machines, objects, or their parts are meant to raise and convey ideas. These are ultimately what Estévez is interested in, given his work's strong conceptual leanings.

Estévez's *Bottles to the Sea* is a unique and original work of art that serves as a source for the exploration of many dimensions of human experience. Its uniqueness and interpretive value are rich and argue for a permanent place in the history not only of the theme of throwing bottles with messages to the sea, but also of art.

Naturally, a project such as this must depend on the cooperation of others. First and foremost is that of the artist himself, who apart from giving his permission for the publication of the images, helped with many of the technical and artistic aspects of getting the book in print. I am also indebted to David E. Johnson and Paula Cucurella for having translated into English the Spanish texts that are part of the drawings. And I am particularly grateful to Francis Acea, an artist in his own right, who designed the book. Finally, I am grateful to Beth Bouloukos from SUNY Press for her interest and support of the project, and to Laurie Searl for her attention to detail and helpful suggestions in the production process.

The Editor

INTRODUCTION

significance and interpretation

Jorge J. E. Gracia

The theme of launching bottles to the sea is not new. Like most good ideas, this is an old one, with a long and distinguished history and many different facets. It has been explored in works of literature, such as the poem by the Uruguayan poet Mario Benedetti, entitled "Botella al mar," the anthology of poems *Botella al mar* by the Cuban poet Nancy Morejón, and the novel *Message in a Bottle* by Nicholas Sparks. Many visual artists also have created works in which they depict bottles with messages. Indeed, there is an entire genre in China that involves writing messages inside bottles. But the idea has also been used with utilitarian purposes in mind. Scientists have thrown bottles to the sea as a way of tracking ocean currents; explorers have used it as a means of communicating results of their travels; and sailors have employed them when seeking help, particularly in times of war, when other means of communication have been unavailable to them. There are even those who throw bottles to the sea just for the sake of communication, without any literary, artistic, or scientific aim in mind. What we have in Carlos Estévez's installation, however, is something quite different.

Many works of art that depict bottles do so in the context of a still life whose purpose has nothing to do with the function of bottles as a medium of a message sent by the sea. Bottles have interesting shapes and the fact that they are usually made of glass makes them intriguing motifs for paintings. Major artists throughout history have used them. Bottles have been commonly included in drinking or homely scenes. A well-laid table and appetizing meal asks for a nice bottle of wine to accompany it. We frequently see these used by baroque and impressionist artists. Cubists also seem to have found the depiction of bottles enticing, and perhaps even challenging insofar as their work aims to decompose objects into geometrical shapes and bottles do not easily lend themselves to this purpose. But the drawings that constitute the core of Estévez's installation do not include depictions of bottles. The bottles are part of the installation not because the artist has drawn them, but because he uses them to transport the drawings.

Artists and literary authors who have been interested in the topic of bottles at sea generally consider a particular bottle and the message it carries, as well as its affective significance at both its origin and its destination. They are usually concerned with particular experiences or predicaments that affect those who throw the bottles or those who receive them. On the contrary, Estévez does not focus on any one of the bottles that are part of the installation, the messages they contain, or the impact the bottles have on their receivers. His installation includes one hundred bottles with one hundred messages that cover a rich array of situations and experiences, rather than one overall theme or experience.

In addition, unlike artists who are interested in bottles because of their potentially challenging and interesting aesthetic features, Estévez pays no special attention to these factors. True, he picked particular bottles because they appealed to him in some, perhaps aesthetic, ways but he does not especially focus on the aesthetic dimensions that other artists have found in bottles. The rationale for the use of bottles is conceptual. Estévez is interested in the bottles as carriers of messages traveling by sea to an unpredictable destiny. He also is not interested in the utilitarian or scientific angle the bottles may have, or the act of throwing them to sea. It is not aesthetics, science, or any other of their common uses that leads him to the bottles; it is the human condition.

The project is surprising in part because the probability that any one of the bottles in the installation, and even less that more than one, would be recovered by someone who will understand and be interested in its content is very low. Imagine the vicissitudes that these bottles face in an ocean full of large animals that may swallow them thinking they are food, ships that accidentally ram and break them, rocks against which the waves and currents can throw and shatter them, and well-meaning ocean cleaners who pick large aggregations of garbage and dispose of them in garbage dumps. Some bottles might land in uninhabited lands, deserts, or in Antarctica, and so languish in solitude for centuries before they are found, if they ever are. Even if someone finds any of these bottles and opens it, what is the likelihood that the person will understand its contents or sympathize with them? It is possible that those who find the bottles come from cultures that forbid creating images, and so they might consider the drawings blasphemous or idolatrous, and destroy them. Still others might regard the images as uninteresting or useless, and thus proceed to discard them. Yet, some bottles thrown to the sea have been found, often many years after they have been at sea. The Internet is full of bizarre stories about such cases. But the odds that the bottles thrown to the sea by Estévez will be found and kept are minimal. Indeed, of seventeen bottles that Estévez has thrown to the sea, only one is known to have been found.

Estévez's installation is an original work of art with quite a different aim from that pursued by artists who have previously explored the themes of bottles, messages in bottles, or messages in bottles thrown to the sea. It is in part because of these differences that the installation uniquely serves to investigate many dimensions of human experience, some of which have been ignored in the past. The core of *Bottles to the Sea* are the one hundred drawings contained in the bottles (Temin 2002). This might be taken to suggest that these drawings are intended as a series of art works devoted to the exploration of a theme or set of interrelated themes, as happens frequently with the work of many artists. The theme or themes may be conceptual, such as a certain human passion or idea like love, death, or justice. Or it may be plastic, such as a certain style or technique whose various dimensions are tested. Other Cuban artists, for example, have created series around the topic of the *balseros,* Cubans who have attempted to escape the island in *balsas* or rafts. And much medieval art consists of series depicting the lives and miracles of Christ and the saints.

Estévez's *Bottles to the Sea,* however, is not a series in this sense. The unifying theme of the installation is the idea of bottles being thrown to the sea and traveling through perilous conditions to undetermined destinations. But none of the individual drawings contained in the bottles explores such an idea or any dimension of it. Moreover, although some themes are explored more than once in the work, they are not related to the general idea behind the installation. Nor can we say that the unifying factor of the drawings is a certain style or technique initiated in it. Of course, it does not take much to notice that the drawings do have a unique style that is quite evident and recognizable by an observer. However, this is not new, proper to the drawings, or intended to be explored in these drawings in particular. Rather, the style and techniques revealed in the drawings are simply the style and techniques idiosyncratic to the work of Estévez as a whole. There is nothing stylistically unique that separates the drawings in the installation from the rest of Estévez's work.

In many ways, *Bottles to the Sea* is like a notebook of ideas that echoes some of the artist's past work but, more significantly, charts a course for future work. Indeed, although the ideas it explores are drawings, an examination of past or subsequent instances of Estévez's art show that some of the drawings revisit previous work or have served as blueprints for future projects, often in different media. For example, the sculpture-installation *Nadie puede ver por mis ojos* (No One Can See Through My Eyes) that Estévez created in 1994 (see Gracia 2009a, 27-33) served as inspiration for a message with the same name in *Bottles to the Sea*, whereas the message "*Escenas del circo. El manipulador*" (Circus Scenes: The Handler) was the source of a work on paper, *El malabarista* (The Juggler) in 2002 (see Gracia 2009a, 91-97), and the idea explored in "*Tratado de los puentes del amor*" (Treatise on Love's Bridges) was revisited and developed further in *Las distancias entre nuestros vecindarios* (Distances Between Our Neighborhoods) in 2001 (see Gracia 2009a, 115-23). This makes *Bottles to the Sea* an important document for understanding Estévez's work, apart from its significance as a work of art in its own right.

The installation is complex, including diverse elements and different media. Among these are artifacts, actors, actions, records of actions, and various contexts, all important for a grasp of its significance. Its core is constituted by the one hundred drawings created on narrow pieces of paper of various kinds intended to be placed inside the glass bottles that are to be launched to the sea. The drawings are referred to as "messages" and each is assigned a number from one to one hundred. Estévez used tracing paper for the foundation of the drawings; pencil for the texts; and tempera, sanguine, and water color pencils for the drawings. Although the works consist primarily of images, some also include texts. The artist mostly composes these, although sometimes they echo the ideas or quotations from authors whom the artist considers influential, such as Jorge Luis Borges, Ernesto Sábato, and St. Augustine.

Apart from the drawings, the installation includes the one hundred bottles of various sizes, shapes, and colors in which the drawings are placed before they are launched. Estévez sometimes picked these because of their uniqueness, whereas at other times he did so precisely because they are common. The bottles are always sturdy pieces meant to withstand stress, despite being made of glass. None of the bottles has been especially made with this installation in mind. The way Estévez went about collecting them illustrates an important component of his modus operandi, for he frequently uses objects he randomly finds in such places as flea markets, antique shops, and the like, and integrates them into his works.

Informative materials accompany the drawings placed inside the bottles. These contain details about the project, a statement to the effect that the drawings belong to whomever finds them, as well as instructions about how to get in touch with the artist so he can record the finding and how far and to which places the bottles have traveled. The actors who are part of the installation include the artist who created the drawings and launched the bottles, as well as the individuals who find them. The actions involve the launching of the bottles by the artist and their reception by those who find them. These actions are meant to be recorded in films, photographs, and whatever means those who find the bottles use to preserve the moment of discovery. The contexts include the places from which the bottles are launched, the seas they travel, and the locations where they land and are picked up.

In exhibitions, the drawings are displayed hanging from strings along walls, as if they were wet laundry set out to dry, thus emphasizing the connection with water and the perilous journey that they are intended to undertake. Below them, on a ledge, the bottles are placed, one for each of the drawings. On the floor, some sand is scattered, to indicate that the bottles are launched on the shore and might be picked up on a beach. A description of the project accompanies the installation, and pictures and films of the launchings as well as the recovery of the bottles, when available, are included in the installation.

The seminal idea for the installation came to Estévez through his son, as he explains in his statement in this book. The early 1990s was a difficult time in Cuba. The aid that the country had enjoyed from the Soviet Union had come to an end, and the island found itself without proper resources, with a bankrupt economy, and isolated from the international community. Estévez, his wife Amarilys, and their son Carlitos, lived on Havana Bay and every day would walk along *El Malecón*. This promenade is a central gathering place for Cubans. It is the place where they gather when some significant event occurs, to exchange ideas, and romance (see Schneider Enríques 2002).

Once the idea of launching a bottle to the sea to establish a tie with the outside world was planted in Estévez's mind, the details of the installation followed easily. The first launching took place in Havana, at *El Malecón*, on December 16, 2001, where a bottle with the drawing of Message 54, "Everything is Written in Heaven," was launched. In all, eighteen bottles have been launched from the following countries: six from the United States; one each from Portugal, Italy, Mexico, Cuba, and Switzerland (in the Rhine); two each from Brazil and France; and three from Spain. So far, only one bottle has been recovered whose receiver communicated with Estévez. It is possible that other bottles have been found, but the artist has not had any news of them. An uncertain fate is certainly one, and perhaps the most obvious and significant, aspect of this work of art, but there are others. Let me turn to a few that easily suggest themselves.

IDEAS BEHIND THE WORK

As mentioned previously, the idea that unifies *Bottles to the Sea* does not seem to have anything to do with the particular messages in the bottles. However, it is significant that the title of the first drawing is *Dwellings of the Spirit*, and the last *Every Ending is a New Beginning*. The first suggests that the messages conveyed by the images are spiritual, that they have to do with what is ethereal and finest in humans, rather than with the ordinary concerns that worry people in the most pedestrian aspects of their lives. The title of the last message suggests that the process intended with these one hundred images is just a starting point. There is no end to the process, no ultimate conclusion reached, no final work. In a Faustian turn, Estévez seems to suggest that it is in the doing that we find what we are looking for, not in the completion of any kind of task. The task, as Borges would perhaps say, is infinite.

The idea that unifies the installation is that of an act, the throwing of a bottle with a message to the sea. This raises the question of its significance, the motive behind it, and the circumstances that gave rise to it. Why would anyone throw to the sea a bottle containing a message that, in this case, is expressed in a work of art? Note that the overall title of the installation is not "message in a bottle," "messages in bottles," or "messages to the sea," but *Bottles to the Sea*. There is an important difference between these. The first two titles put the emphasis on the message or messages and what they say. But the actual title puts the emphasis on the entire phenomenon, the bottles being thrown into the sea and, perhaps indirectly, on someone finding them. This opens a richer field of interpretation in that the object of interpretation becomes complex. Most other uses of this metaphor fail to explore many of the various dimensions possible in the case of Estévez's work because they focus on the messages, and messages are usually rendered in texts, involving a linguistic mode of communication that restricts their significance. But if the emphasis is not exclusively or primarily on the message, and the message is expressed through art, then a multitude of other interpretive possibilities open up.

A bottle is usually made out of glass or some such fragile material. So, from the very beginning, the message is in peril. If the bottle breaks, both its remnants and its message end up at the bottom of the sea. Obviously, there is something very fragile in the attempt to communicate through a message in a bottle, so why would anyone attempt it? Stories of such attempts constitute almost a genre in literature. Usually they involve a shipwreck and a lonely survivor on an island, separated from the rest of the world, but longing for communication made difficult or impossible by any other means. Most often, the shipwreck is a Robinson Crusoe, a man who finds himself isolated and threatened by circumstances far from those he could ever have envisioned; a man who is both trapped and forced to face the unknown. This brings to mind a sense of imprisonment, of being locked in a situation from which it is not easy, and might even be impossible, to break free. He is in a prison of sorts, although the character of the prison or the means that prevent escape are not part of the metaphor of throwing the bottle to the sea. And he is accidentally placed in an unknown environment, full of dangers and perhaps lethal challenges.

We have, then, several areas from which the act of throwing bottles with messages to the sea acquire significance. The bottles themselves, the identities of those who throw them, the conditions in which those who throw the bottles find themselves, the motivations for throwing the bottles, the places of origin from which the bottles are thrown, the intended destinations of the bottles, and the actual destinations at which the bottles arrive.

The significance of a bottle in particular lies to a great extent in its character. Bottles are generally made of glass, and indeed Estévez has often used this traditional medium in his art. But glass is easily broken. An impact with any hard object shatters it. Still, there is considerable strength in a glass bottle. Its shape makes it nimble and adaptable to different circumstances. It floats easily in water as long as it is corked properly. And it offers little resistance, so that it can be carried swiftly by a current, adapting itself to the waves, and moving with a grace generated by its dynamic design.

Bottles are meant to be filled with liquids and can float on liquids. But a bottle with a message written on paper, another very fragile medium, adds another dimension to our understanding of the installation's metaphor. The fragility of the bottle is replicated, although in a different way, by the fragility of its content, while the strength of the bottle is also replicated, *mutatis mutandis*, by the strength of its content: Paper is both fragile and tough. It can be easily destroyed but it can also last for a long time. We have two-thousand-year-old papyri whose condition of survival is a dry environment. This is precisely what a bottle provides: An enclosure that is dry despite being surrounded by water. Safety inside, peril outside.

Now we may surmise one place where this leads us. Bottles may be taken as symbols of the individuals who throw them, of their fragility and strength, and of the perilous situations in which they may find themselves. Their circumstances may be idiosyncratic, or they may be similar to those of Robinson Crusoe, to those of Estévez, or to those that apply to readers of this book or to this writer. We become the bottle. On the one hand, there is the fragility of our bodies. We can be killed; we can die; we can be sick. Our lives are easily terminated and our existence is limited.

But we are also strong in that we are adaptable to different circumstances; we are made to survive under changing situations, some of which may be extremely difficult. We are, like a bottle, tough and resilient. And like it, we have secrets that may make us vulnerable. As individuals we are bundles of thoughts, emotions, ideas, beliefs, and goals. And although much of this will pass, we also, as Averroes would say, reach divine immortality through the universal ideas we are able to understand. Through these, we transcend our particularity. The understanding of unity, truth, and goodness makes us immortal insofar as those thoughts are the same for everyone and, as Plato argued, imperishable.

The bottle becomes a symbol for me and for you, for our selves, revealing something important about our nature and our identity. The bottle contains a drawing, and a drawing is a construction of an artist, which suggests that our selves are also constructs. We become the artist who selects the bottle, draws the picture, and folds the paper to fit the bottle. We establish the conditions of our identity, and create it. The question of whether we create our identity or whether we have little to do with the process of its creation, is one that philosophers most frequently debate. Are we self-made or are we the result of circumstances and forces out of our control? Are we created by nature or by nurture? The idea of the self understood as a bottle thrown into the sea that contains a message helps us meditate on who we are and how we have come to be it.

But there is another dimension of this symbolism that should not escape us, because just as each bottle guards its secret, so do we. A bottle is one, alone, and its content is not revealed unless it is opened and someone looks inside it. Indeed, even if the bottle is opened, whoever looks inside it must have some way of understanding its content. Estévez often has added texts to the drawings he has placed inside the bottles, and the texts are in Spanish. This means that whoever wants to understand the meaning of the messages carried by the bottles has to know or learn Spanish, or use a dictionary to decipher the text. Bridges have to be built between the sender and its message on one side and those who find it on the other, and this is true of us as well. There must be a bridge between us, otherwise, nothing will happen. Bottles with messages symbolize our loneliness and illustrate the difficulties of trying to break out of it.

A bottle may symbolize not just each of us as human beings, trapped in our particular existence, but our attempt to move beyond our isolation and communicate with others. This idea is universal because we all share a similar condition. We are born alone and die alone. And between birth and death we are constantly attempting to share with others who we are, our inner thoughts and feelings, but it is hard to penetrate the thoughts and reality of others. This is why novels that narrate the inner struggles of their characters are so enticing. They tell us about the other, that foreign being who is also a brother or sister in our predicament. We are islands, lonely souls that struggle to communicate throughout our lives. We want to break through, to get into the thoughts of others, to analyze them, to shatter the bottles in which we are trapped, and which contain something we need to communicate but never quite succeed, for we see each other only through a glass darkly. And when we succeed in breaking another bottle in order to look into its contents, we often find that the inside hides something we cannot read, and at best consists of a picture that could mean many things. We want certainty, the imaginary certainty we often think we have of ourselves, but what we find is more elusive, escaping us the moment we think we have it.

And yet, the mere act of throwing the bottle to the sea indicates both the situation of the one who throws it and the desire and intention to communicate with another. Loneliness forces us to make the effort to communicate with others.

And a lack of effective means of communication leads us to use a bottle. Lonely survivors of shipwrecks throw bottles to the sea. People on the mainland don't usually throw bottles with messages to the sea because they think they can easily communicate with others. They are part of a continent, not isolated islanders. It is only when one is stranded, in one way or another—isolated, separated or segregated, secreted from and by others—that one seeks help by throwing a bottle to the sea. The act of throwing the bottle indicates an involuntary imprisonment and a desire to escape. Indeed, the motivating idea of *Bottles to the Sea* was, as Estévez explains in his statement in this book, a reaction of his son to the claustrophobia they were experiencing in Cuba at the time. As an island, the seas surround Cuba. A walk along El Malecón both reminds Cubans how close they really are to the rest of the world, while at the same time how difficult it is to cross that sea and be part of the mainland. And this image reminds us of our own particular situation.

Often, there is an intended destination, or kind of destination if not a particular one, for a bottle thrown into the sea. Survivors of shipwrecks want the bottles to reach those who can rescue them and take them away from the cursed isolation in which they find themselves. Yet, they do not know where the bottles will end up, or who, if anyone, will find and open them. This uncertainty is disquieting, and even frightening. Perhaps the wrong person will get the message. Maybe those who are responsible for the imprisonment of the person who threw the bottle will find it and use that knowledge to exact revenge. No one knows where a bottle thrown into the sea will end up, or when, if in fact it does not break, it will be found. The where and when it does is a matter of currents, winds, tides, and human actions. Ultimately, it is a matter of chance. And thus we return to the cluster of themes that have to do with human destiny and how chance rules our lives. We are bottles at sea, humans immersed and barely floating in a world of forces we cannot control but that affect our destiny. Where will we end up? What will become of us? We think that we control much in our lives, but perhaps the only thing we truly can control is what we think, what is inside us, just as the content of a bottle is the only thing that is controlled by the bottle. But perhaps not even that, because our passions and unconscious drives often derail the plans we have for ourselves. If there is anything that jumps at us in the messages that *Bottles to the Sea* carry, it is the centrality of chance in our lives.

The references to an origin and destination bring out another dimension of the metaphor, namely, the journey of the bottle, and through it, of ourselves. With the increasing process of globalization and the numerous individuals who are on the move throughout the world, the notion of a journey has become common place in literature and art. Cuban art itself has explored this notion in various ways. One of these, to which I have already referred, is the *balsas* that have been used by Cubans seeking to leave the island and travel to the United States in search of refuge. Many Cuban artists have created works of art that are interpretations of this theme, including Luis Cruz Azaceta and Alberto Rey, who have explored many dimensions and aspects of this experience (see Bosch 2004; Gracia, Bosch, and Alvarez Borland 2008). Another is the thought of abandoning one's origins and migrating to an unknown place, fleeing from danger and facing challenges of a different sort than those in the place of origin. The image of the traveler is again found frequently in the art and literature of the twentieth century in particular. In Cuban art it is ubiquitous; we find it, for example, in the well-known interpretation of José Bedia in *Siguiendo su instinto* (Following His Instinct; see Stavans and Gracia 2014, 123-137). The notion of a perilous journey that can end in disaster and death, or in success and a new life, is easily associated with the journey of a bottle. The journey involves discovery by those who undergo it and by those at the receiving end. The bottle finds a new place, but it is also found by someone whose encounter with it may be enlightening or distressing. Travelers may bring good or bad news, and they may turn out to be dangerous or benign. The journey can be that of life itself—beginning in birth and ending in death. For after all, when a bottle reaches a destination and is taken out of circulation, it resembles death insofar as death also is a kind of ending of our journey.

A journey may also function as a metaphor for the trip that artists undertake. The entire life of artists, and the path of exploration and discovery in which they are engaged, is a trip that begins at some point and ends in an unforeseeable destination. Artists do not know quite how their work will evolve and change, or the reception it will elicit, and I am sure that Picasso, despite all his bravado, never really thought that his art was going to succeed in the way it did. The realistic early work of Picasso does not anticipate the transformation of cubism. Even in each work under creation, an artist cannot anticipate the shape the finished product will take. Artistic creation does not work that way. Art does not have predetermined destinations for the most part. It is in the act of creation that the details of the journey and its fate are worked out in part through accidental currents and winds of inspiration, and through the overcoming of unanticipated obstacles and happy coincidences.

A bottle is thrown into the sea, and the sea itself is full of connotations and symbolism. The sea stands for the subconscious, that which is below the surface of our awareness, a dark and foreboding place that is part of us but to which we have dubious access. It is the habitat of monsters that appear and disappear at unexpected times, sometimes propitious and sometimes not. It is a place of storms and danger, of adventure, sacrifice, and heroism. It is a place of survival and struggle. It is, like life itself, a mixed bag of good and bad. It can lead to the sublime and the pedestrian, to triumph and tragedy. It surrounds lands and it is surrounded by land, depending on how one looks at it. And the places where we access it may be rocky or sandy, and thus break us or help us survive. The shore itself is a line, an imaginary landmark that disappears in the sea. Sand also is unstable. It moves, comes and goes, and is regularly sinking into the depths of the sea or surfacing on a beach. A constant indecision permeates it. We cannot build enduring, let alone permanent, structures on it. To build on sand is to be doomed to destruction.

Water itself has suggestive qualities associated with it. It is generally translucent, but not frequently transparent. We see something through it, but unclearly, and what we see gets distorted by the visual effects created by movement in the water and by its volume. It is a malleable medium that in itself seems to be nothing in particular. It takes its color from something else, from the sky, a bottom, or a wall, as does its shape. Yet, water is fundamental. Ancient philosophers considered it one of the basic four elements, together with fire, air, and earth. Water's changing shape makes it stand for the emotions, whereas fire stands for love, air for thought, and earth for solidity. The uses of water are multiple. It is essential to our bodies and it quenches thirst. It is a vital component of our mass. But even more important perhaps, it cleans, so it has been used as a metaphor for getting rid of sin. Immersion in water is a sign of joining a group, of dying and being born again, and of washing away our transgressions. Water serves as an offering to the gods, and it is the basis of many of our drinks. To throw a bottle into water is to open up these possibilities, for bottles can be washed clean and turn toward new directions, and this can be the mark of a new beginning.

And what are bottles used for? To transport valuable substances, such as olive oil, perfume, medications, potions, and wine. Oils serve to soothe. Medications are curative. Perfumes are mysterious substances that appeal to our sense of smell, arousing our imagination, our thoughts, and our passions. Potions make us do things for which we are not responsible, having magical effects that can end in death or love. And wine makes us happy by helping us forget; it brings us together with others in fellowship, and it serves religious and ritual functions. Wine looks like blood, the substance of life, and drinking wine unites us in a community and reminds us, in the Christian faith, of the divine blood spilled for our sins. Bottles seldom contain money. Their function is the preservation of something more basic than money, something precious and vital. In Estévez's installation the bottles are filled with something dear, the drawings that stand at the core of this work of art. They are unlike oil, medications, potions, or wine, but they can do what these also do, soothing, making us healthy, appealing to our senses, and uniting us with others. They are expressions of thought, images preserved for others.

The fact that in Estévez's installation bottles contain images drawn on paper is significant. The choice of paper is particularly important because, as mentioned earlier, it duplicates the fragility of the bottle as well as its toughness. Paper can be ruined by water or destroyed by fire. Paper can be, but is not necessarily, fragile, just as glass, but it is more ephemeral. Paper is not like stone or metal that can last an eternity. But paper is tough in the sense that it can stand pressure, some of it is difficult to tear apart or break, and it endures difficult conditions. It gets wet and it dries; it is flexible and molds itself to its surroundings. And it can support images. In the bottles, it becomes the counterpart of our minds, where our thoughts, just as images on paper, are drawn.

The number of bottles, one hundred, may also be taken as significant apart from the fact that it commemorates the one-hundredth anniversary of the *Malecón*. One hundred has been a number associated with longevity and even immortality. To live to one hundred has always been a feat for human beings. In the Judeo-Christian tradition, this number has been significant from ancient times. Most notably, Abraham, the founder of the ancient Hebrews, was one hundred when his son Isaac was born. It marks a beginning, as the title of the last drawing states. The number has also been associated with individuality. Presumably, one could surmise that the use of this number of bottles indicates a desire for individual longevity and immortality. Both the significance of the installation and the messages contained in the bottles are an attempt by the artist to achieve both.

THE LINE

So far I have been writing about what we might call the elements that play a significant role in Estévez's installation, such as the artist and the receivers, the bottles, the journeys, and the contents of the bottles in general, and I have ignored the images of the drawings that are placed inside the bottles. Yet, this is surely a most important part of the installation insofar as it is those drawings, and the images they form, that are guarded inside the bottles and intended to reach audiences. Now I turn to the drawings, beginning with some observations about a fundamental structural feature of the drawings: the line.

Estévez is a multifaceted artist who has created sculptures, assemblages, combines multimedia, watercolors, pastels, oils, acrylics, installations, ceramics, and works on paper, canvas, and other surfaces. He is particularly fascinated by different kinds of papers and has explored and made use of them in his works.

Some of the drawings included in *Bottles to the Sea* include details in other media. Because the drawings are intended to be placed in bottles, they are created on relatively narrow pieces of paper to make it possible to roll and fit them in the bottles. As one would expect of drawings, a fundamental element in them is the line. The line divides spaces, creates areas of interest, and establishes a hierarchy of importance and value.

Generally, we do not believe that lines are imaginary objects. We think we see them. If I ask readers to point to a line in this book, they will have no difficulty in doing so, finding them both in the images of the works presented in it and also elsewhere, including the letters that compose the texts. Indeed, the drawings in the bottles are full of lines, and some consist primarily of lines: straight lines, curved lines, wiggly lines, all kinds of lines. Some lines are black and others have other colors. They have been made with color pencils or sanguine, and because they are drawn on narrow pieces of paper, there is a marked verticality to them, similar to what happens with some medieval stained glass windows. This leads the observer to move up and down, rather than side to side or in any other direction when considering them, opening a spiritual dimension to the installation that goes with the title of the first drawing. Indeed, this is quite evident in some other drawings, such as Messages 8 and 12: "Man is a Project of God" or "On Lighthouses."

In spite of our common belief that lines can be seen and pointed to, their nature and reality are questionable. A line, if we are going to go by what Euclid tells us, is simply the intersection of two planes. And what are the planes? Again according to Euclid, they are not really visible and have no existence separate from something else. The surface of this desk is a plane, but it is nothing separate or separable from the desk. Yet, it is not a part of the desk, as its drawers are.

At the beginning of the sixth century of the Christian era, Boethius speculated that lines do exist in things, although we know them through a kind of abstraction. He used this metaphor to argue that universals, such as "cat" and "justice," also exist in things: Cat exists in this cat and that cat, and justice exists in this and that human. But he was not successful in convincing many others of his position. If a line is something like the meeting place between the horizontal surface of this desk on which my laptop is resting and the vertical surface of its side, I am not sure I can argue cogently that I see the line as anything other than the surfaces or the sides of the desk. And if I do not see the line, can it be said to exist? Indeed, where is it? Some philosophers have argued that such things as lines are merely in our minds, not outside them. As such, they are tools that we use for thinking about the world in which we are immersed, but are not really anything in the world. So perhaps Boethius's view that lines are known through a kind of abstraction is right after all, although perhaps qua abstractions they are not really things in the world, but rather are inventions or conceptions we create for pragmatic reasons.

Of course, the careful investigation of such questions is well beyond what is appropriate for a discussion such as the one in which we are engaged here. But the consideration of the dubious status of lines in the world contributes to a better understanding of the nature of drawing and of Estévez's work. It suggests that the lines he draws are not really lines as they exist in the world, but representations of ways in which he conceives and manages what he sees. A drawing of a head is in fact a set of lines that demarcate spaces and suggests something like what we think we see, but what we see in the drawing is certainly nothing like what is outside. The images of the art we have in this book, then, would have to be considered creations by Estévez that make us think of things he has not copied. There would not be any realism in the work, although it is far from being abstract. The tension between reality and unreality is one of the most provocative aspects of the work insofar as it points to interpretive avenues that may differ from observer to observer.

What we have here is a parting of the ways in terms of art. Some artists, such as Renoir and other impressionists, were trying to capture what we see. That is why their paintings do not have lines. Renoir in particular seems to have erased boundaries and instead presents us with merging colors on canvas in ways that suggest what we actually see. Where does the shade of green on this leaf begin and the shade of yellow end?

The entities that populate Renoir's world have no limits, no boundaries, whereas those in Estévez's world do. Because of this, we must consider Estévez to be on the side of the Cubists, for the line was fundamental in their work. The art of Picasso, Braque, and Gris had lines galore. The images they created are divided and united by lines that take us where the artists want us to go. They did not set out to reproduce what we see but rather to reproduce what we think. And so is the case of Estévez. His is a world of ideas not of visual images, although it is through visual images that we enter it.

Estévez's world is also close, perhaps closer, to the work of artists who have drawn extensively. Among these, Leonardo da Vinci stands out not only because of his use of the line, but also because of his themes. Estévez, unlike da Vinci, is not an inventor of machines, but he often draws imaginary machines. Even the images of living subjects he draws, such as those we see in many of the drawings included in this book, have a mechanical dimension that aligns the work with that of the great inventors and draftsmen of the past. These are visual images of ideas and inventions, a visual world dominated and directed by concepts rather than images.

Behind this emphasis on the line is the desire to get at the true structure of things. The Cubists were certainly motivated by a similar goal. The reduction of the images of actual objects to a limited number of basic geometrical figures occupies an important place in their agenda. And something similar is clearly evident in the work of Estévez, particularly in what we have in *Bottles to the Sea*. So much, then, about the overall characteristic of the images contained inside the bottles. Now let me turn to the particular motifs of the drawings and the themes that they tend to explore.

KNOWLEDGE

The depiction of humans, animals, plants, machines, objects, and their parts in *Bottles to the Sea* are used to raise and convey ideas. These, of course, are ultimately what Estévez is interested in, given the strong conceptual leanings of his art. These ideas tend to repeat themselves and often have a metaphysical dimension (Gracia 2009a, 63-87; Luis 2002).

One particular example of an idea that Estévez explores repeatedly is that of knowledge. In *Bottles to the Sea* we have a substantial cluster of drawings that address issues related to knowledge. Estévez has been fascinated with epistemic questions throughout his career (e.g., see Gracia 2009a, 21-59). Philosophers consider many different questions concerning knowledge, but there is one in particular that is regarded as generally fundamental and is frequently explored in Estévez's art. This is the question of source: What is the source of our knowledge? The answers that philosophers have given to this question fall roughly into three categories. One is that the source of our knowledge is to be found within ourselves. This is the kind of view that Rationalists, such as Plato and René Descartes, gave. Plato was puzzled by the fact that our acquaintance in the world is with particular things, say this triangle or that one, but our knowledge is universal, not about this or that triangle, but about trangularity. Because of this, he thought that knowledge cannot derive from experience, but must come from within us, because experience is always of the particular. And Descartes was especially concerned with achieving certainty, for which he disparaged the reliability of sense perception.

Another answer is that all knowledge comes from sensation. British Empiricists, such as David Hume and John Locke, thought this is the proper answer to the question of source. They resolved the difficulty encountered by Rationalists, by arguing that our universal ideas are simply perceptions that have lost their strength or sharpness. Our universal idea of triangle is simply a vague idea of this and that triangle that has lost its precision and force, becoming a vague memory of the immediate perceptions of the individual triangles we had.

A third alternative is to argue, with Aristotle, that our knowledge comes from experience, that is, from our sensations and perceptions, but that it is not reducible to experiences insofar as it goes through a process of abstraction and generalization that turns it universal. Our knowledge of triangles comes from the sensations or perceptions we have of this and that triangle, but it is not reducible to those sensations or perceptions. These sensations and perceptions are only the raw materials out of which the mind abstracts essential common characteristics to form the universal idea of triangle.

Estévez addresses the question of origin in a variety of works. In Message 7, "*Observatorium*," he begins by quoting Augustine: "Do not depart from yourself, return to yourself, the truth dwells inside man. . . ." Estévez follows this by noting the untransferability of the knowledge that each of us has, which is a theme to which he comes back frequently. In the text for this drawing, Estévez ties it to the stars and their movement.

The drawing is divided into two parts, each of which shows the outlines of a human head, followed by a text. The top is a face depicted frontally, but most of whose cranial area, all the way to the bottom of the nose, is occupied by a dark circle covered with inscriptions, resembling the circle of the heavens, with stars and planets and symbolizing the inner universe of each human being. The relation of the human mind to the universe is a frequent motif found in Estévez's work. Each of us constitutes an entire world, a microcosm, if you will, using the ancient Greek metaphor, and it is in it that we find the knowledge that we seek and need (see Gracia 2009a, 83-87). The connection with knowledge is drawn in the second figure, also an outline of a head. This, however, is depicted in profile and it is drawn over a building covered with a dome that resembles an observatory, which takes us back to the title of the work. The Rationalist message is clear: Knowledge comes from within. Its key is "to know oneself."

A second step in this exploration of the sources of knowledge is presented in Message 12, "On Lighthouses." Here we have the outline of a lighthouse with seven levels, a number with great significance in that it is the sum of the second odd number and the second even number, three and four. Inside it we see the stairs that lead to the observation platform at the top of the building and the machinery that works the light that illuminates the night and the ocean, providing a path for ships. Do we have the power to know, and in what does this power consist? The lighthouse symbolizes the natural capacities that we have as human beings to penetrate to the truth. Going all the way back to the ancient Greeks and before, the intellect has been traditionally portrayed as a light. To know is to illuminate; casting light on darkness that makes possible sight. The reference to da Vinci in the text, one of Estévez's most important influences, and the comparison of him to a light, support the notion that knowledge is made possible by the capacities of those whose intellects provide the light for them and others to decipher the puzzles of the universe. These lights transcend their contemporaries and their times. But Estévez comes back to the loneliness of knowers. Knowers live in an world that is neither land nor sea, surrounded by a horizon they want to supersede but whose limits are difficult to transcend.

In Message 25, "At the Bottom of the Sea," he pursues further these themes by depicting a machine whose purpose is to dredge the bottom of the sea. At the top, on the shore, a building houses the motor that moves the machine's very long arm that dips into the water and reaches the bottom. Again, knowledge is to be found within, but deep into ourselves, where no one but ourselves can reach. But even for us, to get at it we need more than an easy reach. We need heavy equipment that will go down and dig through deep waters that obscure that bottom where the valuable minerals are accumulated. For Plato, the way to get to these treasures, the valuable raw materials he called Ideas, was through a process of recollection made possible because in a prior life we had been acquainted with them. Estévez does not follow Plato in this, but he accepts the difficulty of uncovering knowledge that only each of us individually can access. It is in hidden thoughts, archived in difficult to access spaces and territories, that the immensity of our true selves is revealed through strenuous and repeated efforts.

In Message 74, "No One Can See Through My Eyes," Estévez retakes the theme of the unique perspective that each of us has on the world and what we know. Just as no one can see through my eyes and see what I see, so no one can know what I know as I know it. In the drawing, we are presented with a man standing, erect, and nude, with arms hanging on his sides and looking straight ahead of him. Important points are highlighted with circles, as is frequent in Estévez's works: the hands, the knees, the feet, the pelvis, the belly, the heart, the junctures on the arms, the eyes, and the forehead. From his eyes come out lines that have ties to each other and eventually reach the floor. These lines form a kind of cage in which the man is encased. The man's senses function as a prison that traps him. He can see, he has knowledge, but his eyes give him a unique perspective. He cannot transcend the information and point of view that his eyes provide for him. There is no escape. We can see only what is concordant with our knowing powers and our unique situation. Transcendental knowledge can only be a hypothesis that can never be verified. We can only know what is possible for us to know with our senses and intellectual powers. Of course, we can speculate about what is out there, beyond ourselves. But this is not the same as actually transcending our limitations and reaching it.

The view of knowledge that Estévez presents us with is quite consistent. Our knowledge is ours, the result of our perspective and our condition. And this knowledge is to be found only by looking inward, into the depth of our selves. Still, although there is no hope of transcending it, there is the possibility that, as part of the universe, as the microcosm we are, we can in fact know the universe outside of us, precisely because knowing ourselves is also knowing the other. So what seemed at first like a Kantian prison may in the end be superseded.

FREE WILL

Another common topic that may frequently be raised in the context of Estévez's art is the question of free will and determinism (see Gracia 2009a, 133-51). Are human beings free or are they determined in some ways, either by physical causes or by a higher will? Again, philosophers have given different answers to this question. Determinists such as the Stoics, or materialists such as Karl Marx, have answered that human will is always determined. Freedom is a mere illusion. The only thing in which we may be free is in the realization that we are determined to do what we do. This jeopardizes moral responsibility, a reason why other philosophers, such as Thomas Aquinas, reject this point of view. For them, humans are free to act as they wish.

At least four works in *Bottles to the Sea* raise the question of free will and determinism, although they do it in different ways. The first is Message 8, "Man Is a Project of God." The work depicts sixty three male figures: a large figure towering over two smaller ones, which in turn tower over four smaller, which in turn tower over eight, and so on all the way down, suggesting a never ending series. The fingers of each figure, the feet, and the head are tied to the fingers of the figure or figures above it. In short, each of the figures is a puppet controlled by some other figure all the way up. Even the largest figure is tied to something above it, although we do not know what that is. Presumably, that highest figure, invisible as it is, is God, whereas the others are human beings. The implication is that we are puppets, controlled by higher powers and wills. The piece does not tell us whether we have any freedom.

Obviously, it might be possible that the higher figures, and God ultimately, give some slack to the figures below them. But even if they do, the control is in the hands of the higher figures and ultimately God. But we do not see God's hands or anything that suggests who or what He is. Nor do we know whether it is possible for him to give lower figures some freedom.

Message 35, "The Chosen One" raises an interesting theological question also related to the freedom of the will. A well-known Christian doctrine teaches that God chooses those He will elect for salvation. This is known as the Doctrine of Predestination. Some humans are predestined to salvation, whereas others are not chosen to be saved. The drawing has a group of nine men in outline in the act of walking, presumably going about their business. They all look alike and are engaged in the same sort of activity, although they are not all going in the same direction. In the sky we see stars and among them a hand points to one of the men. From the index finger of this bodiless hand comes a blue ray that radiates from the place on the head of the man it is touching to the rest of his body, like a kind of electrical current that is beginning to transform the body. The observer surmises that this is the hand of God and the man it indicates is the one chosen for salvation. He alone has been picked and he has also received something from above, perhaps what Christians refer to as grace. One interesting thing is that, just as the Doctrine of Predestination holds, there is no apparent reason given why the elected man has been chosen because he is like the others. The Christian doctrine explains this shocking fact, that seems to go against justice, by saying that God has His reasons, but Estévez's work leaves it for us to speculate.

Another drawing, Message 36, "The Invention of Destiny," presents us with another idea. This is the notion that the very Doctrine of Determinism and Predestination, or whatever other forms this view takes, is just a human invention. The picture could not be clearer. We have a puppet similar in some ways to the puppets in the other drawings and, like other puppets, this one has strings tied to his head, hands, and feet that control his movements. But unlike the case of the other puppets, the strings go up and meet the hands of the very puppet that is controlling his own movements. There is no God that has predestined us, nor are we subject to the laws of physical nature in such a way that we lose our free will. We are in fact free, and have invented the doctrine that we are not. Perhaps because we want to do away with moral responsibility? Obviously, this is the next logical question for us to ask, but Estévez leaves it to us to formulate and answer.

An interesting variation of this theme is found in Message 52, "*Creatoris*." In it, we see a man looking up. He is holding a glass in one hand that is extended upward, and is holding another glass upside down in the other hand that is extended downward. The contents of this second glass are being emptied. The glass at the top is receiving something presumably precious, judging from the expression on the face of the puppet, and the one below is being emptied of something presumably useless, judging from the carelessness with which it is being emptied. The text that accompanies the message speaks of how man dreams of creating something valuable. This work goes beyond raising the question of someone or something controlling us and determining our actions. Humans appear to be free, creators, the artists who are free despite imbibing in the nectar of originality from the muses. Freedom comes from inspiration, determinism from drudgery.

PHILOSOPHICAL DIMENSIONS

The conceptual and philosophical depth of Estévez's art naturally leads to the question: Is this philosophy? Is what we have found in Estévez's works philosophy? Can art express a philosophy or be philosophical, and if so in what sense?

These questions are pertinent in this context because of Estévez's own convictions and the nature of his work. Indeed, how many other artists have considered as many philosophical topics and ideas as he has?

Elsewhere, I have argued that Estévez's art is highly philosophical (Gracia 2009a). But what does it mean to say that the art is philosophical? Does it entail that it is a mode of expression that uses linguistic tools, such as words? If this were the criterion of being philosophical, then some of Estévez's works would be philosophical whereas others would not be, because some of them include writing and others do not. The problem with this criterion is that it also applies to enterprises that are clearly not philosophical, like religion and science. More than the medium of expression, then, we might surmise that it is the content of a work that makes it philosophical. Is the content of Estévez's works philosophical because it tells us something akin to what philosophers tell us?

The answer, like any good philosophical answer, is both yes and no. No, because Estévez's art does not articulate for us any particular view. An examination of any piece of art by Estévez does not yield a position with respect to a philosophical problem that one can unambiguously attribute to the piece or to Estévez. The consideration of the art may lead us to think of philosophical problems and answers, but the art itself does not make any such claims. The art simply presents images that are subject to interpretation and may lead in different directions. The paths to which they lead are not fixed, although they are not completely indeterminate. Using a famous metaphor found in Borges, we might say that they are like gardens of forking paths. When confronting Estévez's works, we find ourselves in concrete, if complex, situations defined by sets of images that suggest alternative interpretive strategies but do not force us to choose any one of them. And the moment we choose one, that very choice in turn opens for us further possible choices, other paths, from which we also have to choose which to follow.

But there is more to it than this, for the themes that Estévez's art suggest are traditionally favored by philosophy. They come from the plight of human experience, the predicaments that we all face. As one interpreter put it, they are existential (Damian 2009). Some are deadly serious and some are humorous, but all of them are authentic. This might suggest that Estévez's work should be classified as conceptual art if not philosophy. After all, from what we have been saying, the art is clearly about concepts, they are at the center of it and seem to override other concerns. There is a conceptual structure to each piece that speaks to us, not necessarily in words, although occasionally Estévez includes words in his works, but through images. However, there are major differences between standard conceptual art and Estévez's art. Contemporary conceptual artists seem to have in mind only the concepts that they are trying to convey or explore in their art. Aesthetic considerations such as balance, symmetry, weight, composition, harmony, technique, and the like, which have been traditionally the province of visual art, disappear on the face of the need to communicate concepts. The result is that most conceptual art lacks aesthetic qualities as traditionally understood and technique becomes irrelevant—indeed, many conceptual artists employ craftsmen to carry out their projects. Notions such as beauty do not arise, and it would be a mistake to judge a work of conceptual art on such bases. Some conceptual artists seem to make great efforts to show that they ignore such traditional aesthetic values as beauty and harmony and have no particular interest in technique, which they associate with craftsmanship rather than art.

The case of Estévez's art is quite different because some traditional aesthetic considerations still play roles in much of Estévez's art and he is a hands-on artist for whom technique is important. The result is that a considerable part of his art is aesthetically attractive and exquisitely crafted. His work not only tries to convey a concept but does so in ways that tie the art to some of the great currents of traditional Western art, the medieval period, the early Renaissance, and folk art from different ages, among others, where visual pleasure and technique played a role.

INTERPRETATION

The strong philosophical profile of Estévez's work leads us to ask whether it is acceptable to provide interpretations of it that are not philosophical. This is an important question because its answer would determine to a great extent the value of the interpretations and ultimately of the art. First, we need to be clear that an interpretation, broadly taken, is a kind of understanding that we have of something, whether an event, an idea, or a thing. But it can also be an instrument, such as a text or a picture used to make others grasp it. Witnesses of an accident have understandings of what happened—this is interpretation in the first sense—and they also may produce drawings of the accident for the police—this is interpretation in the second sense. So an interpretation of a work of art is an understanding of the work of art or an instrument to make others understand it.

To judge the value of an interpretation it is essential that we consider its purpose. It would not do, for example, to judge an interpretation that is intended to make us understand what the author had in mind with the same criteria we would use to judge an interpretation whose purpose was not to understand what the author had in mind, but how some particular audience understood it.

Interpretations come in various kinds (see Carvalho 2010; Gracia 2010, and 2012, 185-206; Ortega 2010). Particularly important are the following interpretations: authorial, audiential, work-based, and relational. An authorial interpretation seeks to understand what the author of a work had in mind by the work. For example, it seeks to grasp how Estévez understands "*Creatoris*." An audiential interpretation seeks to grasp what a particular audience of a work understood by it. For example, it seeks to grasp what Cuban Americans residing in Miami understand by "*Creatoris*." A work-based interpretation seeks to grasp the meaning of the work regardless of what Estévez or any particular audience take it to mean. And a relational interpretation seeks to grasp the relation of the work or its meaning to something else that the interpreter brings into the process of interpretation. A relational interpretation seeks to grasp how "*Creatoris*" can be understood philosophically or historically, for example.

Philosophical interpretations are, of course, relational in that they bring into the interpretive process a philosophical idea, concern, problem, or disciplinary dimension. This means that surely they are not the only valid interpretations of Estévez's works, even if it turns out that Estévez had in mind philosophical ideas or concerns when he created *Bottles to the Sea*. But it is perfectly valid to give philosophical interpretations of Estévez works. Each type of interpretation uses different criteria to reach its goal and should be judged according to those criteria. If some readers of this book are interested in authorial interpretations, they should try to figure out what Estévez thought the images in this book mean, and their efforts should be judged according to how successful the persons in question are in achieving that end. But if the aim is audiential, work-based, or relational, then different criteria would be applicable. There is considerable freedom of interpretation for the interpreter of Estévez's works, but the freedom is not complete license. Obviously, the brief interpretations of some of the drawings that are part of *Bottles to the Sea* that I gave earlier are philosophical, insofar as my interest in them is philosophical and I have brought that interest to bear on my understanding of the art pieces (for more examples, see Gracia 2009a). But readers of this book may have other interests in mind and therefore legitimately seek to understand the works differently.

As Aristotle reminded us at the beginning of his *Metaphysics*, it is in human nature to desire to know. We crave knowing not only for its own sake, as he meant, but I would add, because knowledge is a necessary condition of every intentional human enterprise. Nothing is possible for us without knowledge. To cross a deep river, we need to know how to swim; to feed ourselves, we need to pick food; and to love, we need to identify its object. But we have many avenues of knowledge, each of which provides something that is unique and that we need. This applies to such different epistemic enterprises as physics, psychology, chemistry, literature, religion, and the arts. With respect to the arts, I venture to say that one of their most important and idiosyncratic contributions is that they introduce an element of interpretive freedom missing in most other fields.

In science, we cannot let our imagination run free when confronted with the interpretation of its object. Scientific knowledge is good only if it is supported by empirical evidence and our inferences follow the laws of logic. Religion also has constraints, although in this case they have nothing to do with empirical evidence or even logic, insofar as most religions are concerned with a knowledge that transcends both. The constraints of religion come from authority and law, regulations and beliefs that cannot be violated or superseded.

Art is different from science and religion in that both the artist and the interpreter of art are free to understand in ways that these other epistemic paths are not. Yes, the artist is constrained by materials and the observer of art is constrained by the objects of artistic appreciation. But both the materials and the objects are mere points of departure rather than interpretive prisons within which the interpreter must remain. Artists can make whatever they want and is possible out of the elements they have at their disposal. And interpreters can go in interpretive directions that extend beyond the artist's explicit intentions (e.g., Damian 2008; Gracia, 2009a). Instead of constraining observers, works of art set them free. Art is one of the few ways in which humans can overcome the chains that enslave them. Rousseau's famous remark that "man is born free, and everywhere he is in chains" was intended in a different sense, but it is applicable here nonetheless. Art can cut those chains. Even if we live under totalitarian regimes, even if we are forced to bow to authority, even if we must recognize the truth of facts, we can still dream and imagine through art. Art makes it possible for us to fly in spite of gravity. Art opens our eyes to a world that has no limits. And indeed, this is the function of Estévez's installation *Bottles to the Sea*. It sets us on a journey whose end we do not know, but which will be guided by our dreams and imagination.

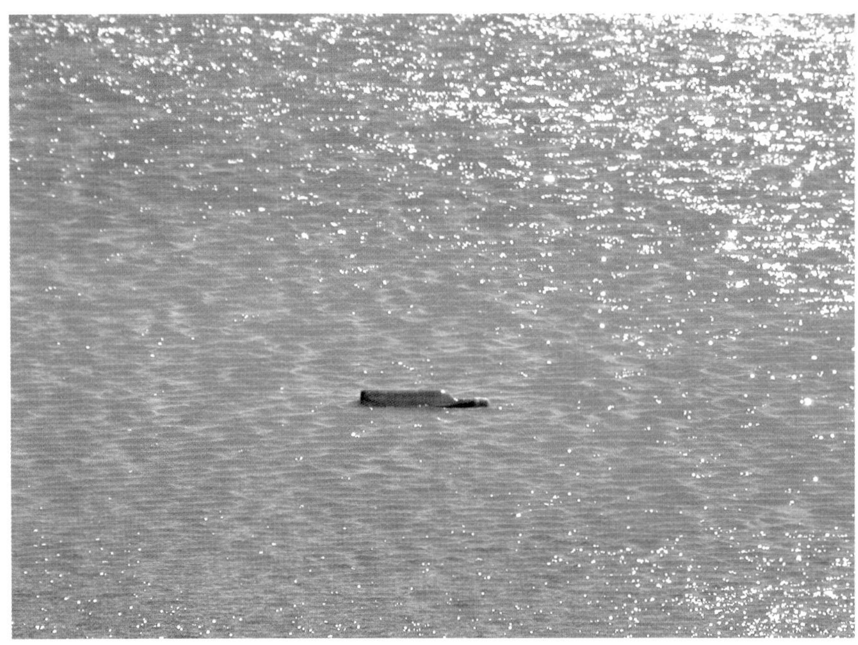

ARTIST STATEMENT

Carlos Estévez

When my son was young, he left a plastic Pepsi bottle with a message in it on the windowsill of my studio. The note—written in the childish calligraphy proper to his age—was a plea for medicine and food for the Cuban people. That simple object, which to me seemed so beautiful and full of meaning, immediately became the point of departure for one of my works.

In the complex process of creation it often happens that a simple element becomes the detonator for a series of complex ideas that later coalesce into a definite image. It was then that I began to elaborate *Bottles to the Sea*. At that time I was working on a group of paintings about the relation of the individual to the place in which he lives; how it is that one creates and modifies the other in an extremely complicated and dynamic process of mutual interaction. Each of the paintings alluded to a specific place. *Bottles to the Sea* arose as homage to the *Malecón*. This is a wide avenue with a wall on the seaward side where people go to sit and contemplate the horizon. For me, this confrontation has a strong symbolic connotation in that Cuba, in addition to being an island, is politically isolated, and the majority of Cubans have no possibility of leaving the island or ever knowing what the world is really like. On the other hand, and paradoxically, only 90 miles from the Cuban coasts are the Florida Keys and a little further north the city of Miami, where a great number of Cubans live. When I lived in Cuba, each time I passed by the *Malecón* I thought of my mother who lived on the other side of the sea and of other Cubans who, just like me, suffered because their families were divided by political circumstances. Havana's seawall constitutes a barrier; it is the limit that restricts the reach of an island and its inhabitants.

To throw a bottle into the sea with a personal message means to go beyond those limits, to escape in some form, if only symbolically. Later, as I developed the idea, I realized that the work could escape its context and its original circumstances and become something more universal. To throw a bottle into the sea meant, then, to escape the spiritual limits of the human being.

In 2001, the *Malecón* celebrated the one hundreth anniversary of its construction. It seemed to me a perfect opportunity to convert the piece into a homage of its centenary. Thus, I completed one hundred drawings, which, in the form of illuminated manuscripts, consisted of a compilation of texts and images taken from the notebooks that have accompanied me throughout my career. Thus, the piece became a compendium of my personal experiences, of my ideas and drawings of every kind, which were mixed with the history of the city where I was born, educated, and grew up.

The installation unfolded in space is also an allusion to the wall and the sea. The piece consists of a long shelf that supports a sequence of one hundred bottles. The bottles, all of different sizes and colors, contain the messages that later are thrown to the sea. Every bottle on the shelf also contains its respective drawing, all of which were done on light blue paper as an allusion to the sea. Each drawing possesses a number corresponding to the order of its realization, but that does not necessarily correspond to its order in the installation. The work has a ludic character and is always mounted differently, adapting itself to the space.

The messages are conceived to be cast into the sea. The work's method is chance. It attempts to simulate existence itself, in the way human events happen following the incalculable course of what we call destiny. Each time I go to a place near the sea, in any point around the world, my son chooses one among many pieces of folded paper kept in a small box. Each paper has a number between one and one hundred, which of course corresponds to the numbers of the messages. It is here where the play of chance and meanings begins. Each drawing has a title whose election will begin a relation with the destined place. Once thrown to the sea, the possibility of the encounter of this message with an unexpected receiver begins, at an indefinite time and in an unforeseen place. In turn, the person who finds the message becomes an active element in the work, forming an indispensable part of its play of meanings. With the drawing-message, I have included a note. The first line reads: "This drawing is yours." After this, I explain briefly the project and the importance of having a response from its bearer. Fundamentally, the expected commentary is where and when the message was found and if this has some meaning for or connection to the person. Like the book *I-Ching*, the messages are symbols with their meanings that are found by chance and from there a bridge is created.

In addition to the bottles and drawings, the installation includes a map on which are marked the launching points and their trajectories in the case of a message being found. Also the work includes a photographic and video documentation of all the launchings. Over time, this documentation will be the complete and unique testimony of the installation. The documentation of the launchings takes the place of the launchings, so that the installation is always changing; each time it is shown it is different, until the point that, when all the drawings have been thrown to the sea, only the visual documentation of photographs and video will remain.

The work was exhibited for the first time at the VII Biennial of Havana, together with the first launch on the Havana seawall in the year 2001. Since then, the piece has been shown in the United States, Mexico, and Switzerland. As of the end of 2014, there have been eighteen launchings: Cuba, the United States (on the Pacific and Atlantic coasts), France, Portugal, Spain, Switzerland (the Rhine), Italy, and Brazil. Only one message has been found. It was launched in the port of Barcelona, Spain, and it was found by a German tourist on the beach in Alcudia, Mallorca.

PRESENTACIÓN DEL ARTISTA

Carlos Estévez

Cuando mi hijo era pequeño dejó en la ventana de mi estudio una botella plástica de Pepsi cola con un mensaje dentro. La nota—escrita con caligrafía infantil propia de su edad—era una solicitud de medicinas y alimentos para ayudar a los cubanos. Aquel objeto tan simple me pareció tan hermoso y lleno de significados que inmediatamente se convirtió en el punto de partida para una de mis obras.

En el complejo proceso de la creación muchas veces ocurre que un simple elemento se convierte en el detonante de una serie de complejas ideas que más tarde confluirán en una imagen definitiva. Fue entonces cuando comencé a elaborar la pieza *Botellas al mar*. En aquel momento estaba trabajando en un grupo de obras sobre la relación entre el individuo y el lugar donde este habita; cómo es que uno crea y modifica al otro en un proceso de interacción mutuo sumamente complejo y dinámico. Cada una de las obras hacía alusión a un lugar específico. *Botellas al mar* surgió entonces como un homenaje al Malecón. El Malecón es una amplia avenida con un muro al lado del mar donde la gente va a sentarse y a contemplar el horizonte. Para mí esta confrontación tiene una fuerte connotación simbólica pues Cuba además de ser una isla está aislada políticamente, donde la mayoría de los cubanos no tienen la posibilidad de salir de ella y saber cómo es en realidad el mundo.

Por otra parte, y paradójicamente, del otro lado a sólo 90 millas de sus costas están los cayos de la Florida y un poco más al norte la ciudad de Miami, donde viven una gran cantidad de cubanos. Cada vez que yo pasaba por el Malecón—cuando vivía en Cuba—pensaba en mi madre que vivía del otro lado del mar y que al igual que yo, otros cubanos sufrían de familias dividas por circunstancias políticas. El Malecón de La Habana constituye una barrera, es el límite que restringe el alcance de una isla y sus habitantes.

Lanzar una botella al mar con un mensaje personal significa rebasar esos límites; escapar de alguna forma, aunque solo sea simbólicamente. Más adelante elaborando la idea me di cuenta que la obra podía escapar a su contexto y a sus circunstancias originarias y convertirse en algo más universal. Lanzar una botella al mar significaba entonces rebasar los límites espirituales del ser humano.

En el 2001 el Malecón cumpliría 100 años de su construcción; me pareció entonces una convergencia perfecta convertir la pieza en un homenaje a su centenario. De ahí que realicé 100 dibujos, que a modo de manuscritos iluminados consistían en una recopilación de textos e imágenes de mis cuadernos de apuntes que me han acompañado a lo largo de mi carrera desde que era estudiante. La pieza se convertía así en un compendio de mi experiencia personal, de mis ideas y dibujos de todo tipo, que se mezclaban con la historia de la ciudad donde nací, me eduqué y crecí.

La instalación desplegada en el espacio es también una alusión al muro y al mar. La pieza consiste en una larga repisa que sostiene una secuencia de 100 botellas. Las botellas de distintos tamaños y colores contendrán los mensajes que luego serán lanzados al mar. Cada botella de la repisa tiene encima su respectivo dibujo, que fueron realizados sobre un papel azul claro como alusión al mar. Cada dibujo posee un número correspondiente a su orden de realización, pero no necesariamente responde al orden de montaje de la instalación. La pieza tiene un carácter lúdico y siempre es montada de manera diferente adaptándose al espacio.

Los mensajes están concebidos para ser lanzados al mar. El método de esta obra es el azar. Pretende ser un símil de la existencia misma, igual que ocurren los eventos humanos siguiendo el curso incalculable de lo que llamamos destino. Cada vez que voy a un lugar donde hay mar en cualquier punto alrededor del mundo, mi hijo selecciona un papel doblado entre muchos que se guardan en una pequeña caja. Cada papel tiene un número entre el uno y el cien y que por supuesto responde a los números de los mensajes. Es aquí donde comienza el juego del azar y los significados. Cada dibujo tiene un título cuya elección comenzará una relación con el lugar destinado. Una vez lanzado al mar empieza la posibilidad del encuentro de este mensaje con un inesperado receptor; en un tiempo indefinido y en un lugar imprevisto. A su vez esta persona al encontrar el mensaje se convierte en elemento activo de la obra formando parte indispensable de su juego de significados. Junto al dibujo-mensaje he puesto una nota. La primera línea dice: Este dibujo es suyo. A continuación explico brevemente el proyecto y la importancia de tener una respuesta de su portador. Fundamentalmente el comentario esperado es dónde y cuándo encontró el mensaje y si este tiene algún significado o conexión con la persona. Como el libro del *I-Chin*, los mensajes son símbolos con significados que se encuentran por azar y a partir de ahí se crea un puente.

Además de las botellas y los dibujos, la instalación cuenta con un mapa donde se van señalando los puntos de lanzamiento y sus trayectorias en caso de ser encontrado algún mensaje. También la obra cuenta con una documentación fotográfica y de video de todos los lanzamientos. Esta documentación con el tiempo será el testimonio completo y único de la instalación. Los lanzamientos se van sustituyendo con la documentación por tanto la instalación es mutante, cada vez que se muestra es diferente, hasta el punto de que cuando todos los dibujos hayan sido lanzados sólo quedará la documentación visual de fotografías y video.

La obra se exhibió por primera vez en la VII Bienal de La Habana, junto con el primer lanzamiento en el Malecón habanero en el año 2001. A partir de entonces la pieza ha sido mostrada en Los Estados Unidos, México y Suiza. Hasta el momento se han realizado 18 lanzamientos: Cuba, USA, (en la costa pacífica y atlántica), Francia, Portugal, España, Suiza (Río Rin), Italia y Brasil. Solo un mensaje ha sido encontrado. El mismo fue lanzado en el puerto de Barcelona, España y fue encontrado por una turista Alemana en la playa Alcúdia, Mallorca.

MESSAGES

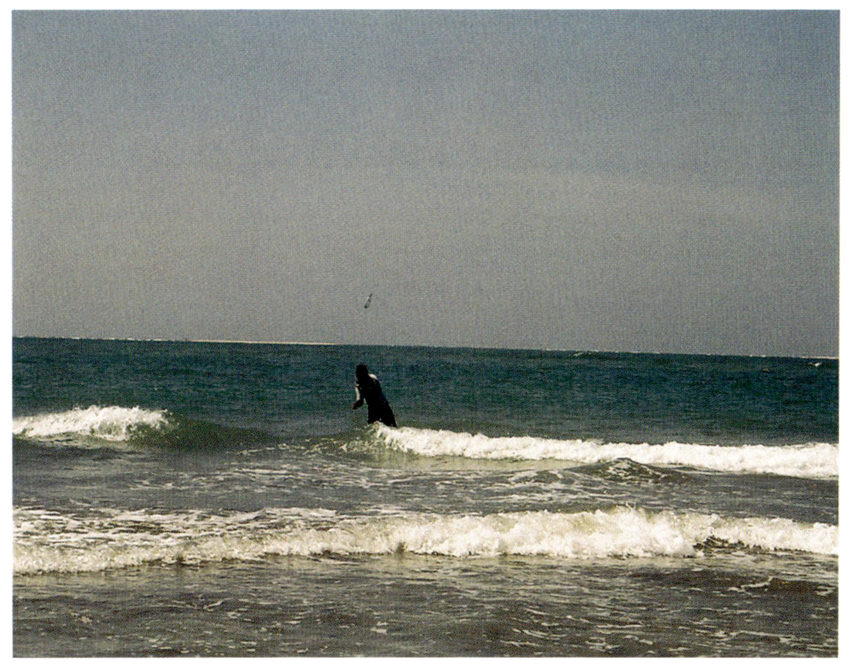

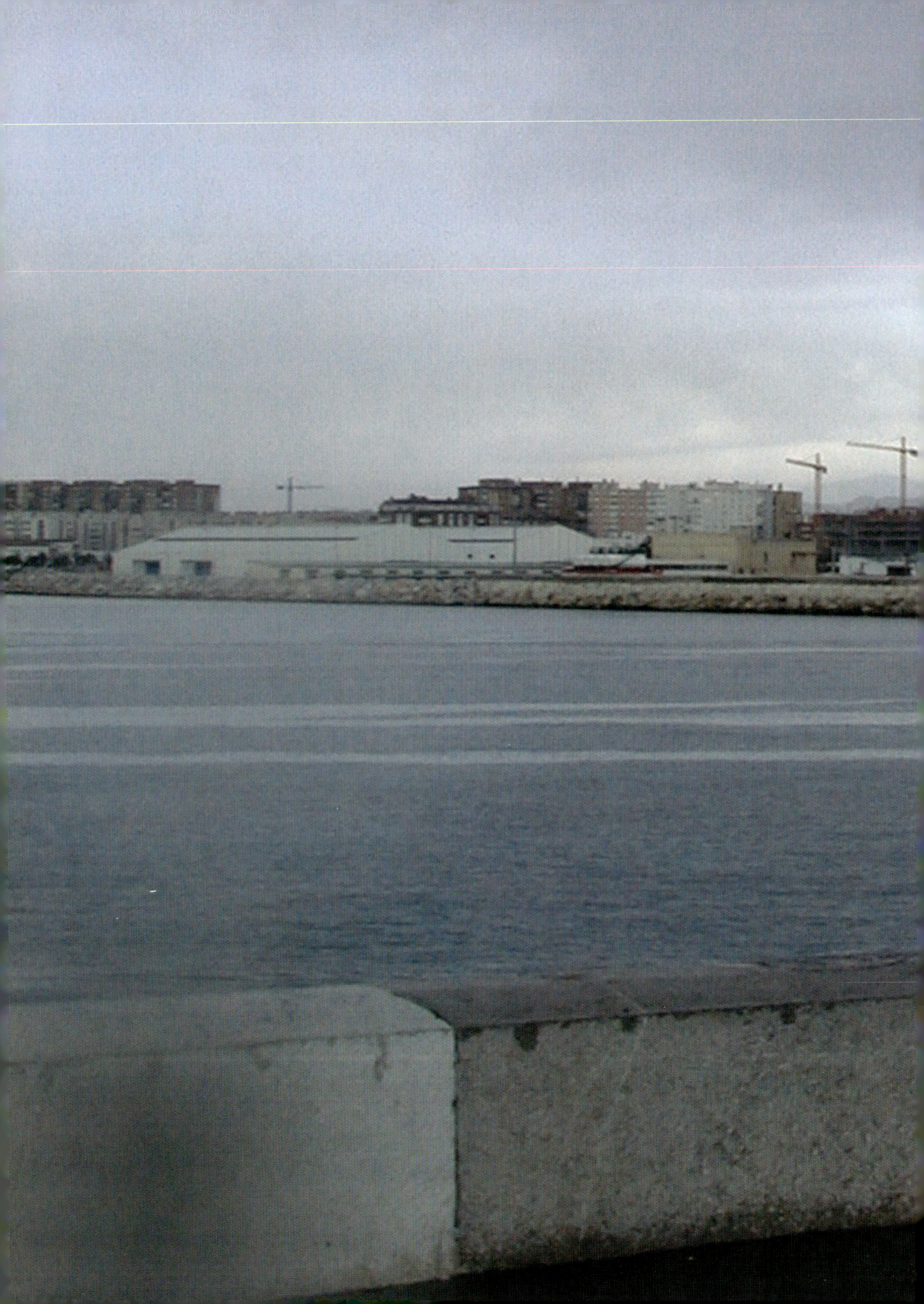

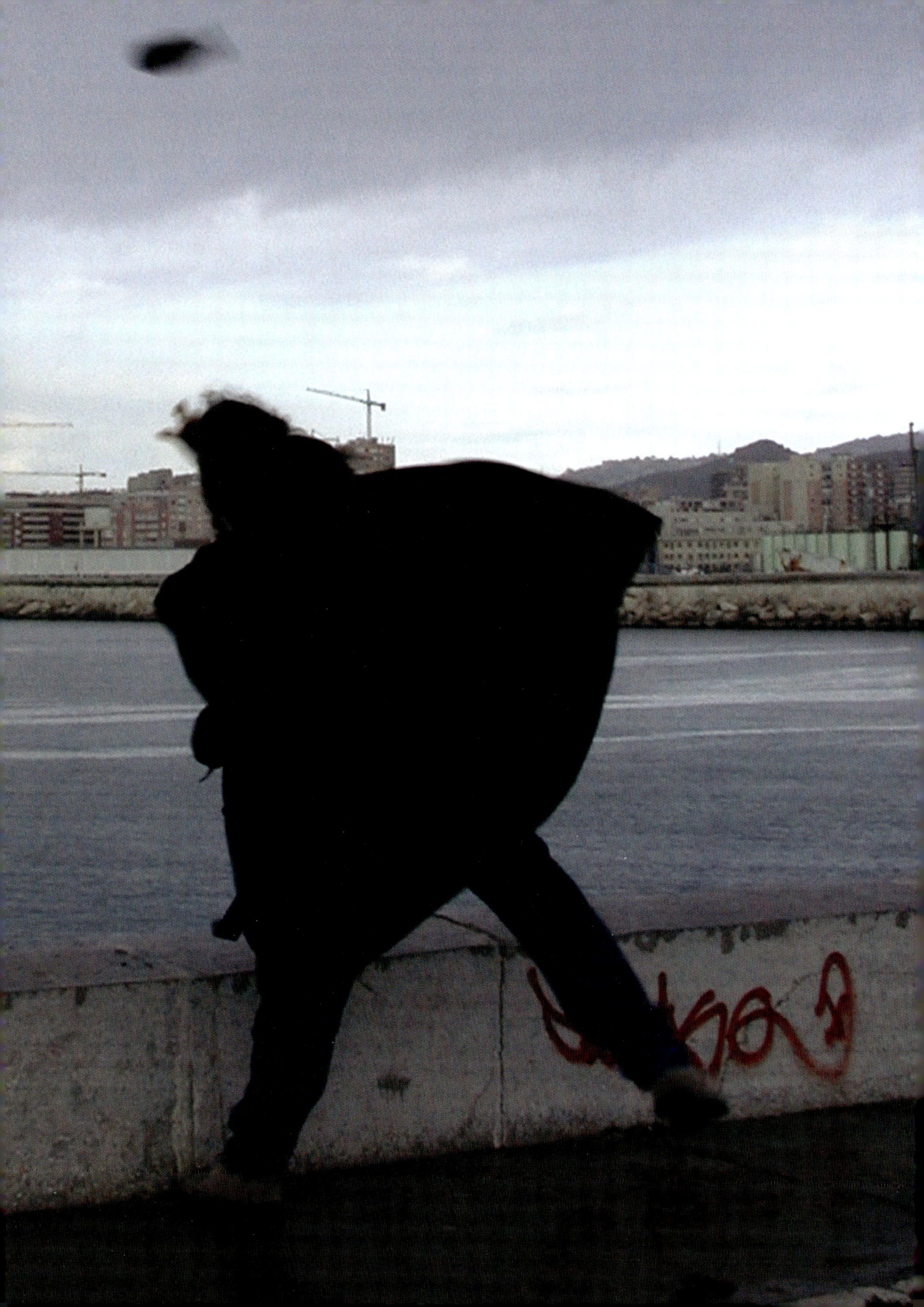

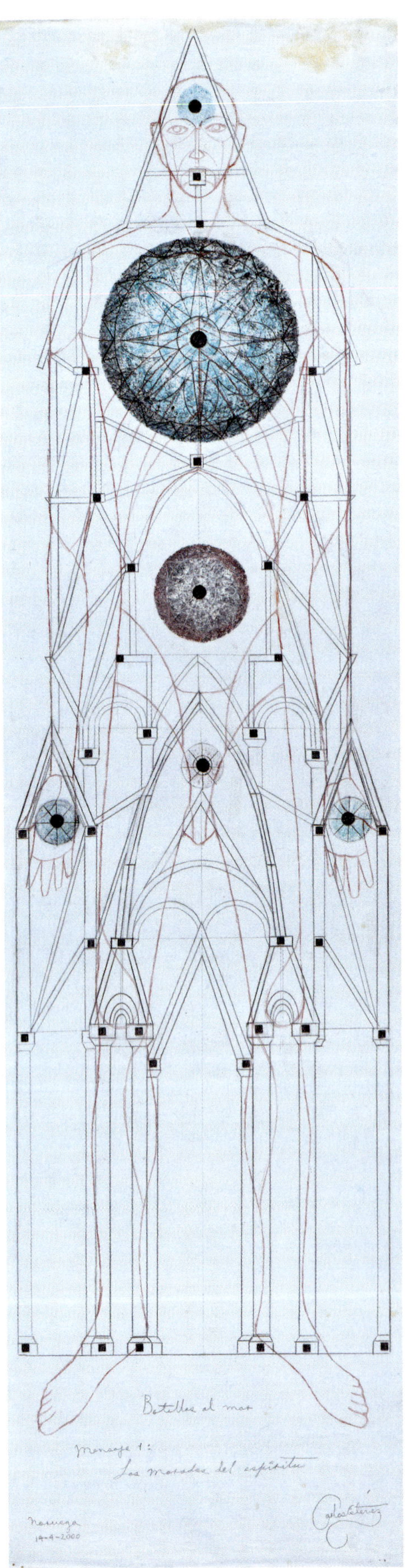

Bottles to the Sea
Message 1 "Spirit's Dwellings"
Norway 4-14-2000

Botellas al mar
Mensaje 1 "Las moradas del espíritu"
Noruega 14-4-2000

Bottles to the Sea
Message 2 "The World in Which We Live"
Norway 4-16-2000

Botellas al mar
Mensaje 2 "El mundo en que vivimos"
Noruega 16-4-2000

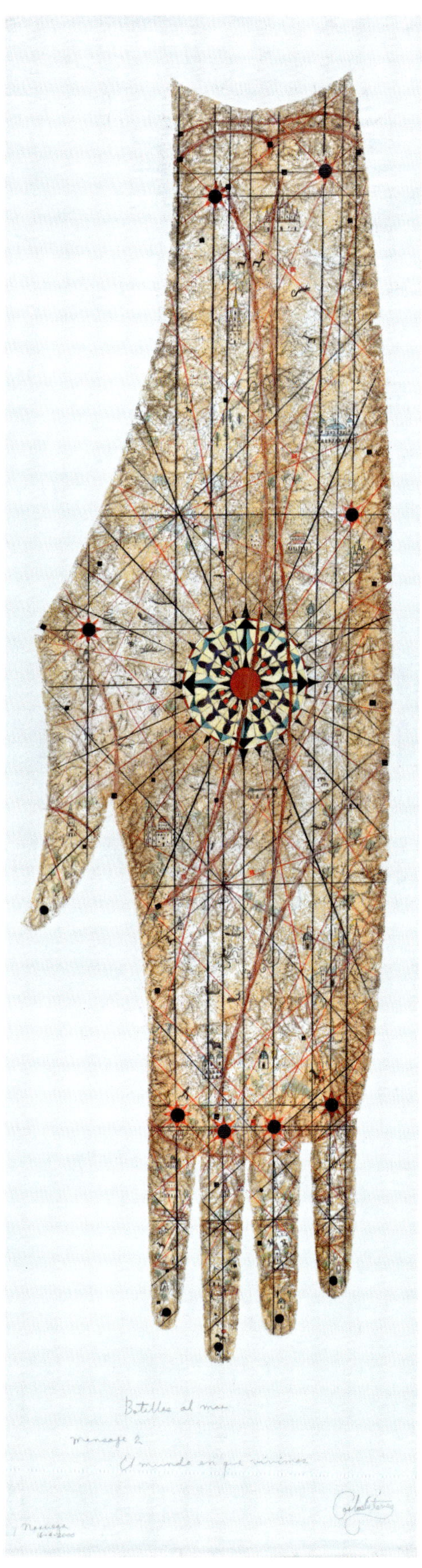

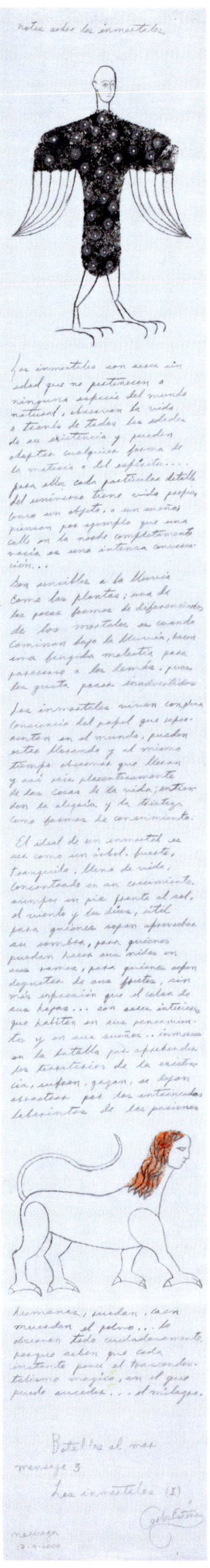

Bottles to the Sea
Message 3 "The Immortals (I)"
Norway 4-17-2000

Notes on the immortals

Immortals are ageless beings that do not belong to any species of the natural world; they observe life through all ages of their existence and can adopt any material or spiritual form . . .

For them, each particular detail of the universe has its own life, as an object, a dream; they think, for example, that a completely empty street in the night is an intense conversation . . .

They are sensitive to the rain like plants; one of the few ways to distinguish them from mortals is that when they walk in the rain they pretend to be bothered in order to seem like everyone else because they like to pass unnoticed.

Immortals live fully conscious of the role they play in the world. They can be crying and at the same time observe that they cry and thus laugh pleasantly at the things of life; they understand happiness and sadness as forms of knowledge.

The ideal of an immortal is to be like a tree—strong, tranquil, full of life, concentrated on its growth, always standing facing the sun, the wind, and the day, useful for those who know how to take advantage of its shade, for those who can make their nests in its branches, for those who know how to enjoy its fruits, without more expression than the color of its leaves—they are interior beings who live in their thoughts and in their dreams . . . immersed in the battle for apprehending the territories of existence, they suffer, enjoy, allow themselves to be carried away by the intricate labyrinths of human passions, they roll, fall, bite the dust . . . they observe everything carefully because they know that each instant possesses magical transcendentalism, in which can happen . . . the miracle.

Botellas al mar
Mensaje 3 "Los inmortales (I)"
Noruega 17-4-2000

Notas sobre los inmortales

Los inmortales son seres sin edad que no pertenecen a ninguna especie del mundo natural, observan la vida a través de todas las edades de su existencia y pueden adoptar cualquier forma de la materia o del espíritu . . .

Para ellos cada particular detalle del universo tiene vida propia, como un objeto, un sueño; piensan por ejemplo que una calle en la noche completamente vacía es una intensa conversación . . .

Son sensibles a la lluvia como las plantas; una de las pocas formas de diferenciarlos de los mortales es cuando caminan bajo la lluvia, hacen una fingida molestia para parecerse a los demás, pues les gusta pasar inadvertidos.

Los inmortales viven con plena conciencia del papel que representan en el mundo, pueden estar llorando y al mismo tiempo observar que lloran y así reír placenteramente de las cosas de la vida; entienden la alegría y la tristeza como forma de conocimiento.

El ideal de un inmortal es ser como un árbol, fuerte, tranquilo, lleno de vida, concentrado en su crecimiento, siempre en pie frente al sol, el viento y los días, útil para quienes sepan aprovechar su sombra, para quienes puedan hacer sus nidos en sus ramas, para quienes sepan degustar de sus frutos, sin más expresión que el color de sus hojas . . . son seres interiores que habitan en sus pensamientos y en sus sueños . . . inmersos en la batalla por aprehender los territorios de la existencia, sufren, gozan, se dejan arrastrar por los intrincados laberintos de las pasiones humanas, ruedan, caen, muerden el polvo . . . lo observan todo cuidadosamente porque saben que cada instante posee el trascendentalismo mágico, en el que puede suceder . . . el milagro.

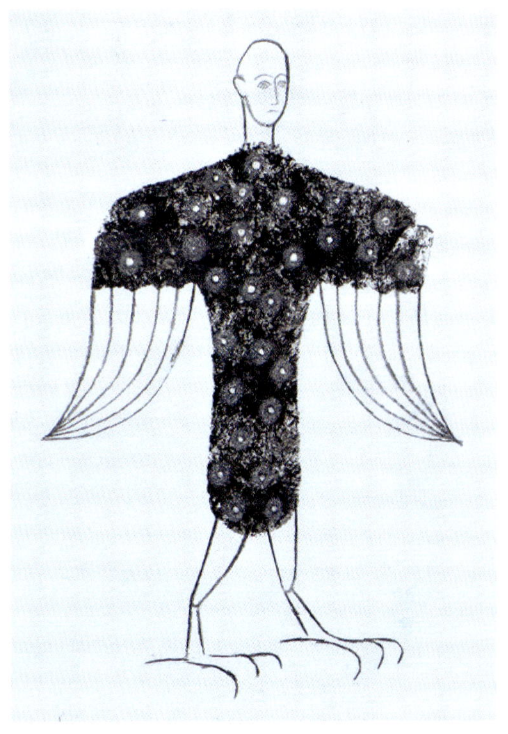

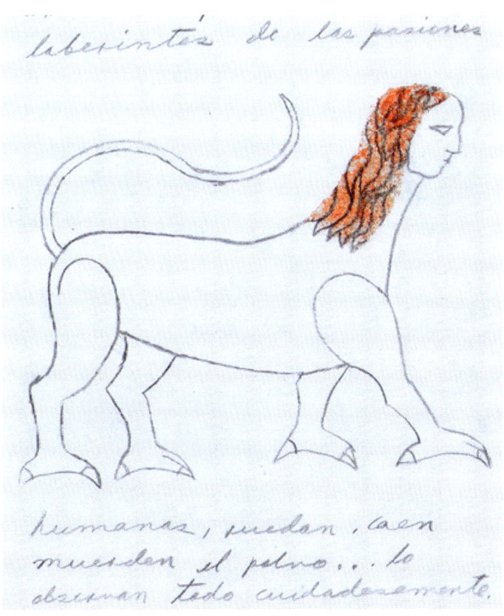

details, Message 3

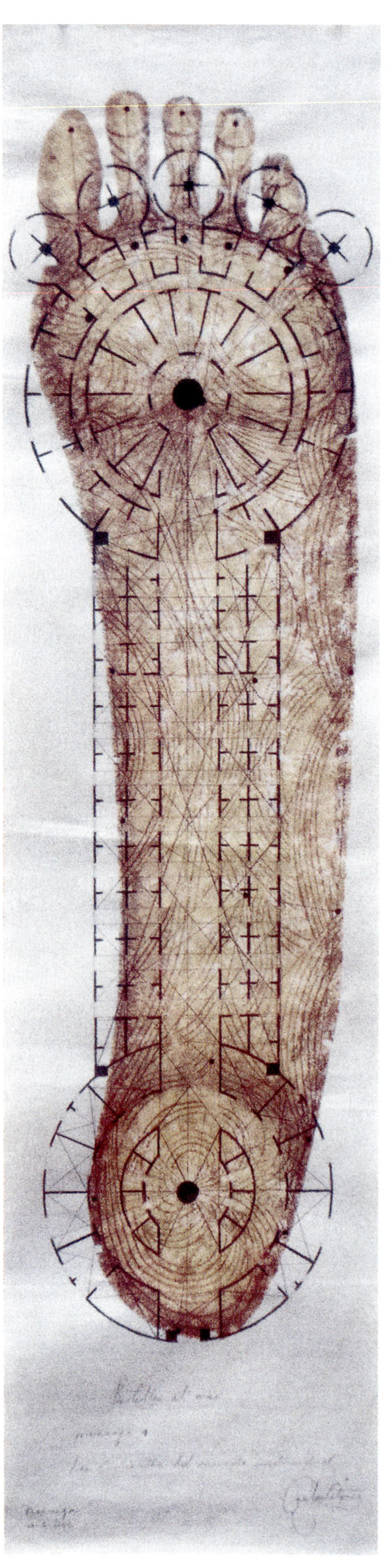

Bottles to the Sea
Message 4 “The Foundations of the Individual World”
Norway 4-19-2000
Launched at La Malagueta Beach, Malaga, Spain. 2-22-2004

Botellas al mar
Mensaje 4 “Los cimientos del mundo individual”
Noruega 19-4-2000
Lanzado en la Playa La Malagueta, Málaga, España. 22-2-2004

Bottles to the Sea
Message 5 "Like the Trees"
Norway 4-20-2000

. . . and the trees from their apparent quietude are everywhere, their leaves fly spreading toward any place, some mark the pages of a book with who knows what history . . .

. . . their branches inspire who knows what fires . . .

. . . their shade comforts who knows what creatures . . .

. . . the plague of impatience and uncertainty has forever closed to us the wise condition of the tree.

The first man was a tree, the wind taught him to move his branches, and the storms how to raise his roots; thus it was that he began to walk desiring to know the world, he walked and walked until losing himself beyond the horizon. When he wanted to return, he was too far away. He never again found his place. It is for this reason that man always moves from one place to another looking for he knows not what, longing for his territory.

Botellas al mar
Mensaje 5 "Como los árboles"
Noruega 20-4-2000

. . . y los árboles desde su aparente quietud están en todas partes, sus hojas vuelan esparciéndose hacia cualquier lugar, algunas marcan las páginas de un libro con quien sabe qué historia . . .

. . . sus ramas alientan quien sabe que fuegos . . .

. . . su sombra conforta a quien sabe que criaturas . . .

. . . la plaga de la impaciencia y la incertidumbre nos ha vedado para siempre la sabia condición de árbol.

El primer hombre fue un árbol, el viento le enseñó a mover sus ramas, y las tormentas cómo levantar sus raíces; así fue que echó a andar deseoso de conocer el mundo, anduvo y anduvo hasta perderse más allá del horizonte. Cuando quiso volver estaba demasiado lejos. Nunca más encontró su lugar. Es por eso que el hombre anda siempre de un lado a otro buscando no sabe que, añorando su territorio.

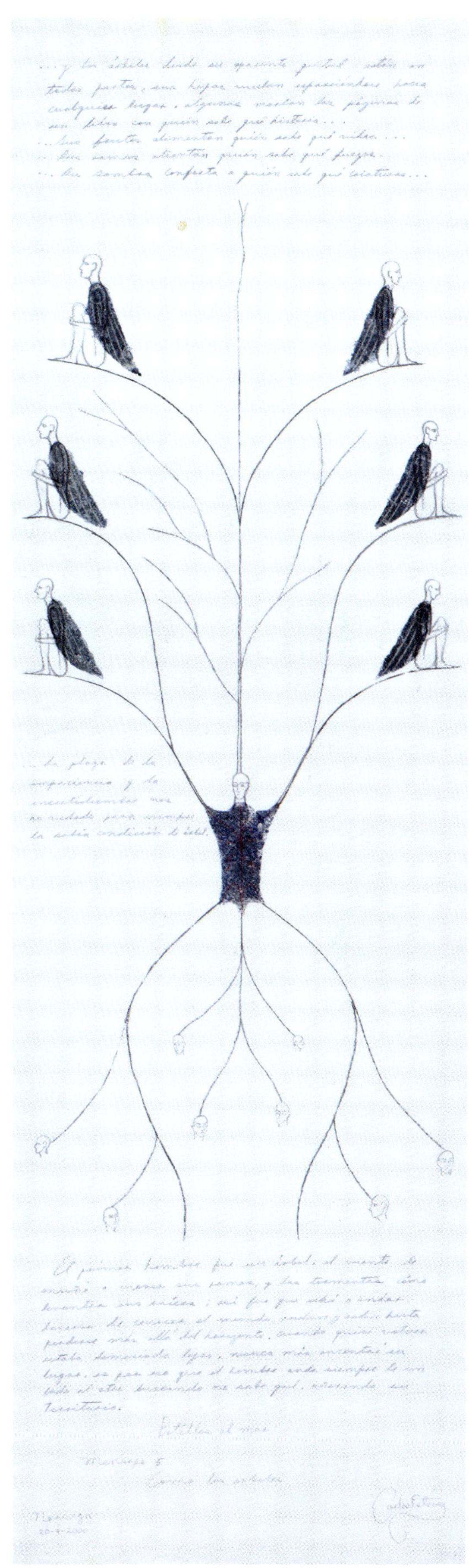

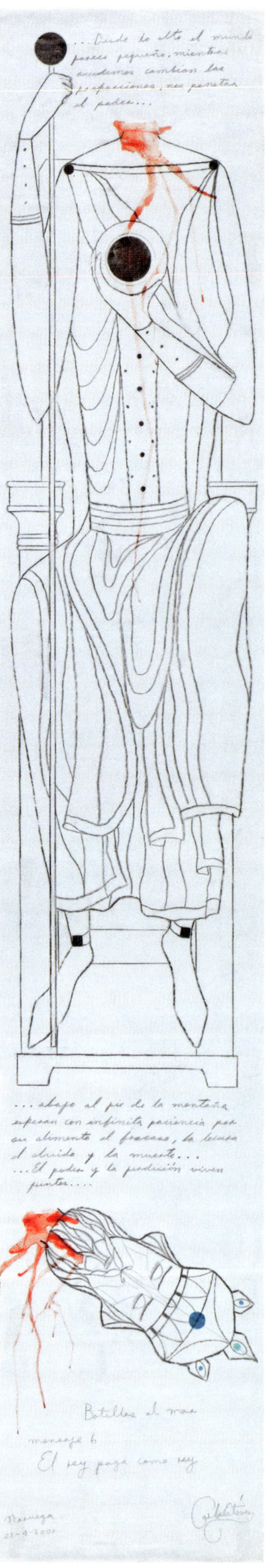

Bottles to the Sea
Message 6 "The King Pays Like a King"
Norway 4-21-2000

. . . from above the world appears small; while we ascend, the proportions change, power penetrates us . . .

. . . below at the foot of the mountain they await with infinite patience their sustenance: failure, madness, oblivion, and death . . .

. . . power and perdition live together . . .

Botellas al mar
Mensaje 6 "El rey paga como rey"
Noruega 21-4-2000

. . . Desde lo alto el mundo parece pequeño, mientras ascendemos cambian las proporciones, nos penetra el poder . . .

. . . abajo al pie de la montaña esperan con infinita paciencia por su alimento el fracaso, la locura, el olvido y la muerte . . .

. . . El poder y la perdición viven juntos . . .

Bottles to the Sea
Message 7 "*Observatorium*"
Norway 4-22-2000

. . . Do not depart from yourself, return to yourself, the truth dwells inside man . . .

Saint Augustine

. . . I feel a profound fascination for the imaginative capacities, that infinite space that every human being possesses in order to make the voyage toward his inner universe, or teaching with his life the map of existence . . .

The most profound knowledge of life, the keys to human existence are untransferable . . . it is for this reason that every being should carefully observe the movement of its stars.

Botellas al mar
Mensaje 7 "Observatorium"
Noruega 22-4-2000

. . . No salgas de ti mismo, vuelve a ti, en el interior del hombre habita la verdad . . .

San Agustín

. . . siento una profunda fascinación por las capacidades imaginativas, ese espacio infinito que posee cada ser humano para hacer el viaje hacia su universo interior, o enseñando con su vida el mapa de la existencia . . .

Los conocimientos más profundos de la vida, las claves de la existencia humana son intransferibles . . . es por eso que cada ser debe observar cuidadosamente el movimiento de sus astros.

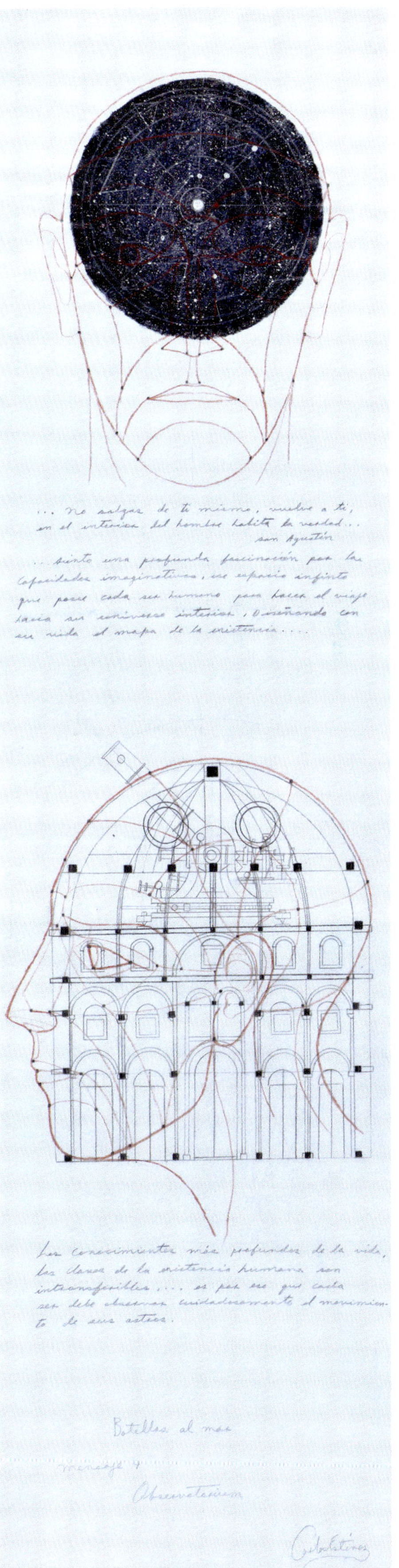

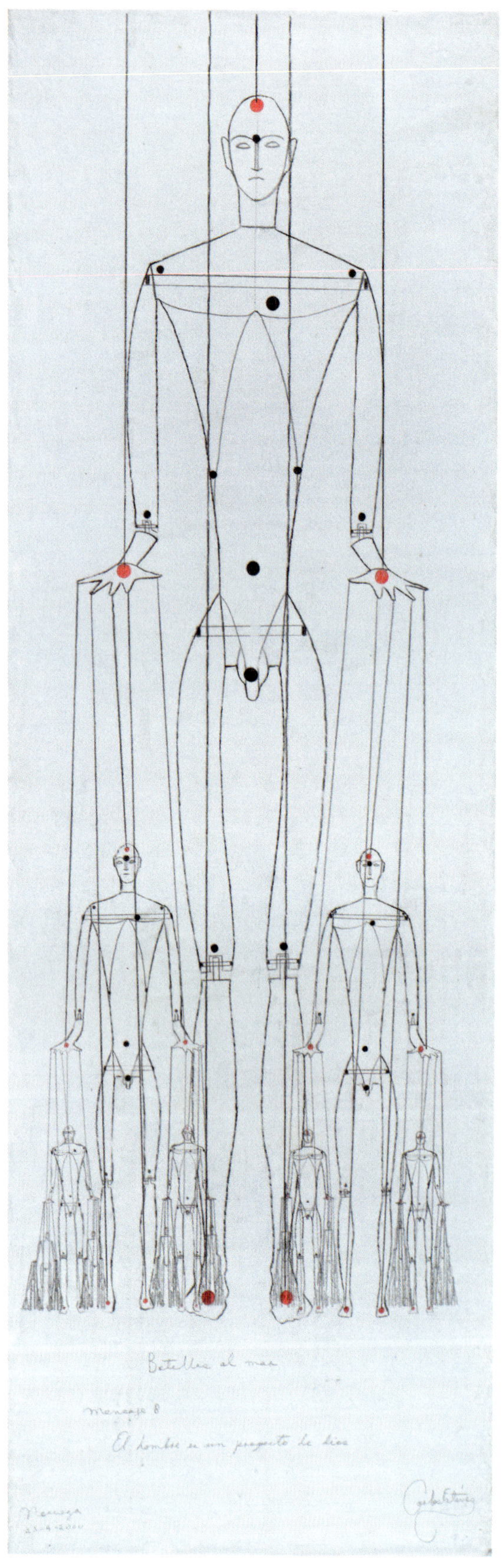

Bottles to the Sea
Message 8 "Man is a Project of God"
Norway 4-23-2000

Botellas al mar
Mensaje 8 "El hombre es un proyecto de Dios"
Noruega 23-4-2000

Bottles to the Sea
Message 9 "The Battle of Life"
Norway 4-24-2000

. . . and he fought in battle with valor . . . he seemed to divine the blows of the adversary, he learned to fight fighting, he grew so much that he unsettled the enemy, he became frightening, he triumphed in victories and defeats, in storms and calms . . .

. . . without suspecting that so many of God's concessions were connected to certain mutations of the soul . . .

When he stopped for an instant to observe his life, he was another and could not recognize himself.

Botellas al mar
Mensaje 9 "La batalla de la vida"
Noruega 24-4-2000

. . . y peleó en batalla con valor . . . parecía adivinar los golpes del adversario, aprendió a pelear peleando, creció tanto que desconcertó al enemigo, se hizo temer, triunfó en victorias y en derrotas, en tormentas y calmas . . .

. . . sin sospechar que tantas concesiones de Dios estaban conectadas a ciertas mutaciones del alma . . .

Cuando se detuvo un instante para observar su vida, él era otro y no pudo reconocerse.

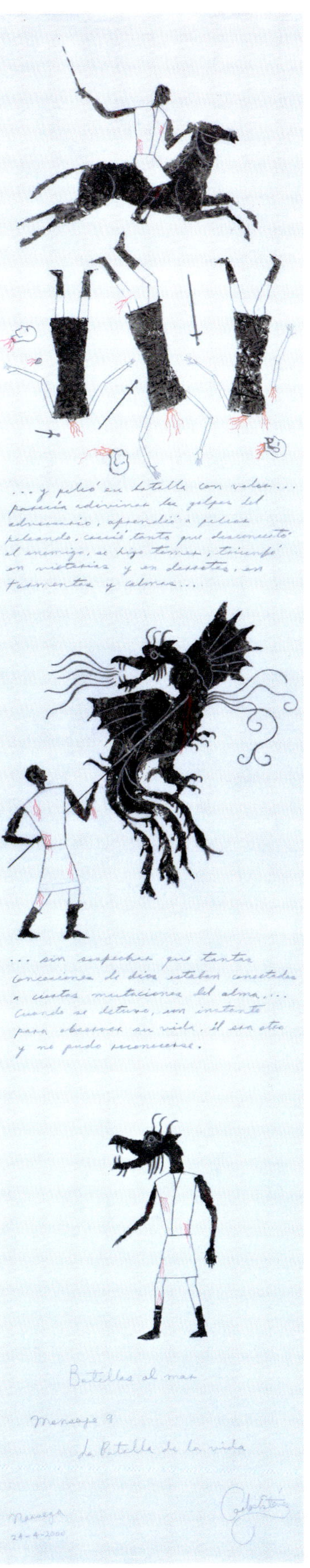

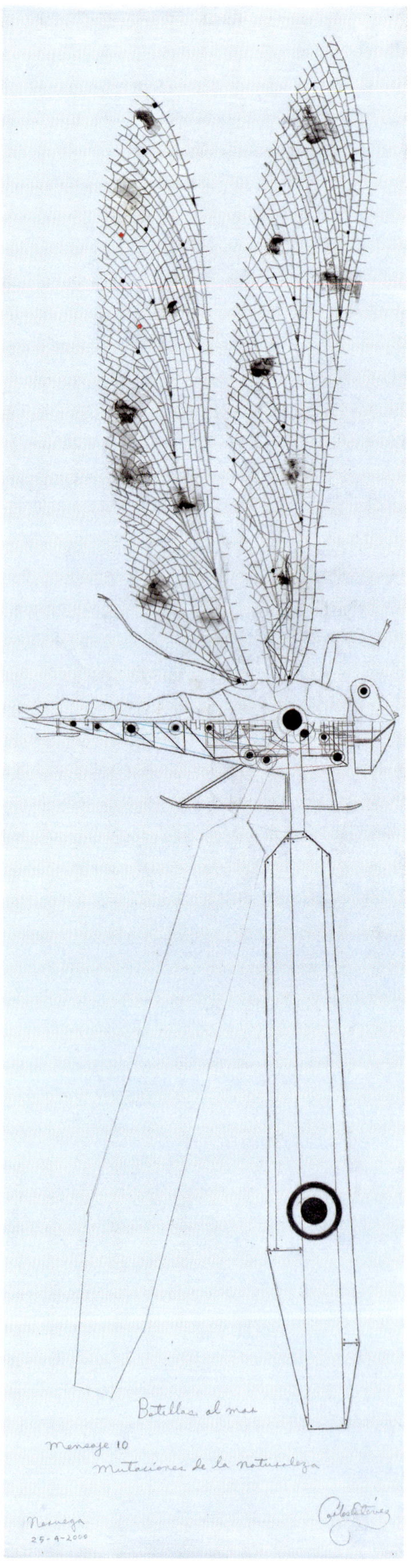

Bottles to the Sea
Message 10 “Mutations of Nature”
Norway 4-25-2000

Botellas al mar
Mensaje 10 “Mutaciones de la naturaleza”
Noruega 25-4-2000

Bottles to the Sea
Message 11 "*Anfiteatrum*"
Norway 4-30-2000

. . . This is the place where the drama of the personal world occurs . . .

. . . no one can see through my eyes the space where I project the maps of my existence . . .

Botellas al mar
Mensaje 11 "Anfiteatrum"
Noruega 30-4-2000

. . . Este es el lugar donde transcurre la trama del mundo personal . . .

. . . nadie puede ver a través de mis ojos el espacio donde proyecto los mapas de mi existencia . . .

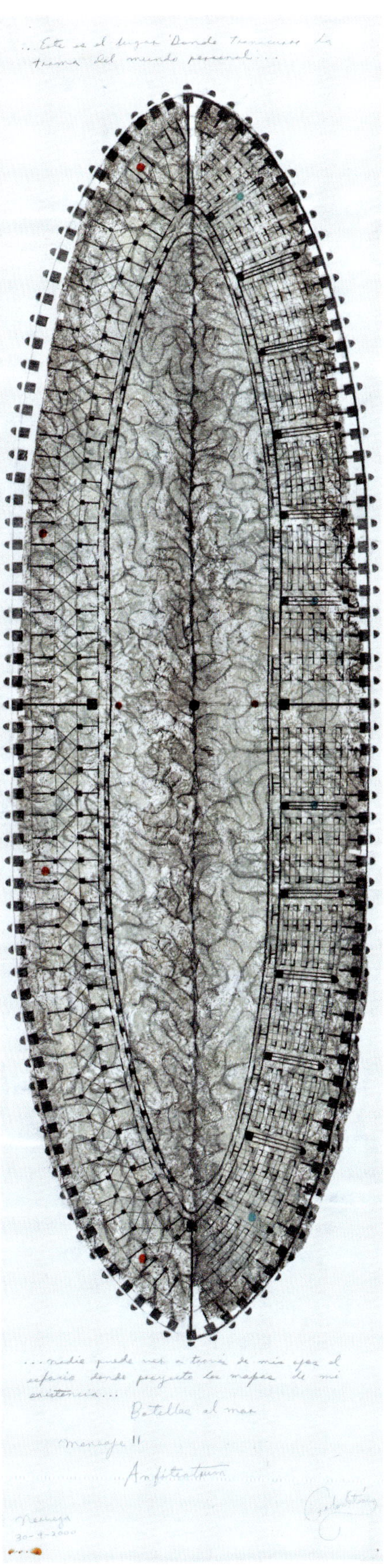

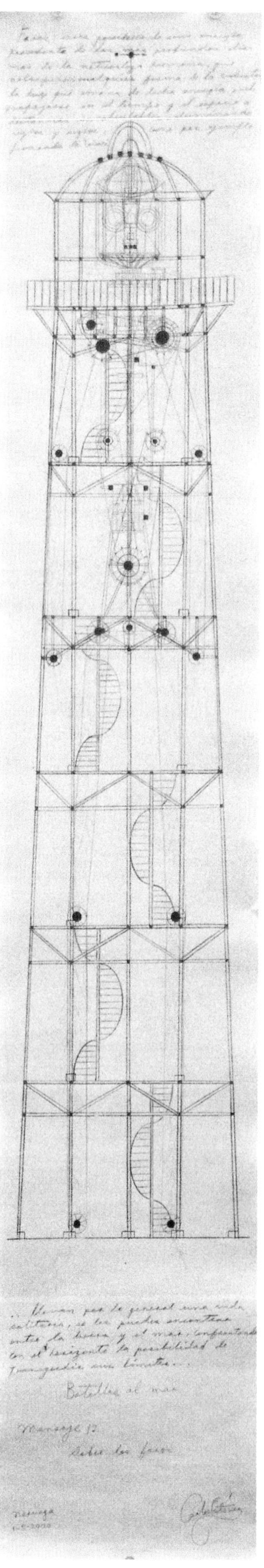

Bottles to the sea
Message 12 "On Lighthouses"
Norway 5-1-2000

Lighthouses: beings possessing an energy proceeding from the most profound abysses of human nature that exceed any form of volition. The light that emanates from said energy can propagate itself in space and time at incalculable distances, illuminating centuries and centuries, as, for example, Leonardo Da Vinci.

. . . they live, in general, a solitary life, they can be found between the land and the sea, confronting with the horizon the possibility of trespassing its limits . . .

Botellas al mar
Mensaje 12 "Sobre los faros"
Noruega 1-5-2000

Faros: seres poseedores de una energía procedente de los más profundos abismos de la naturaleza humana, que sobrepasan cualquier forma de la voluntad. La luz que emana de dicha energía puede propagarse en el tiempo y el espacio a distancias incalculables, iluminando siglos y siglos, como por ejemplo, Leonardo Da Vinci.

. . . llevan por lo general una vida solitaria, se les puede encontrar entre la tierra y el mar, confrontando con el horizonte la posibilidad de transgredir sus límites . . .

Bottles to the Sea
Message 13 "On Windmills"
Norway 5-2-2000

. . . mechanism by which living beings process natural energy, transforming it mostly into shit, and a small part into works, . . . many agree that the human species is the possessor of the highest level of evolution of this process. Opinions divide upon arriving at the point of discerning toward where the balance inclines . . .

Botellas al mar
Mensaje 13 "Sobre los molinos de viento"
Noruega 2-5-2000

. . . mecanismo mediante el cual los seres vivos procesan la energía natural, transformándola mayormente en mierda, y una pequeña parte en obras, . . . muchos coinciden en que es la especie humana poseedora del más alto grado de evolución de dicho proceso. Las opiniones se dividen al llegar al punto de discernir hacia donde se inclina la balanza . . .

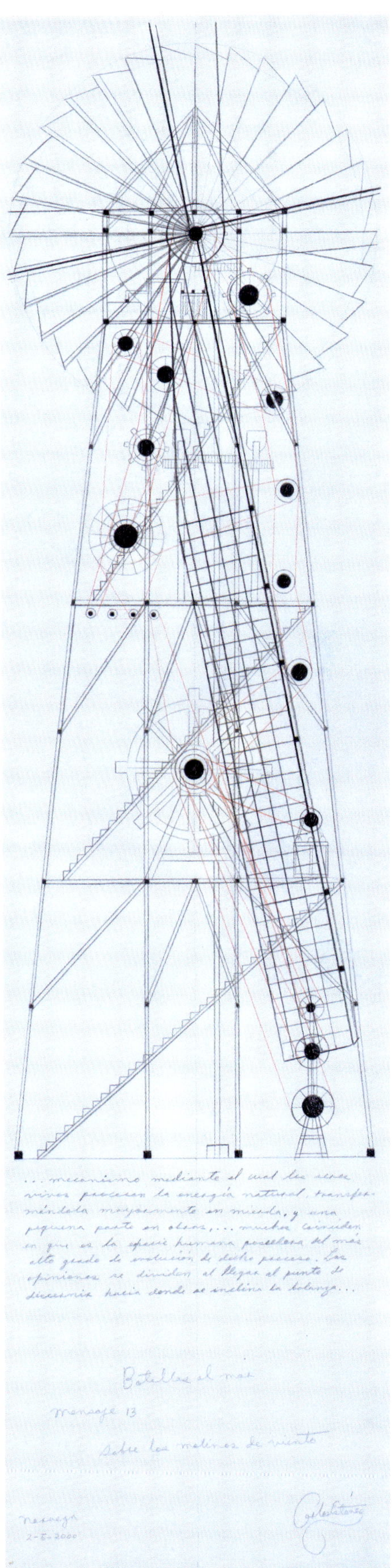

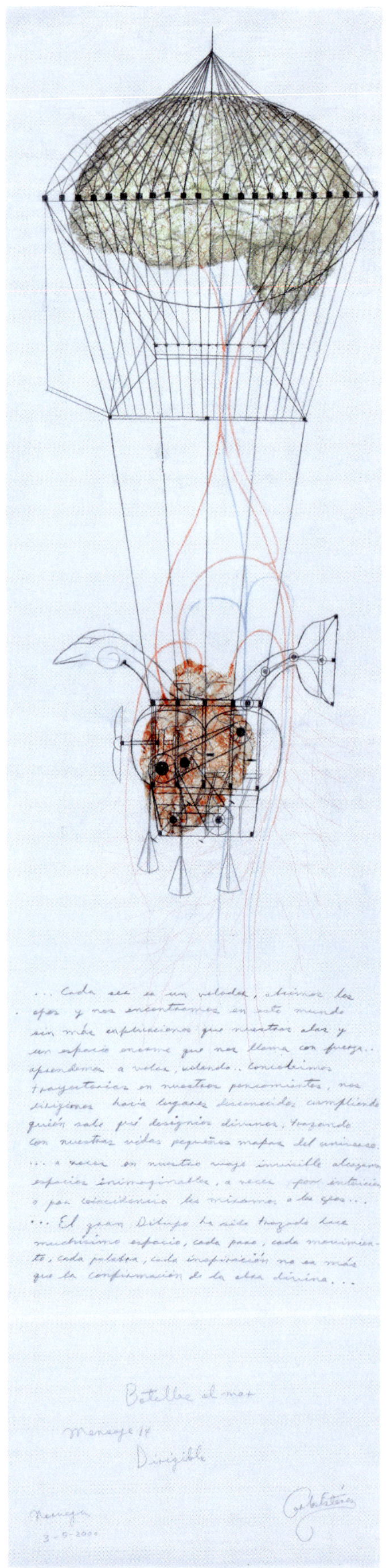

Bottles to the Sea
Message 14 "Dirigible"
Norway 5-3-2000

. . . every being is a flyer, we open our eyes, and we find ourselves in this world without explanation other than our wings and an enormous space that calls us forcefully . . .

We learn to fly, flying . . . we conceive trajectories in our thoughts, we direct ourselves toward unknown places fulfilling who knows what divine designs, tracing with our lives small maps of the universe.

. . . at times in our invisible journey we reach unimaginable spaces, at times by intuition, or by coincidence we look them in the eyes . . .

. . . The great drawing has been traced a long space ago, each step, each movement, each word, each inspiration is nothing more than the confirmation of the divine work . . .

Botellas al mar
Mensaje 14 "Dirigible"
Noruega 3-5-2000

. . . cada ser es un volador, abrimos los ojos, y nos encontramos en este mundo sin más explicaciones que nuestras alas y un espacio enorme que nos llama con fuerza . . .

Aprendemos a volar, volando . . . concebimos trayectorias en nuestros pensamientos, nos dirigimos hacia lugares desconocidos cumpliendo quien sabe que designios divinos, trazando con nuestras vidas pequeños mapas del universo.

. . . a veces en nuestro viaje invisible alcanzamos espacios inimaginables, a veces por intuición, o por coincidencia les miramos a los ojos . . .

. . . El gran dibujo ha sido trazado hace muchísimo espacio, cada paso, cada movimiento, cada palabra, cada inspiración no es más que la confirmación de la obra divina . . .

Bottles to the Sea
Message 15 "Neither Knowledge nor Experience Can Save Us"
Norway 5-4-2000

Botellas al mar
Mensaje 15 "Ni el saber ni la experiencia nos pueden salvar"
Noruega 4-5-2000

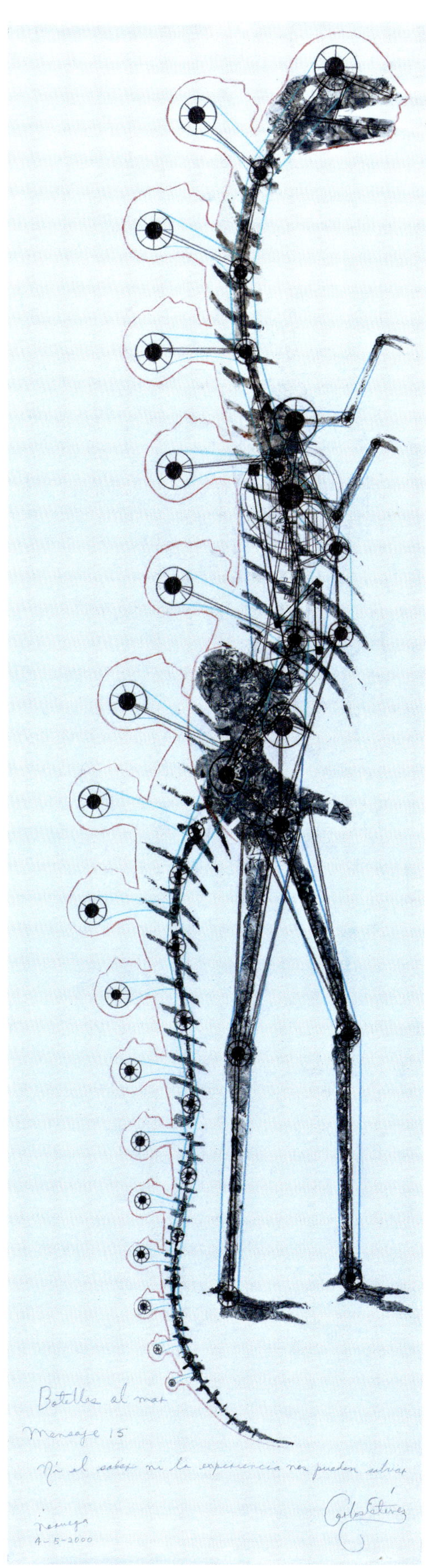

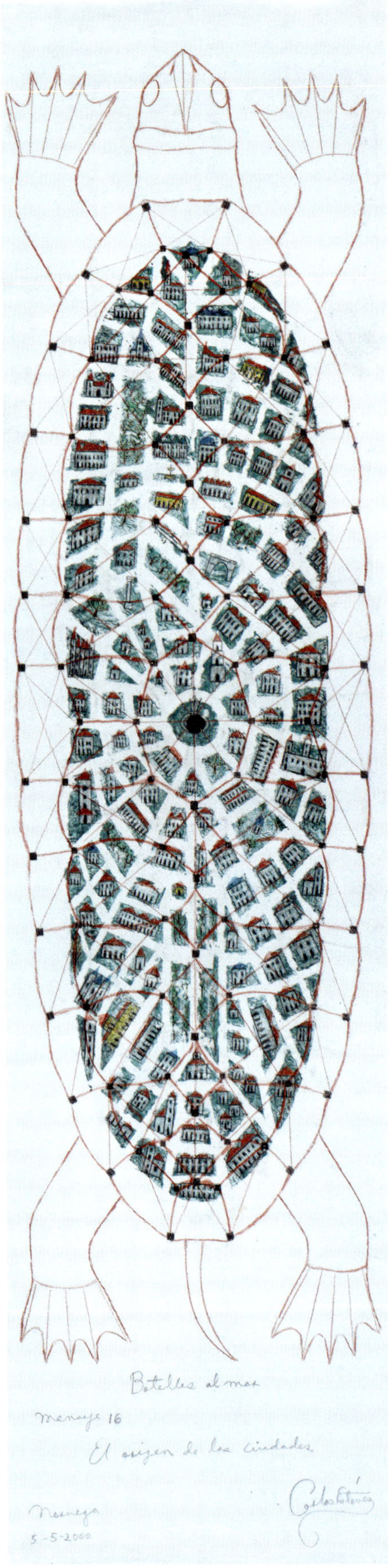

Bottles to the Sea
Message 16 "The Origin of Cities"
Norway 5-5-2000

Botellas al mar
Mensaje 16 "El origen de las ciudades"
Noruega 5-5-2000

Bottles to the Sea
Message 17 "*Cucullus non facit monachum*"
Norway 5-6-2000
Launched at Hull Gut Beach, Boston, Massachusetts, United States. 10-2-2002
Version of the original
Miami 8-14-2013

Botellas al mar
Mensaje 17 "Cucullus non facit monachum"
Noruega 6-5-2000
Lanzado en Hull Gut Beach, Boston, Massachusetts, Estados Unidos . 2-10-2002
Versión del original
Miami 14-8-2013

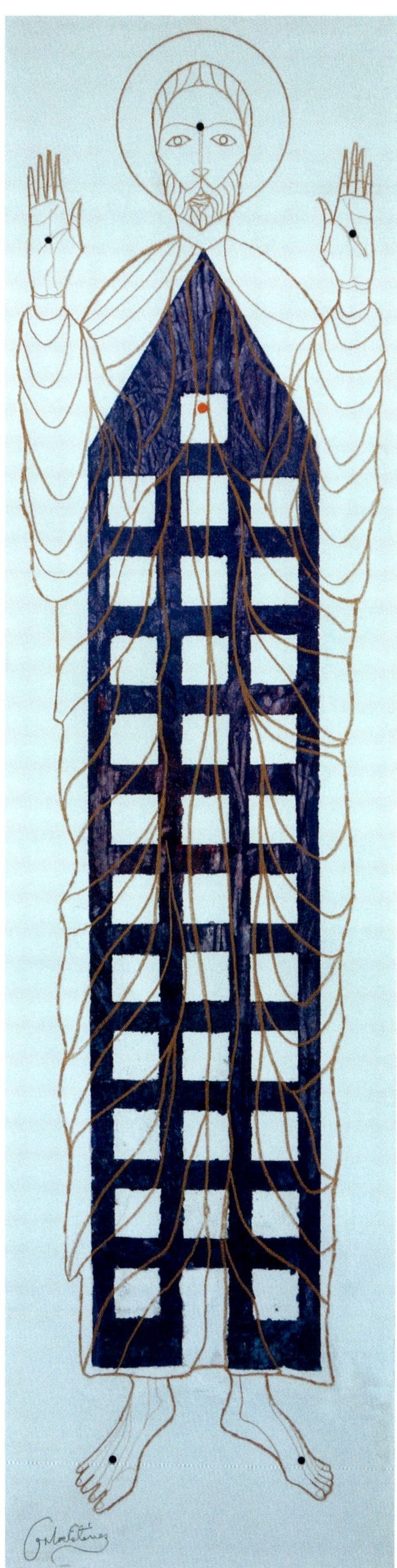

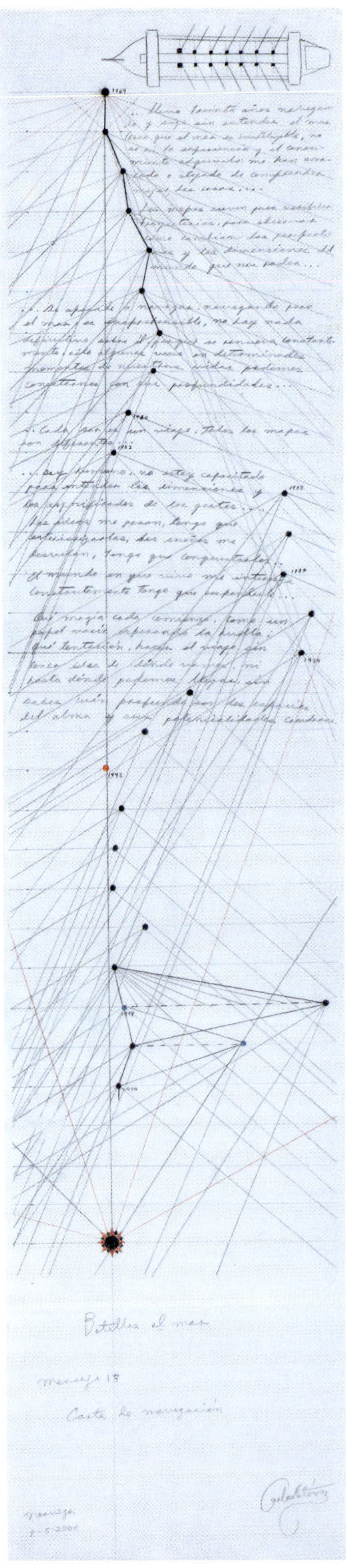

Bottles to the Sea
Message 18 "Navigation Chart"
Norway 5-8-2000

. . . I have spent 30 years sailing and still I do not understand the sea. I believe the sea is unintelligible, I do not know if the experience and the knowledge acquired has brought me closer or taken me further away from comprehending things better . . .

Maps serve to verify trajectories, to observe how perspectives change and the dimensions of the world that surrounds us . . .

. . . one learns to sail sailing but the sea is ungraspable, there is nothing definitive about it because it renews itself constantly. Only some times in determined moments of our lives are we able to connect with its profundities . . .

. . . every being is a voyage, all the maps are different . . .

. . . I am human, I am not qualified to understand the dimensions and meanings of gestures . . .

Ideas weigh on me, I have to exteriorize them; dreams keep me awake, I have to conquer them . . .

The world in which I live constantly questions me, I have to respond to it . . .

How magical each beginning, like an empty paper awaiting the mark: what a temptation, to make the voyage without having any idea where we are going, not even where we could arrive, without knowing how deep are the spaces of the soul and its creative potential.

Botellas al mar
Mensaje 18 "Carta de navegación"
Noruega 8-5-2000

. . . llevo 30 años navegando y sigo sin entender el mar. Creo que el mar es ininteligible, no sé si la experiencia y el conocimiento adquiridos me han acercado o alejado de comprender mejor las cosas . . .

Los mapas sirven para verificar trayectorias, para observar cómo cambian las perspectivas y las dimensiones del mundo que nos rodea . . .

. . . se aprende a navegar navegando pero el mar es inaprehensible, no hay nada definitivo sobre él porque se renueva constantemente. Sólo algunas veces en determinados momentos de nuestras vidas podemos conectarnos con sus profundidades . . .

. . . cada ser es un viaje, todos los mapas son diferentes . . .

. . . soy humano, no estoy capacitado para entender las dimensiones y los significados de los gestos . . .

Las ideas me pesan, tengo que exteriorizarlas; los sueños me desvelan, tengo que conquistarlos . . .

El mundo en que vivo me interroga constantemente, tengo que responderle . . .

Qué magia cada comienzo, como un papel vacío esperando la huella: que tentación, hacer el viaje sin tener idea de dónde vamos, ni hasta donde podemos llegar, sin saber cuan profundo son los espacios del alma y sus potencialidades creadoras.

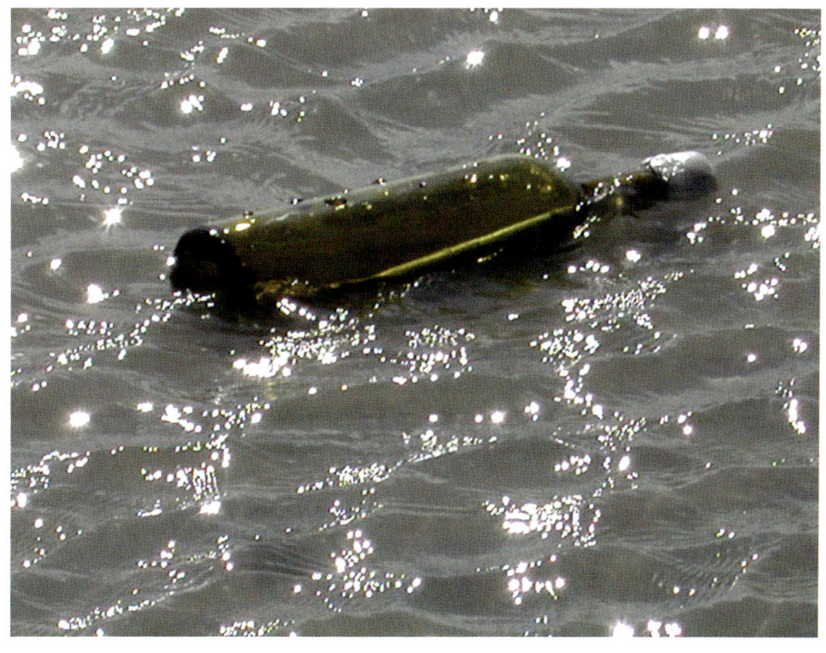

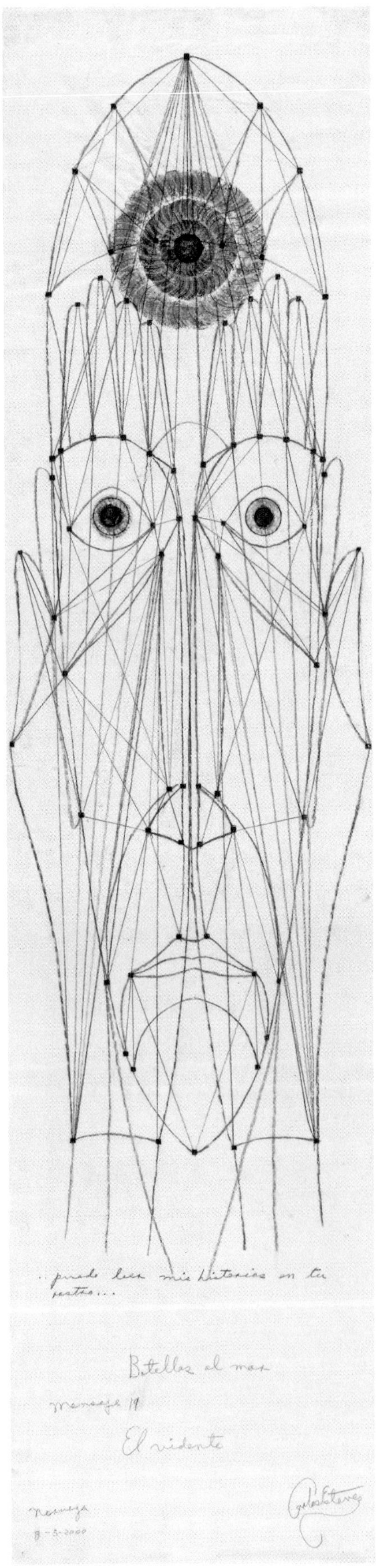

Bottles to the Sea
Message 19 "The Seer"
Norway 5-8-2000

. . . I can read my stories in your face . . .

Botellas al mar
Mensaje 19 "El vidente"
Noruega 8-5-2000

. . . puedo leer mis historias en tu rostro . . .

Bottles to the Sea
Message 20 "To Sail"
Norway 5-15-2000

To sail: to traverse the distances between life and death.

Botellas al mar
Mensaje 20 "Navegar"
Noruega 15-5-2000

Navegar: recorrer las distancias entre la vida y la muerte.

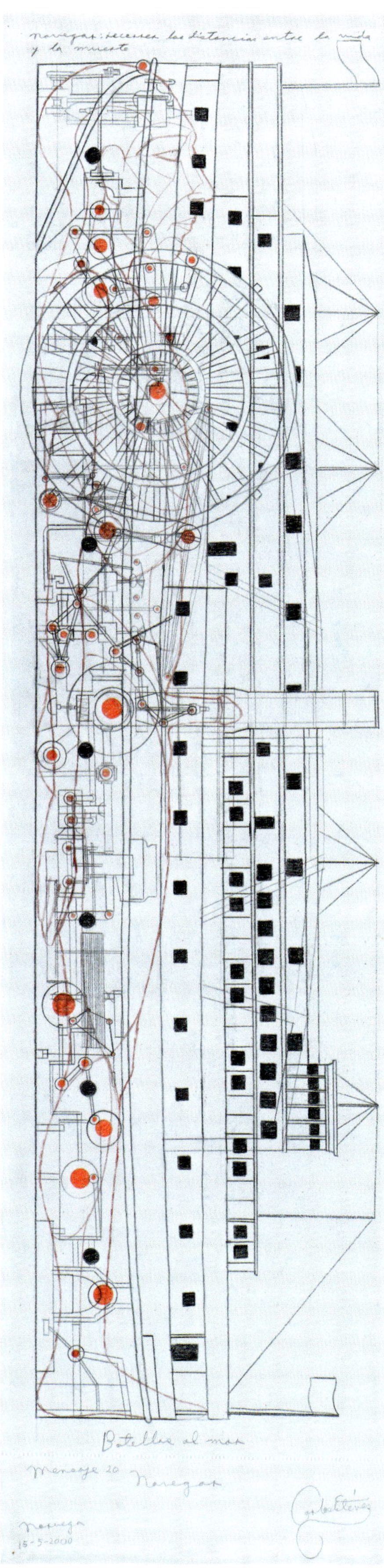

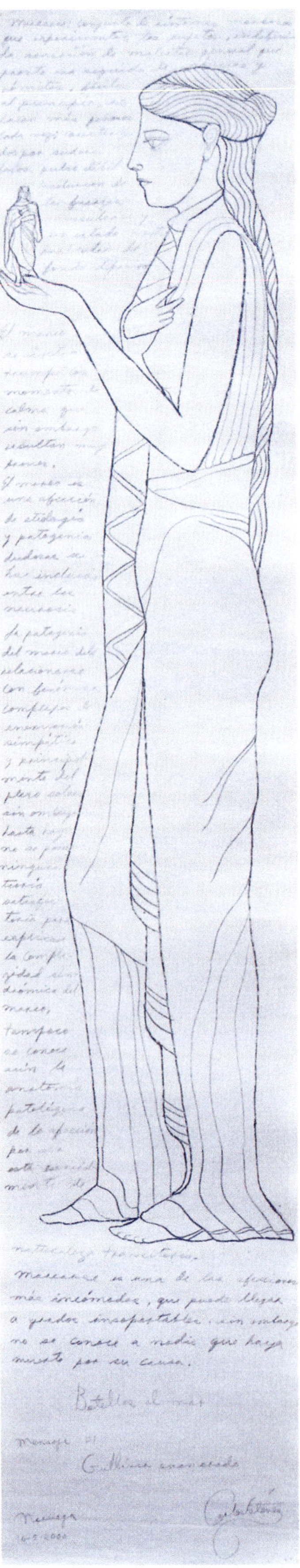

Bottles to the Sea
Message 21 "Gulliver in Love"
Norway 9-16-2000

To become seasick: set of morbid symptoms that subjects experience; undefined sensation of general malaise that is quickly followed by nausea and vomiting, light at the beginning, they become more difficult at the same time; characterized by cold sweats, weak pulse, dissolution of muscular strength and a particular mental state, depressive in essence.

Seasickness is interrupted by moments of calm, which nevertheless turn out to be very brief.

Seasickness is a disease of doubtful etiology and pathogenesis, it has been included among the neuroses.

The pathogenesis of seasickness should be related to complex phenomena of sympathetic enervation and principally of the solar plexus, nevertheless, even today we do not possess a satisfactory theory to explain the symptomatic complexity of seasickness, nor do we know the disease's pathological anatomy for its being essentially of a transitory nature.

To become seasick is one of the most uncomfortable diseases, which can reach intolerable levels. Nevertheless, no one is known to have died from it.

Botellas al mar
Mensaje 21 "Gulliver enamorado"
Noruega 16-9-2000

Marearse: conjunto de síntomas morbosos que experimentan los sujetos; indefinida sensación de malestar general que pronto va seguida de nauseas y vómitos, fáciles al principio, se hacen más penosos a la vez; caracterizados por sudores fríos, pulso débil, disolución de las fuerzas musculares y un estado mental particular de fondo depresivo.

El mareo se interrumpe con momentos de calma que sin embargo resultan muy breves.

El mareo es una afección de etiología y patogenia dudosas, se ha incluido entre las neurosis.

La patogenia del mareo debe relacionarse con fenómenos complejos de enervación simpática y principalmente del plexo solar, sin embargo hasta hoy no se posee ninguna teoría satisfactoria para explicar la complejidad sindrómica del mareo, tampoco se conoce aún la anotomía patológica de la afección por ser esta esencialmente de naturaleza transitoria.

Marearse es una de las afecciones más incómodas que puede llegar a grados insoportables. Sin embargo, no se conoce a nadie que haya muerto por su causa.

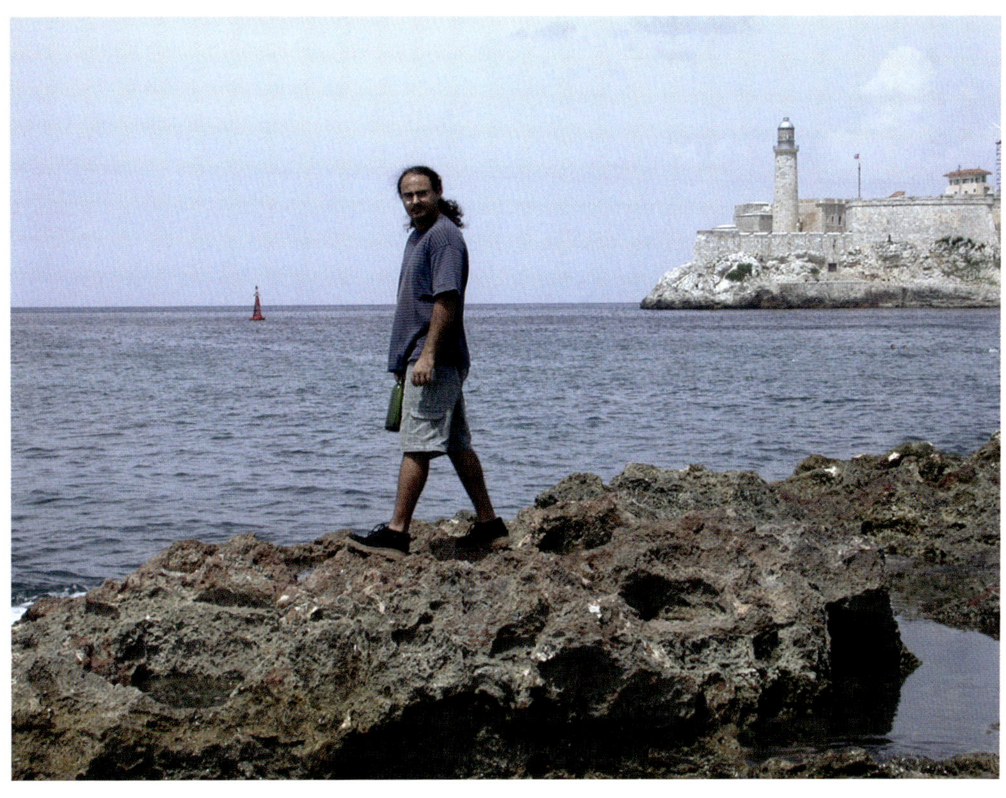

Bottles to the Sea
Message 22 "The Female Cyclops"
Norway 5-26-2000

When I saw her, I immediately thought about those gifts that life does not give, but which we always dream of receiving; for brief spaces of time, the imagination can accommodate everything in a very happy way, thus it was that the illusion clouded my senses, I was possessed by magic.

Perhaps it was the beginning of a great love story, thus becoming conscious of a possible future, I began premeditatedly to observe her.

. . . her feet were small and white, the contour of her legs was perfection itself, each line, each curve articulated itself with a delicacy that I believed only existed in tales about gods; her hips were wide and inspired a tender desire, she tried to cover her body with a fine cloth that very sensually allowed the accentuated chiaroscuros of the pubic triangle to be seen, my eyes never had a better excursion; it slid down her belly, I felt moving around her narrow waist without the necessity of changing my position; she gently moved her hands trying to hide her marvelous breasts, . . . I swallowed saliva, wet my lips instinctively upon seeing her precious pink nipples.

I ascended through the cleavage between her breasts, I rested on her clavicles next to the fall of her reddish hair, I imagined the smells of her neck, I thought about kisses while traversing her jaw, I softly rubbed together my fingers trying to reach, to imagine the texture of her lips, nature's great skill in achieving such variation of color as her nipples, I figured a triangle that became a rhombus, I imagined her sex . . . the skin of her face evinced an intense softness, drawing in the center a very fine nose, I imagined the best Eskimo kiss . . . finally came the moment reserved for finding the complement of such beauty, the moment of penetrating her soul through the expression of her gaze . . . I was blinded by love, and I launched myself in search of the grand end of the new beginning. When suddenly, an overwhelming blow against the solid wall of conventions stopped me: the enchantment vanished as if by magic, upon noticing that she had only one eye in the center of her face.

Botellas al mar
Mensaje 22 "La cíclope"
Noruega 26-5-2000

Cuando la vi, enseguida pensé en esos regalos que la vida no da, pero que siempre soñamos recibir; la imaginación puede por algunos breves espacios de tiempo acomodarlo todo de una forma muy feliz, así fue como la ilusión nubló mis sentidos, fui poseído por la magia.

Quizás era el principio de una gran historia de amor, así que tomando conciencia del posible futuro, comencé premeditadamente a observarla.

. . . sus pies eran pequeños y blancos, el dibujo de sus piernas era la perfección misma, cada línea, cada curva se articulaba entre sí con una delicadeza que creía solo existía en las historias sobre dioses; sus caderas eran anchas e inspiraban un tierno deseo, trataba de cubrir su cuerpo con un fino paño que transparentaba muy sensualmente los claroscuros acentuados en el triángulo pubiano, nunca mis ojos tuvieron mejor paseo; se deslizó por su vientre, sentí recorrer su estrecha cintura sin necesidad de cambiar mi posición; ella movía con suavidad sus manos tratando de ocultar sus maravillosos senos, . . . tragué saliva, humedecí mis labios instintivamente al ver sus preciosos pezones rosados.

Ascendí por la canal entre sus pechos, reposé en sus clavículas junto a la caída de su pelo de color rojizo, imaginé los olores de su cuello, pensé en besos al recorrer su mandíbula, froté suavemente mis dedos tratando de alcanzar, de imaginar la textura de sus labios, gran pericia de la naturaleza al lograr semejante variación de color de los pezones, me figuré un triángulo que se convirtió en un rombo, imaginé su sexo . . . la piel de su cara traslucía una suavidad intensa, dibujando en el centro una nariz muy fina, imaginé el mejor de los besos esquimales . . . al fin llegó el momento reservado de encontrar el complemento de tanta belleza, el momento de penetrar en su alma a través de la expresión de su mirada . . . me cegué de amor, y me lancé en busca del gran final del nuevo comienzo. Cuando de pronto un golpe contundente contra el sólido muro de las convenciones me detuvo: la magia se esfumó como por arte de magia, al notar que solo tenía un ojo en centro de su rostro.

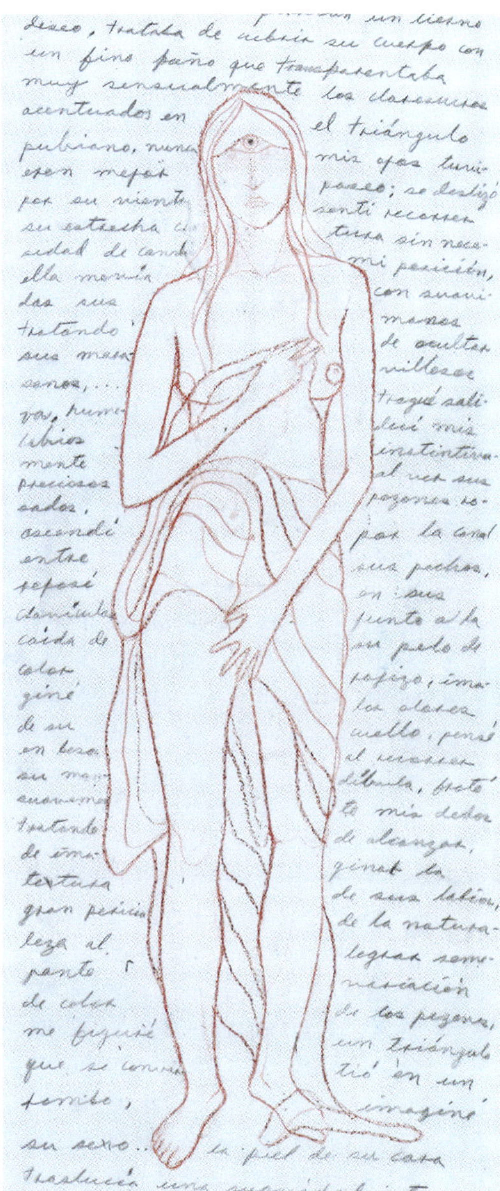

detail, Message 22

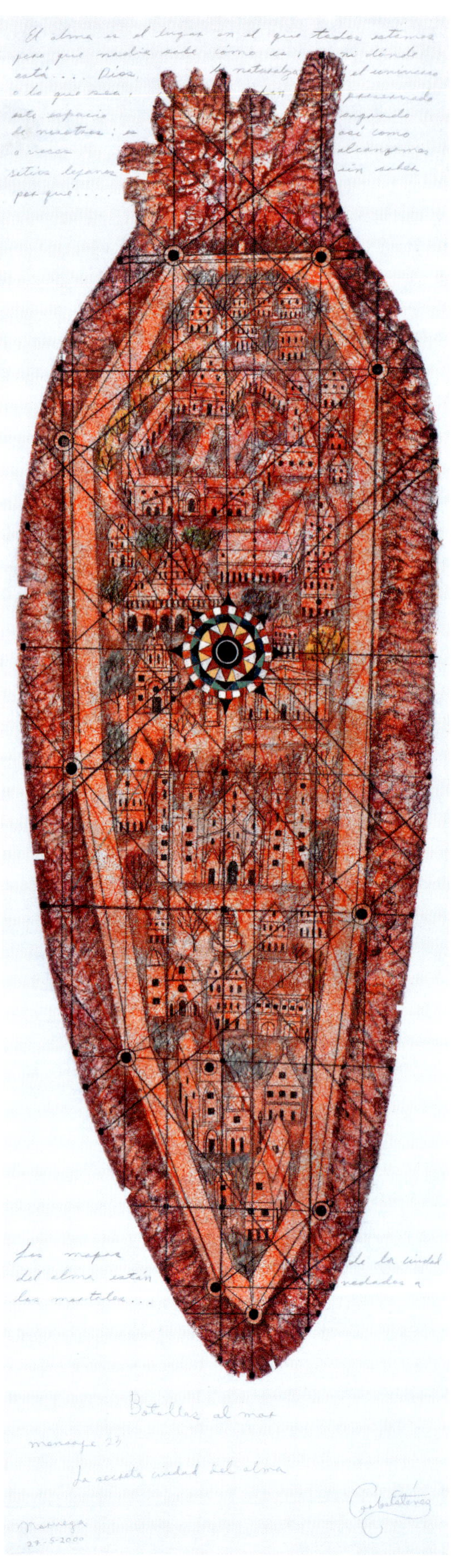

Bottles to the Sea
Message 23 "The Secret City of the Soul"
Norway 5-27-2000

The soul is the place in which we all are but which no one knows as it is, nor where it is . . . God, nature, the universe, or whatever, have preserved this sacred space from us; this is how we sometimes reach distant places without knowing why . . .

The maps of the city of the soul are forbidden to mortals . . .

Botellas al mar
Mensaje 23 "La secreta ciudad del alma"
Noruega 27-5-2000

El alma es el lugar en el que todos estamos pero que nadie sabe como es, ni dónde está . . . Dios, la naturaleza, el universo, o lo que sea, han preservado este espacio sagrado de nosotros; es así como a veces alcanzamos sitios lejanos sin saber por qué . . .

Los mapas de la ciudad del alma están vedados a los mortales . . .

Bottles to the Sea
Message 24 "The World is a Description of the Soul"
Norway 5-28-2000

Feelings: surface, preferably solid, upon which constructions are realized. Foundation of life, invisible spaces where the structures of love and other manifestations of human relations rest and establish themselves. Places beneath the earth to keep secrets. Barely secure way to calculate distances by observation.

Botellas al mar
Mensaje 24 "El mundo es una descripción del alma"
Noruega 28-5-2000

Sentimientos: superficie, preferentemente sólida, sobre la cual se realizan construcciones. Base de la vida, espacios invisibles dónde reposan y se erigen las estructuras del amor y otras manifestaciones de las relaciones humanas. Lugares debajo de la tierra para guardar secretos. Recurso poco seguro para calcular distancias a partir de la observación.

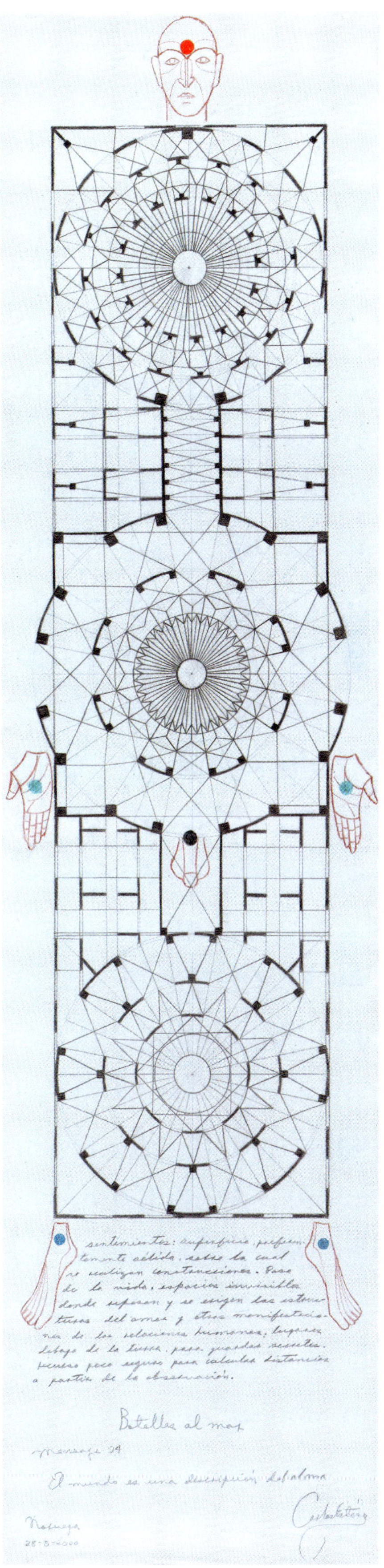

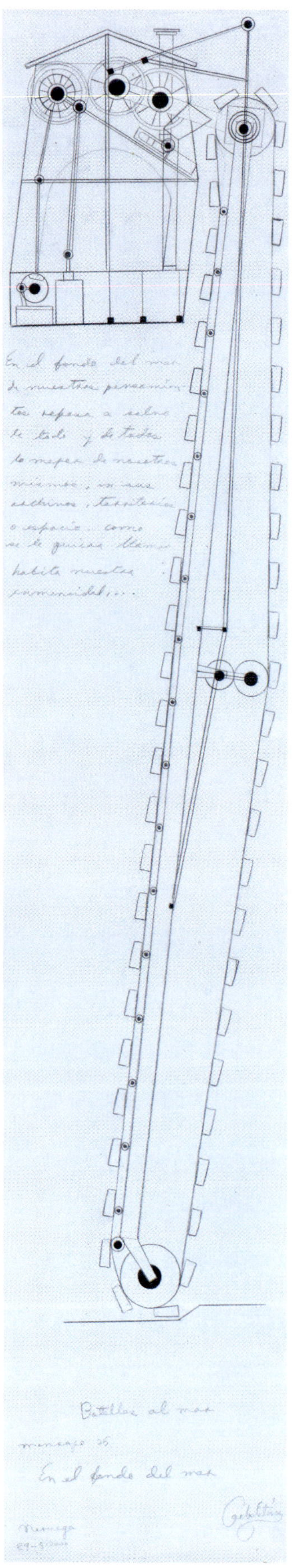

Bottles to the Sea
Message 25 "At the Bottom of the Sea"
Norway 5-29-2000

At the bottom of the sea of our thoughts rest, saved from everything and everyone, the best of ourselves; in their archives, territories or spaces, however one wants to call them, lives our immensity . . .

Botellas al mar
Mensaje 25 "En el fondo del mar"
Noruega 29-5-2000

En el fondo del mar de nuestros pensamientos reposa a salvo de todo y de todos lo mejor de nosotros mismos, en sus archivos, territorios o espacios, como se le quiera llamar, habita nuestra inmensidad . . .

Bottles to the Sea
Message 26 "*Novem cephalus*"
Norway 5-31-2000

Novem cephalus: Creature with nine heads and a single body, each head with total autonomy over the cerebral functions and other organs of sense, that is to say, nine forms of thought, of feeling, of dreaming, etc. The adaptation to the environment of this class of phenomenon is extremely slow and difficult; owing to the fragility of the heart, because of the excessive work, very few make it past the first years of life, and those that do make it pass to the second much more difficult phase of intellectual cohabitation. One is capable of cohabitating with one's own miseries but it is so difficult to accept those of the others. No one knows of any nine heads that has done it, they die of intolerance as soon as they begin the so-called period of immaturity.

Botellas al mar
Mensaje 26 "Novem cephalus"
Noruega 31-5-2000

Novem cephalus: Criatura de nueve cabezas y un solo cuerpo, cada cabeza con autonomía total en cuanto a las funciones cerebrales y demás órganos de los sentidos, es decir, nueve formas de pensamiento, de sentir, de soñar, etc. La adaptación del medio de esta clase de fenómeno es extremadamente lenta y difícil, debido a la fragilidad del corazón por el exceso de trabajo muy pocos sobrepasan los primeros años de vida, y los que lo logran pasan a una segunda fase mucho más difícil que es la convivencia intelectual. Uno es capaz de convivir con sus miserias pero es tan difícil aceptar las de los demás. No se conoce a ningún nueve cabezas que lo haya logrado, mueren de intolerancia inmediatamente que comienzan el llamado período de inmadurez.

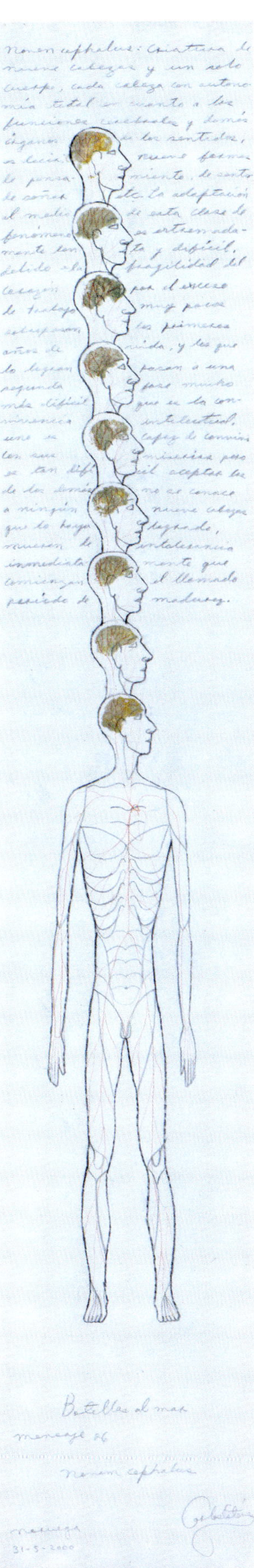

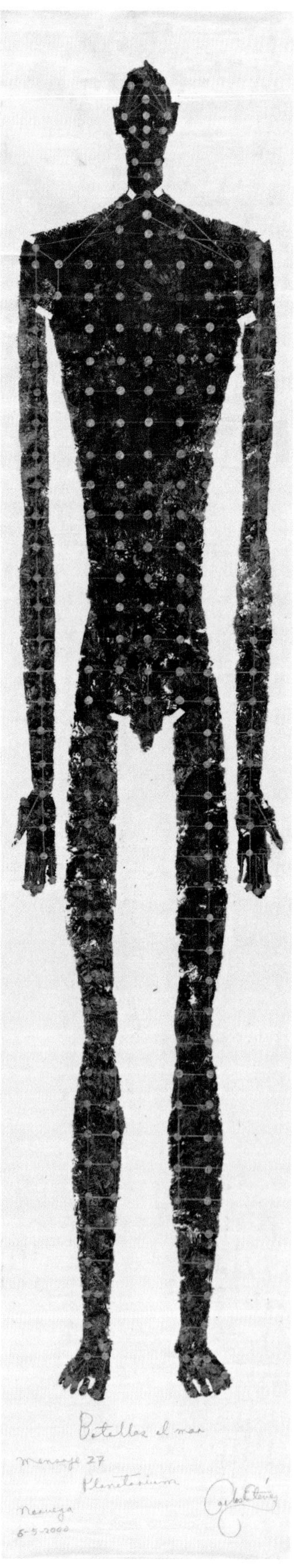

Bottles to the Sea
Message 27 “Planetarium”
Havana 9-16-2000
Launched at the Rhine, Basel,
Switzerland. 8-27-2003

Botellas al mar
Mensaje 27 “Planetarium”
La Habana 16-9-2000
Lanzado en el Río Rin, Basilea, Suiza.
27-8-2003

Bottles to the Sea
Message 28 "Some Notes on the World of Insects"
Norway 6-1-2000

Botellas al mar
Mensaje 28 "Algunas notas sobre el mundo de los insectos"
Noruega 1-6-2000

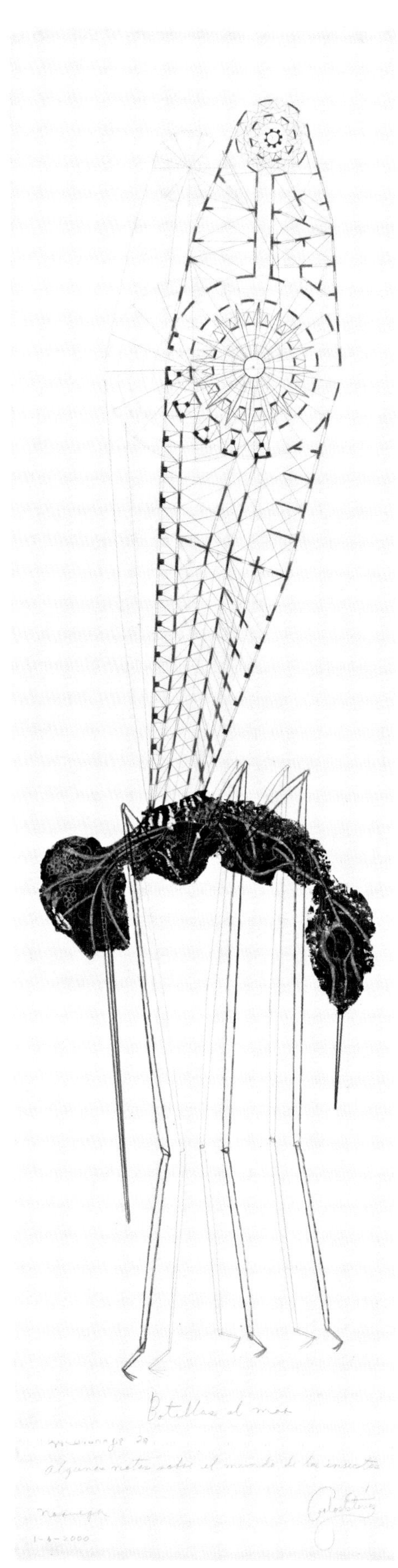

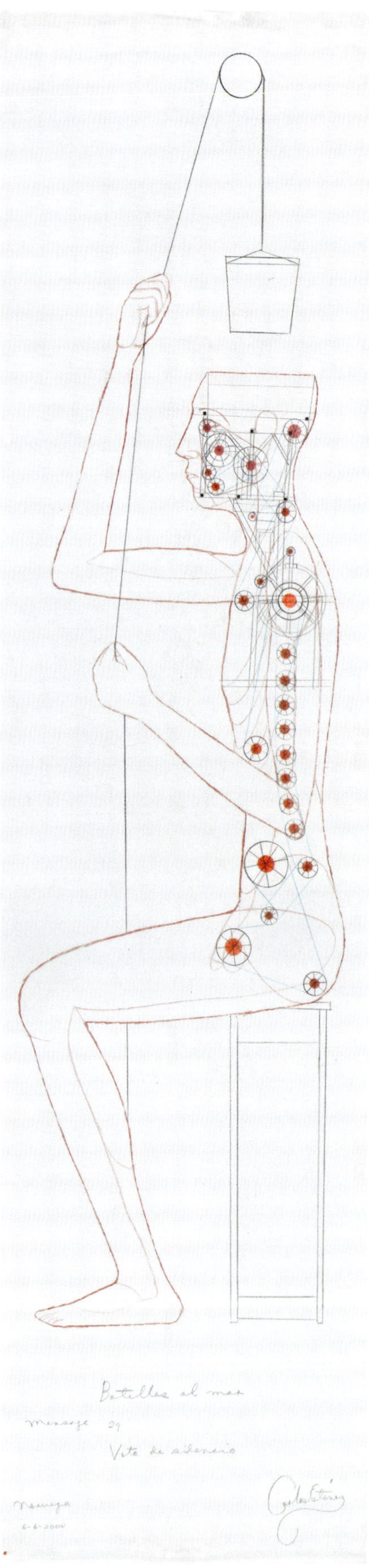

Bottles to the Sea
Message 29 "Vow of Silence"
Norway 6-6-2000

Botellas al mar
Mensaje 29 "Voto de silencio"
Noruega 6-6-2000

Bottles to the Sea
Message 30 "*Sero sevi satum*"
Norway 6-6-2000

Botellas al mar
Mensaje 30 "Sero sevi satum"
Noruega 6-6-2000

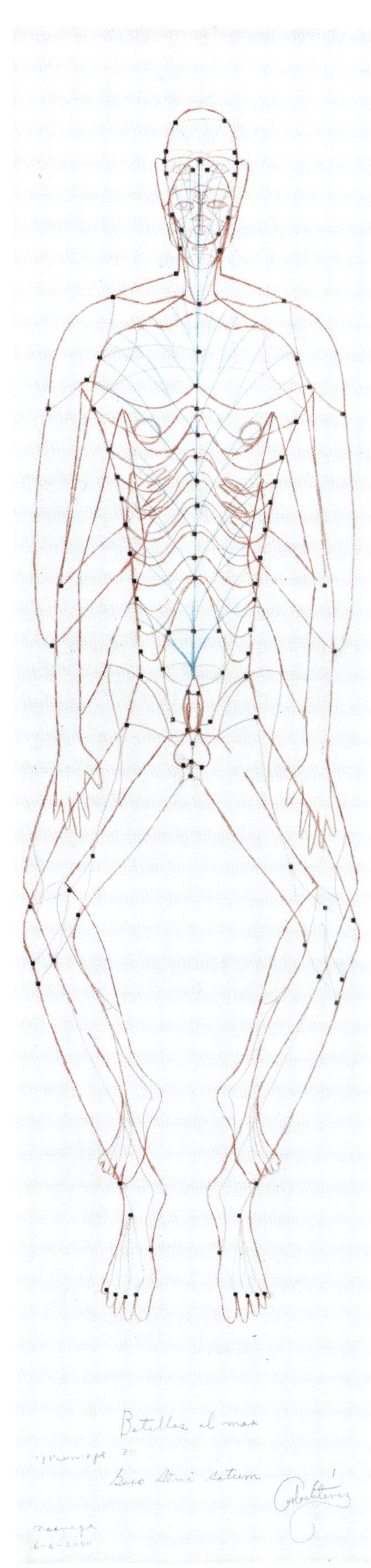

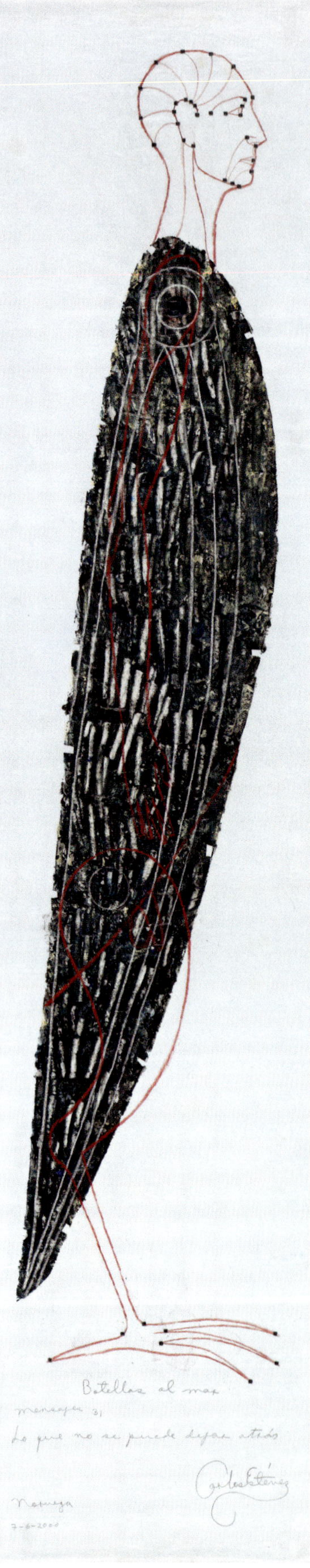

Bottles to the Sea
Message 31 "What Cannot Be Left Behind"
Norway 6-7-2000

Botellas al mar
Mensaje 31 "Lo que no se puede dejar atrás"
Noruega 7-6-2000

Bottles to the Sea
Message 32 "The Spirit of the Night"
Norway 6-7-2000

Night: mood of unknown origin that connects us to the most profound spaces of the universe, it has neither space nor time to appear. Emergency exit, union of two edges, a certain type of transportation for traveling from one day to the other. Party of the stars.

Botellas al mar
Mensaje 32 "El espíritu de la noche"
Noruega 7-6-2000

Noche: estado anímico de procedencia desconocida que nos conecta con los espacios más profundos del universo, no tiene ni espacio ni tiempo para aparecer. Salida de emergencia, unión entre dos orillas, cierto tipo de transporte para viajar de un día al otro. Fiesta de las estrellas.

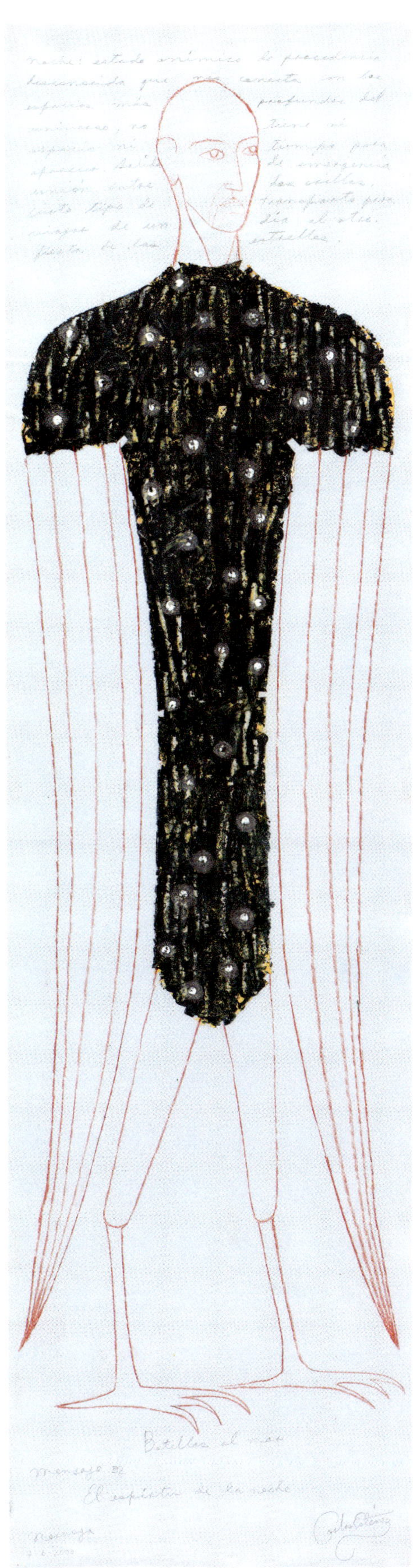

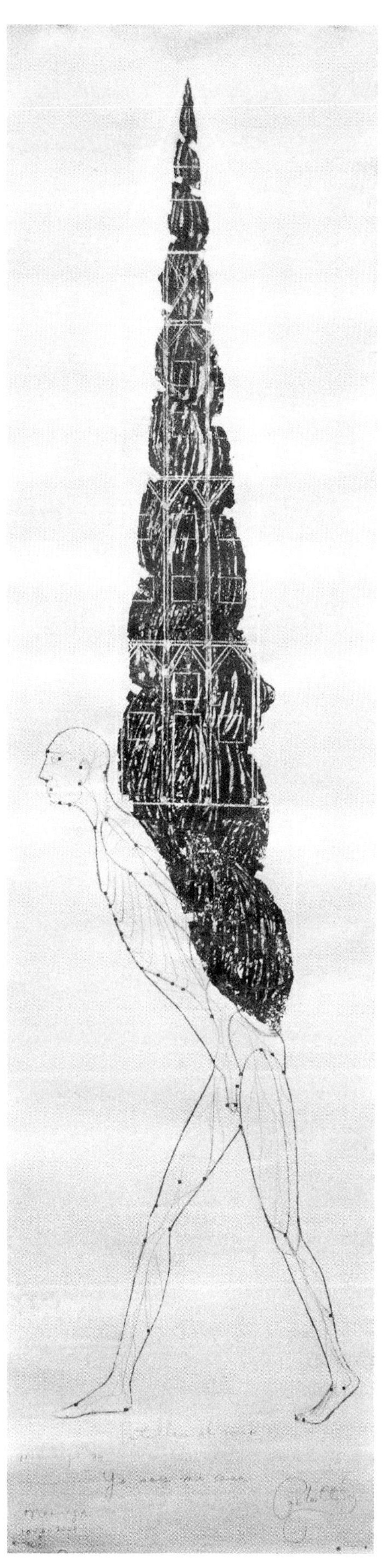

Bottles to the Sea
Message 33 "I Am My House"
Norway 6-10-2000
Launched at Lido, Venice, Italy. 6-19-2006

Botellas al mar
Mensaje 33 "Yo soy mi casa"
Noruega 10-6-2000
Lanzado en la Isla de Lido, Venecia, Italia.
19-6-2006

Bottles to the Sea
Message 34 "The Election"
Norway 6-12-2000
Launched at Le Havre, Normandy, France.
6-19-2004

Botellas al mar
Mensaje 34 "La elección"
Noruega 12-6-2000
Lanzado en Le Havre, Normandía,
Francia. 19-6-2004

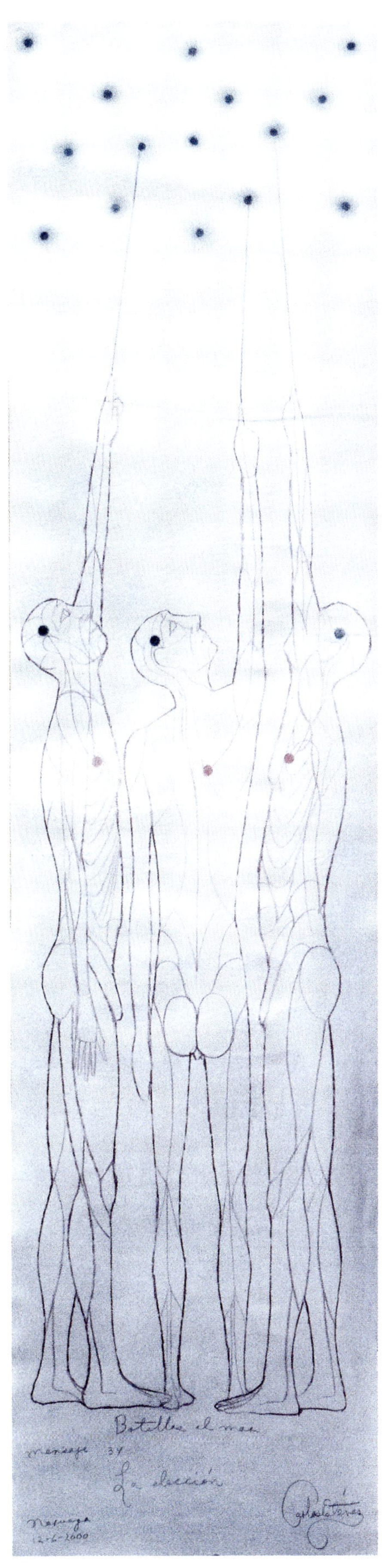

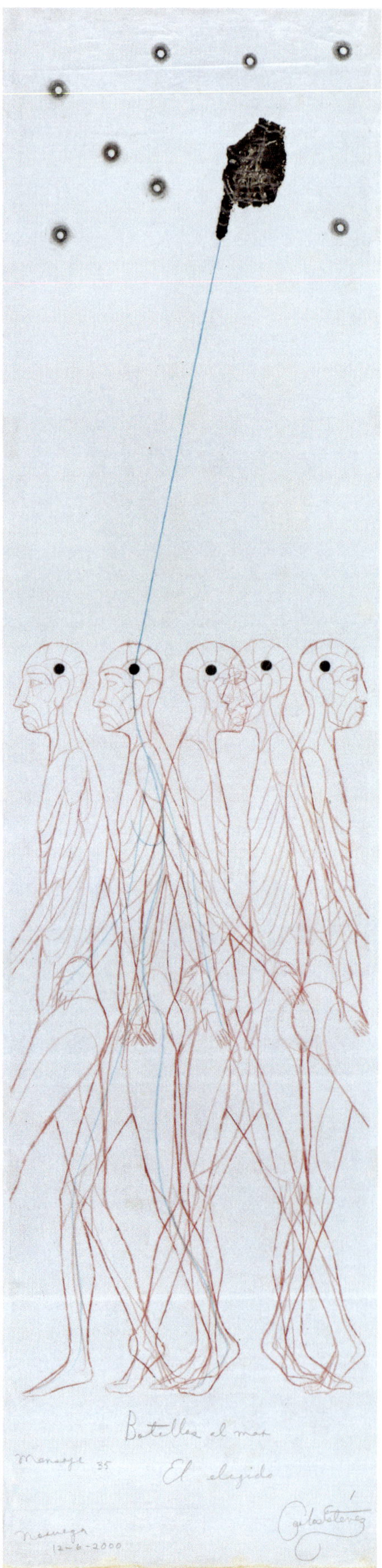

Bottles to the Sea
Message 35 "The Chosen One"
Norway 6-12-2000

Botellas al mar
Mensaje 35 "El elegido"
Noruega 12-6-2000

Bottles to the Sea
Message 36 "The Invention of Destiny"
Norway 6-12-2000

Botellas al mar
Mensaje 36 "La invención del destino"
Noruega 12-6-2000

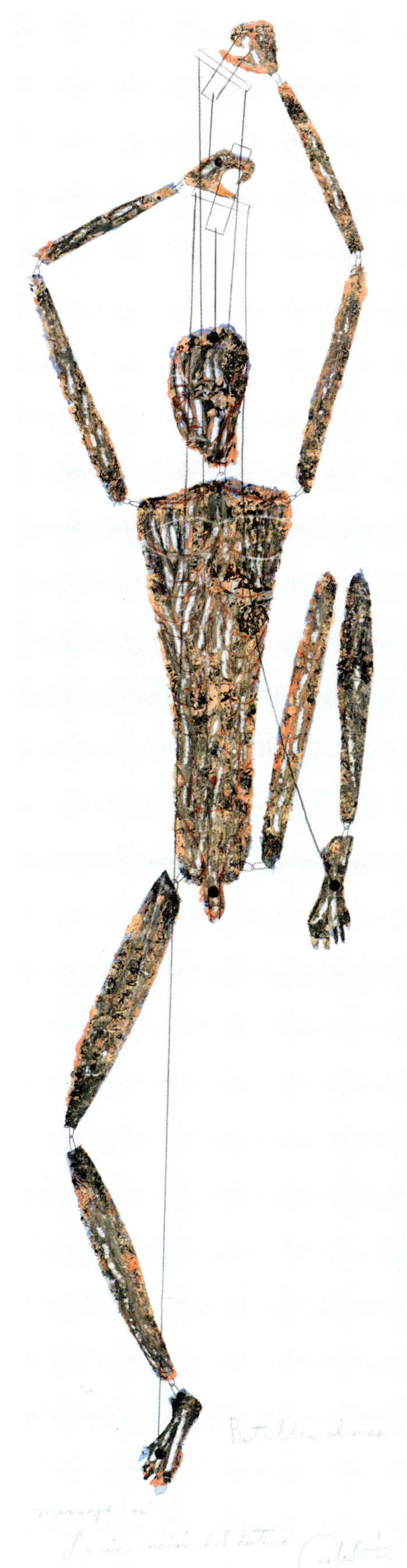

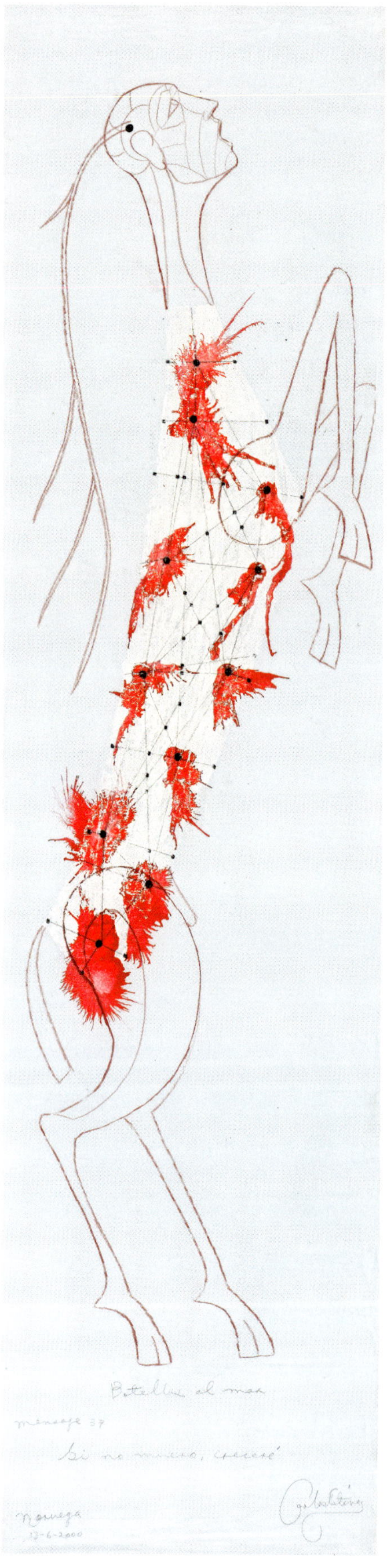

Bottles to the Sea
Message 37 "If I Don't Die, I Will Grow"
Norway 6-13-2000

Botellas al mar
Mensaje 37 "Si no muero, creceré"
Noruega 13-6-2000

Bottles to the Sea
Message 38 "The Rain of the Soul"
Norway 6-13-2000

Botellas al mar
Mensaje 38 "La lluvia del alma"
Noruega 13-6-2000

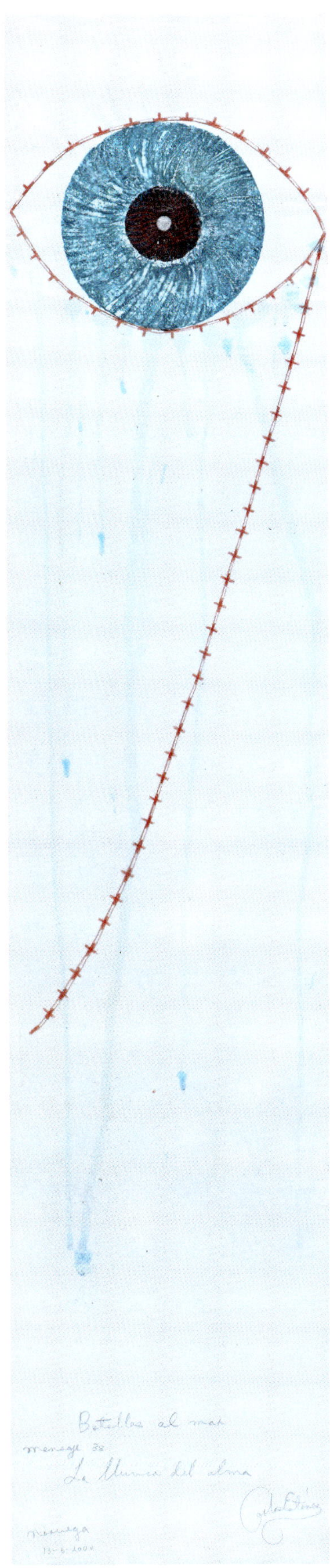

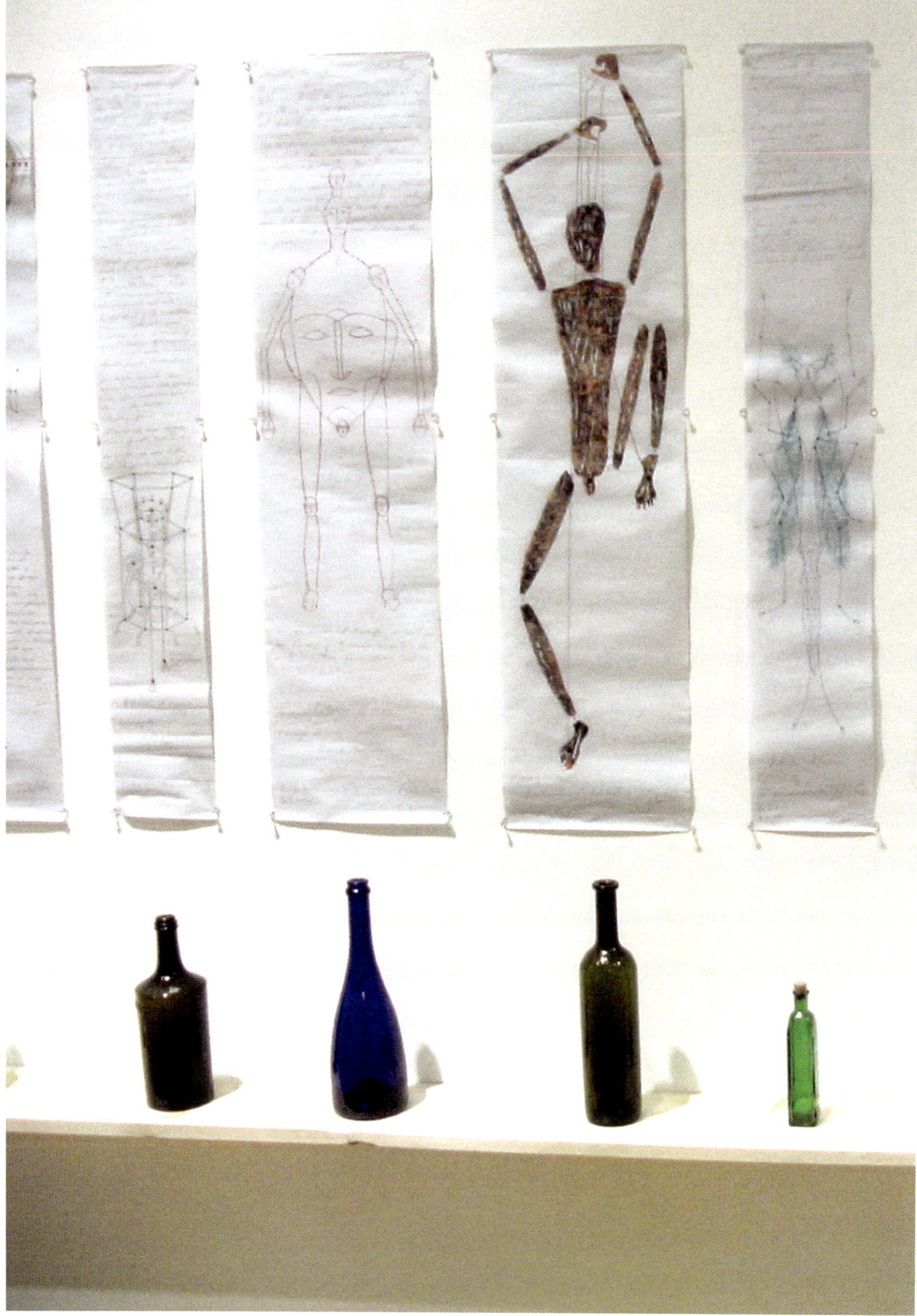

Bottles to the Sea
Message 39 "Autumn Leaves"
Norway 6-14-2000

Botellas al mar
Mensaje 39 "Hojas de otoño"
Noruega 14-6-2000

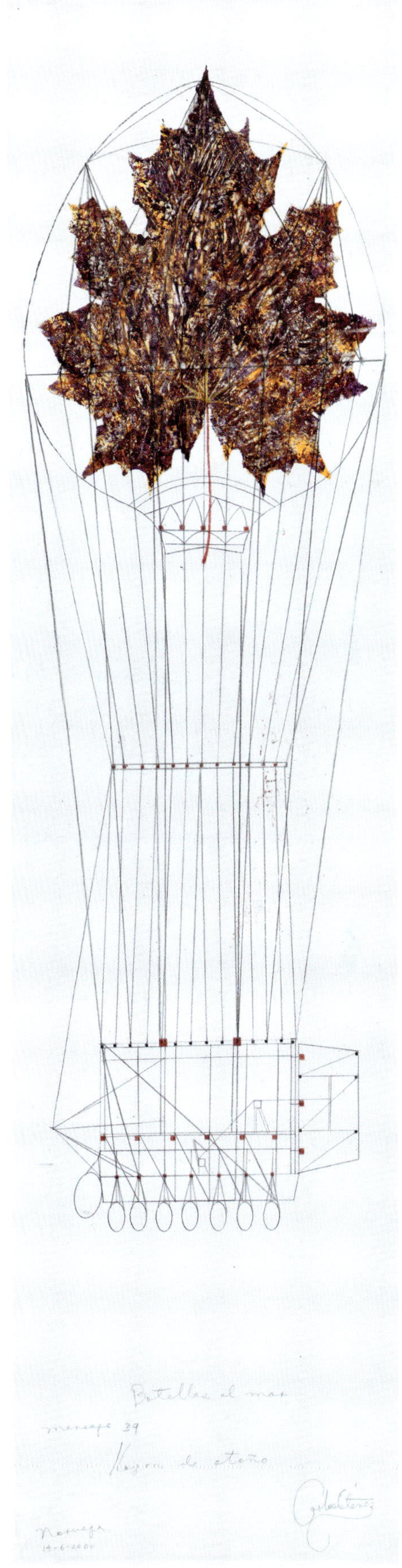

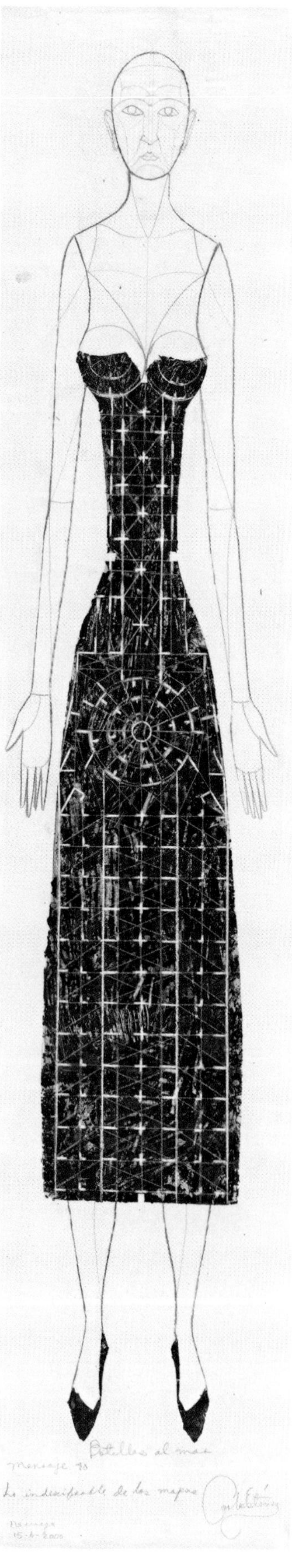

Bottles to the Sea
Message 40 "The Indescribable of Maps"
Norway 6-15-2000

Botellas al mar
Mensaje 40 "Lo indescriptible de los mapas"
Noruega 15-6-2000

Bottles to the Sea
Message 41 "Calculating Distances"
Norway 6-16-2000

Botellas al mar
Mensaje 41 "Calculando distancias"
Noruega 16-6-2000

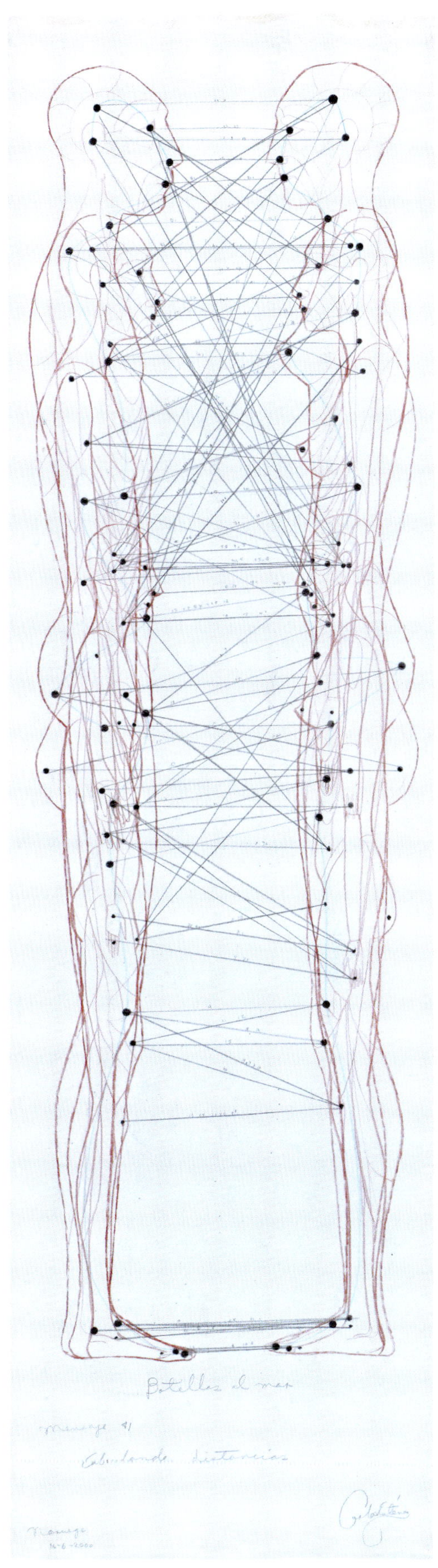

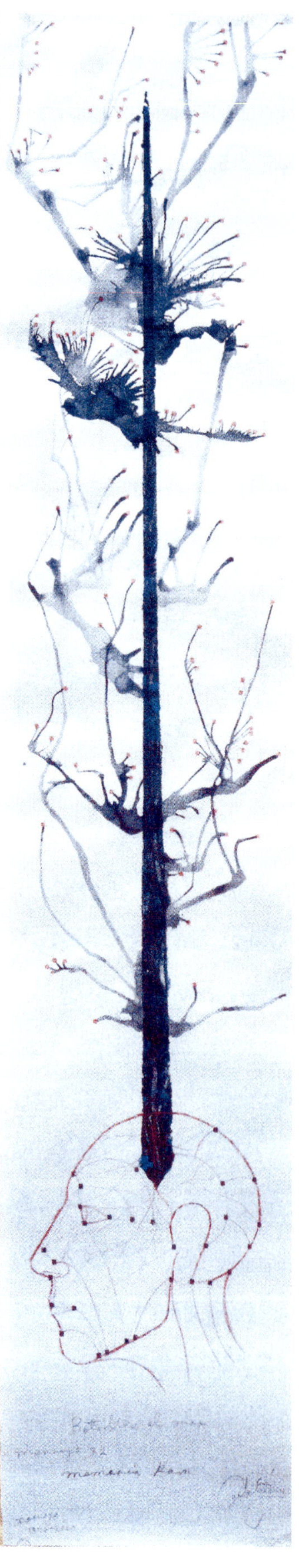

Bottles to the Sea
Message 42 "RAM Memory"
Norway 6-18-2000
Launched at Salvador de Bahia, Brazil.
2-2-2003

Botellas al mar
Mensaje 42 "Memoria RAM"
Noruega 18-6-2000
Lanzado en Salvador de Bahía, Brasil.
2-2-2003

Bottles to the Sea
Message 43 "The Invention of the Constellations"
Havana 9-1-2000

Life is like a mirage, we live in a fog that preserves us, the one who is able to escape from it to the light, will be instantly struck blind . . .

. . . perhaps in the passage of time, in the imperceptible movement of the stars, when this world among many others has been erased, the blurry silhouette of a man would remain in some hidden space. . .

I have spent my life asking myself the same things and I have never obtained definitive answers, perhaps the definitive is silence, the possibility that everything could happen, because our lives are like drawings in the air, without possible errors, without more pretension than that of a gesture in the universe . . .

Botellas al mar
Mensaje 43 "La invención de las constelaciones"
Havana 1-9-2000

La vida es como un espejismo, vivimos en una niebla que nos conserva, el que logre salir de ella a la luz, quedará ciego al instante . . .

. . .quizás al paso del tiempo, en el imperceptible movimiento de los astros, cuando se haya borrado este mundo entre tantos, quede en algún escondido espacio, la borrosa silueta de un hombre . . .

Me he pasado la vida preguntándome las mismas cosas y nunca he obtenido respuestas definitivas, quizás lo definitivo sea el silencio, el infinito, la posibilidad de que todo pueda ocurrir, porque nuestras vidas son como dibujos en el aire, sin errores posibles, sin más pretensión que el de un gesto en el universo . . .

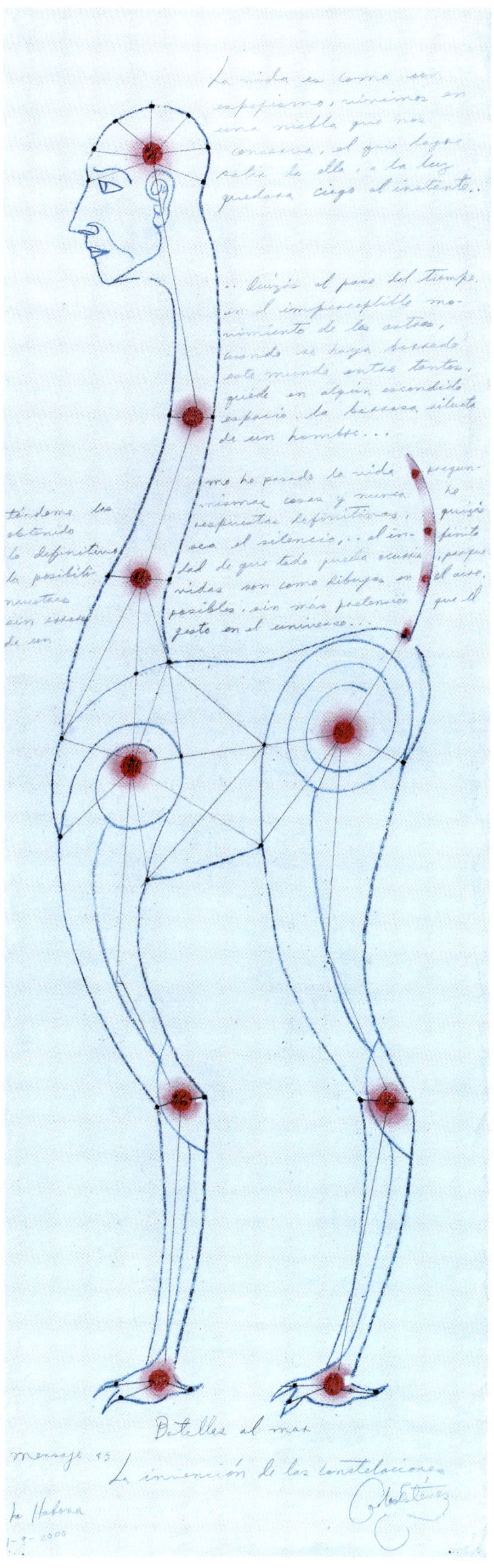

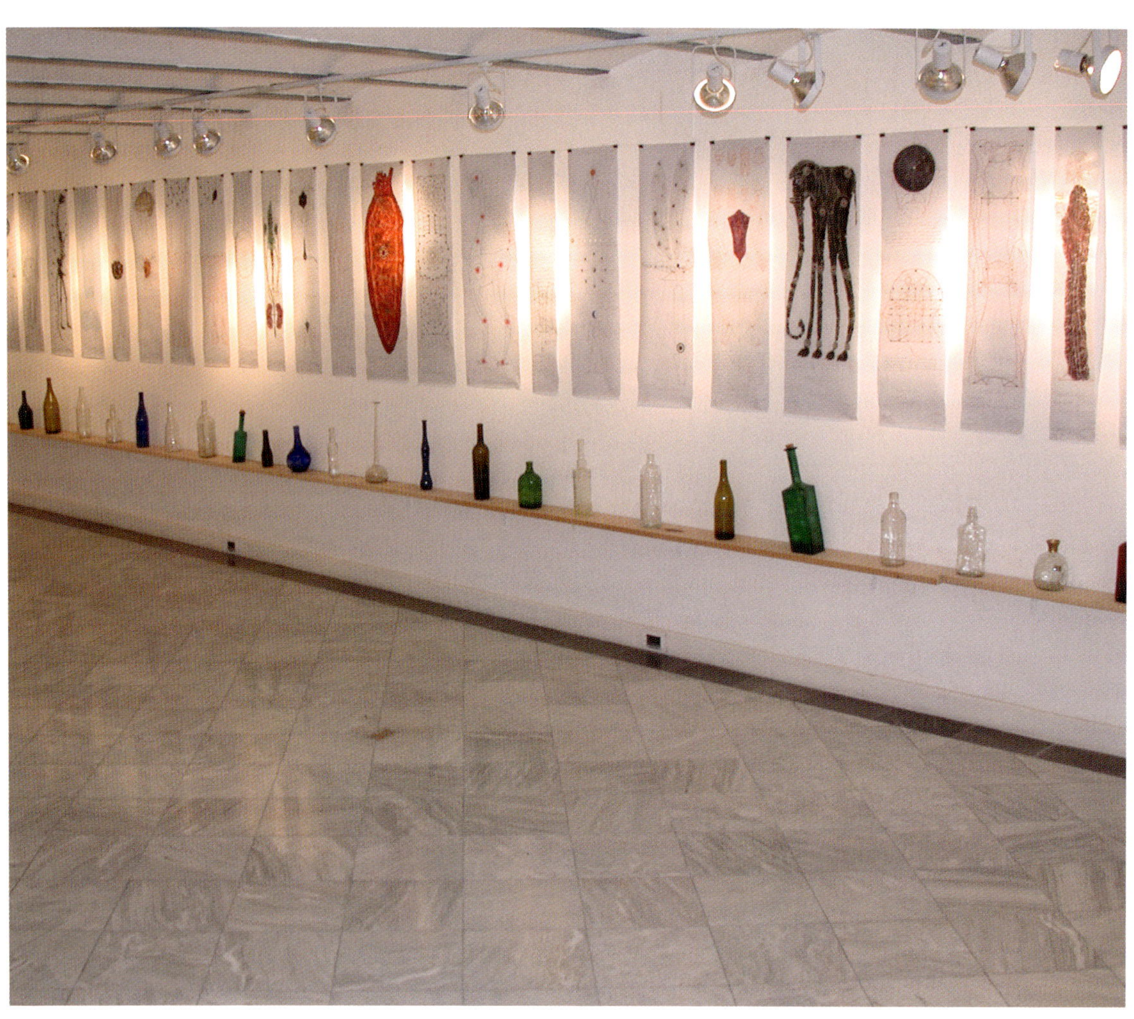

Bottles to the Sea
Message 44 "*Vestigium sacrum*"
Havana 9-2-2000

. . . Each of our marks made in the course of life is as insignificant and, at the same time, as relevant as the movement of the stars . . .

. . . I know that you are always with me despite the fact I cannot see you . . .

Botellas al mar
Mensaje 44 "Vestigium sacrum"
La Habana 2-9-2000

. . . Cada marca nuestra hecha en el camino de la vida es tan insignificante y a la vez tan relevante como el movimiento de los astros . . .

. . . Sé que estás conmigo siempre aunque no pueda verte . . .

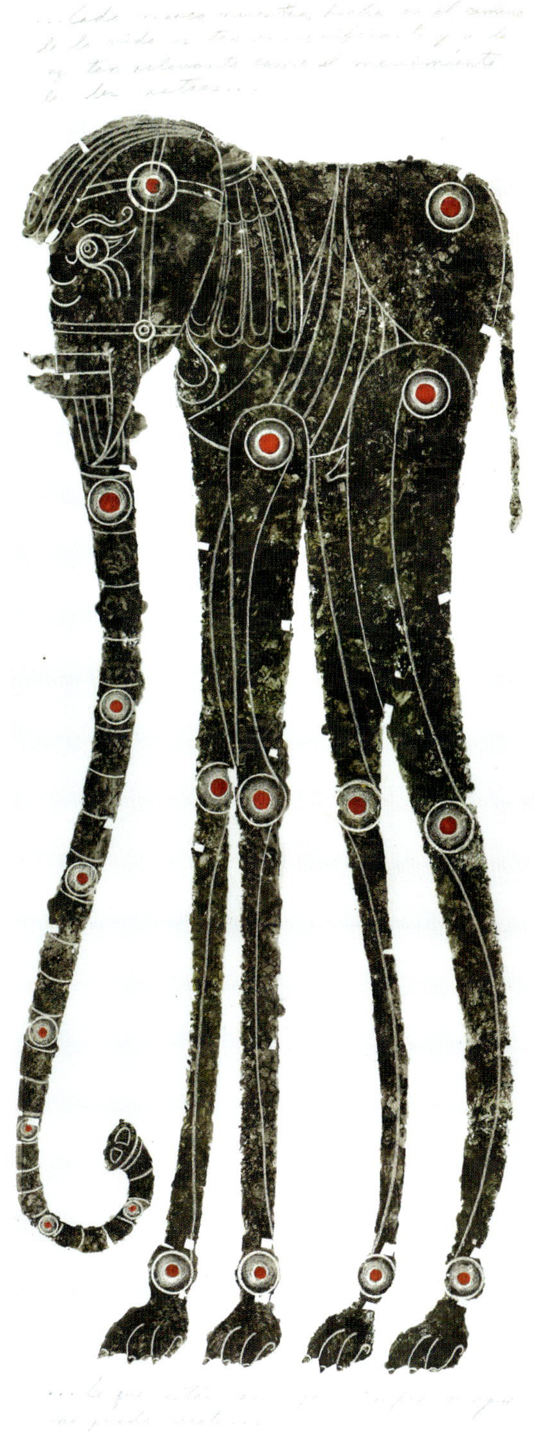

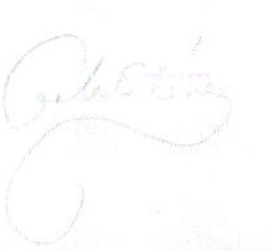

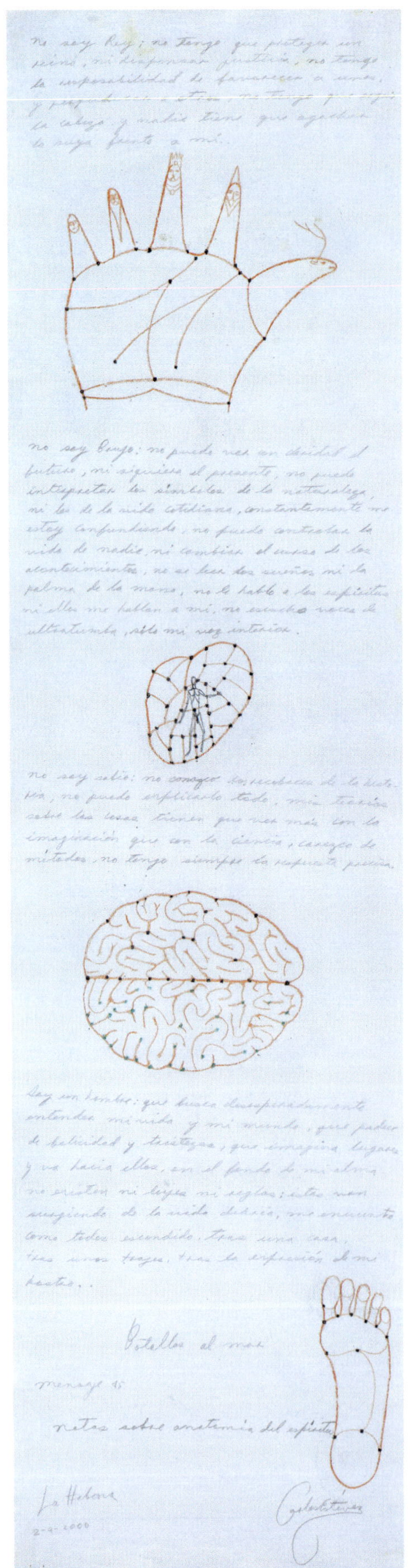

Bottles to the Sea
Message 45 "Notes on the Anatomy of Spirit"
Havana 9-2-2000

I am not King: I do not have to protect a kingdom, nor dispense justice, I do not have the responsibility of favoring some and harming others, I do not have to raise my head, and no one has to lower theirs before me.

I am not a Wizard: I cannot see the future clearly, nor even the present. I cannot interpret the symbols of nature, nor those of everyday life. I am constantly becoming confused, I cannot control anyone's life, nor change the course of events. I do not know how to read dreams, nor the palm of the hand; I do not speak to spirits, nor they to me, I do not listen to voices from beyond the tomb, only my inner voice.

I am not a Wise man: I do not know the ruses of history, I cannot explain everything. My theories about things have more to do with the imagination than with science, I lack methods, I do not always have the precise answer.

I am a man, who desperately seeks to understand my life and my world; who suffers from happiness and sadnesses, who imagines places and goes toward them. At the bottom of my soul there exist neither laws nor rules; these arise from daily life, I find myself like others, hidden, behind a house, behind some suits, behind the expression of my face.

Botellas al mar
Mensaje 45 "Notas sobre anatomía del espíritu"
La Habana 2-9-2000

No soy Rey: no tengo que proteger un reino, ni dispensar justicia, no tengo la responsabilidad de favorecer a unos y perjudicar a otros, no tengo que erguir la cabeza y nadie tiene que agachar la suya ante mí.

No soy Brujo: no puedo ver con claridad el futuro, ni siquiera el presente. No puedo interpretar los símbolos de la naturaleza, ni los de la vida cotidiana. Constantemente me estoy confundiendo, no puedo controlar la vida de nadie, ni cambiar el curso de los acontecimientos. No sé leer los sueños, ni la palma de la mano; no le hablo a los espíritus ni ellos me hablan a mí, no escucho voces de ultratumba, sólo mi voz interior.

No soy Sabio: no conozco los recovecos de la historia, no puedo explicarlo todo. Mis teorías sobre las cosas tienen que ver más con la imaginación que con la ciencia, carezco de métodos, no tengo siempre la respuesta precisa.

Soy un hombre que busca desesperadamente entender mi vida y mi mundo; que padece de felicidad y tristezas, que imagina lugares y va hacia ellos. En el fondo de mi alma no existen ni leyes ni reglas; estas van surgiendo de la vida diaria, me encuentro como todos, escondido, tras una casa, tras unos trajes, tras la expresión de mi rostro.

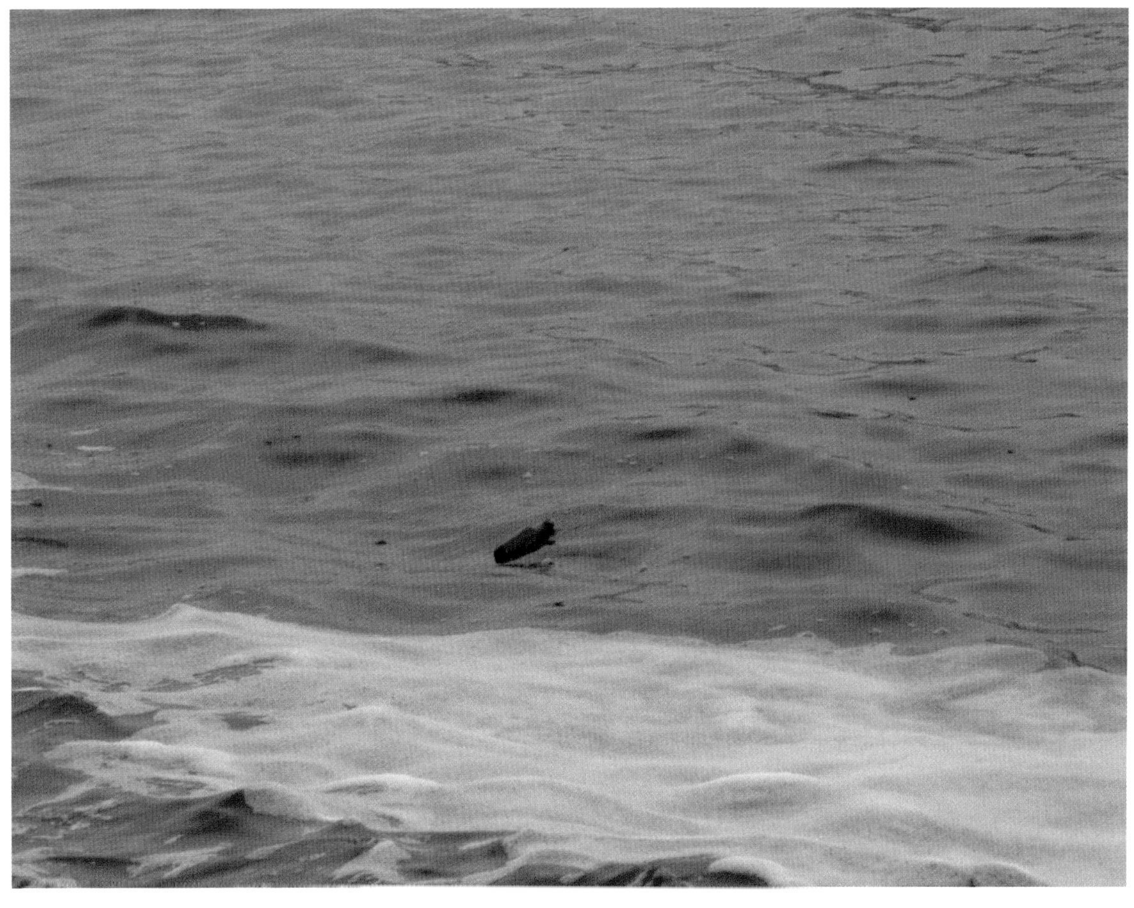

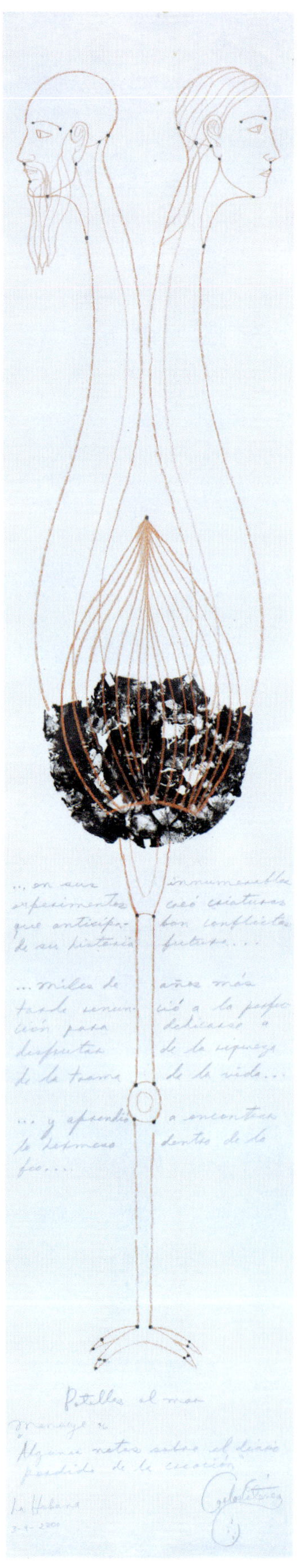

Bottles to the Sea
Message 46 "Some Notes on the Lost Diary of Creation"
Havana 9-3-2000

. . . in his innumerable experiments he created creatures that anticipated the conflicts of its future history . . .

. . . thousands of years later he renounced perfection to dedicate himself to enjoying the richness of the drama of life . . .

. . . and he learned to find the beautiful in the ugly . . .

Botellas al mar
Mensaje 46 "Algunas notas sobre el diario perdido de la creación"
La Habana 3-9-2000

. . . en sus innumerables experimentos creó criaturas que anticipaban conflictos de su historia futura . . .

. . . miles de años más tarde renunció a la perfección para dedicarse a disfrutar de la riqueza de la trama de la vida . . .

. . . y aprendió a encontrar lo hermoso dentro de lo feo . . .

Bottles to the Sea
Message 47 "Plant Man"*
*Notes on the lost diary of creation
Havana 9-4-2000

In the phase project, before arriving at the essential form of the diversity of species, many mixed among themselves, forming strange creatures that later were restored according to their design . . .

While without the least suspicion of the creator, their contents carried out secret exchanges.

Botellas al mar
Mensaje 47 "Hombre planta"*
****Apuntes sobre el diario perdido de la creación.***
La Habana 4-9-2000

En la fase proyecto, antes de llegar a la forma esencial de la diversidad de las especies, muchas se mezclaron entre sí, conformando extrañas criaturas que más tarde fueron restauradas en cuanto a diseño se refiere . . .

Mientras sin la menor sospecha del creador, sus contenidos efectuaban secretos intercambios.

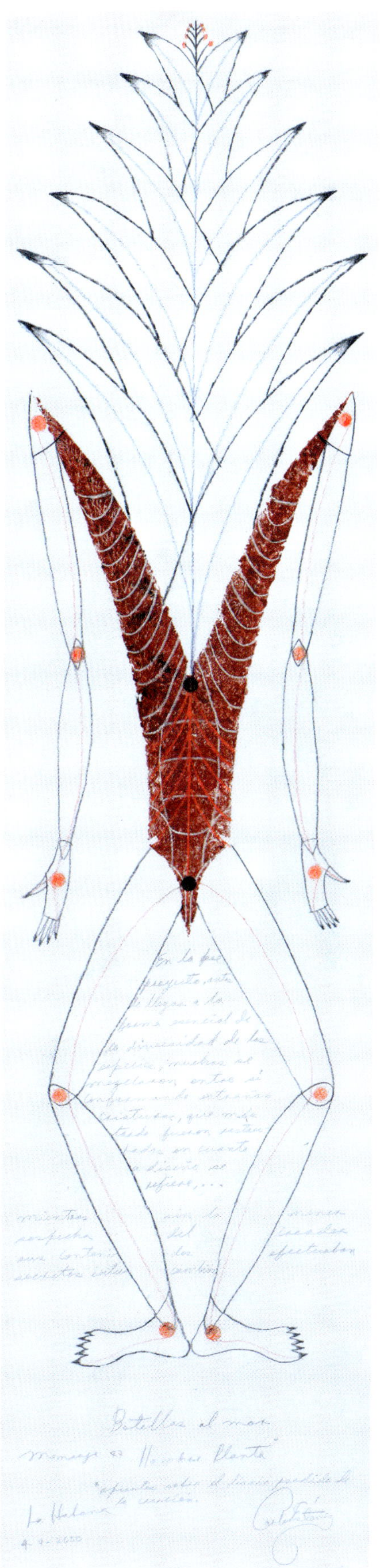

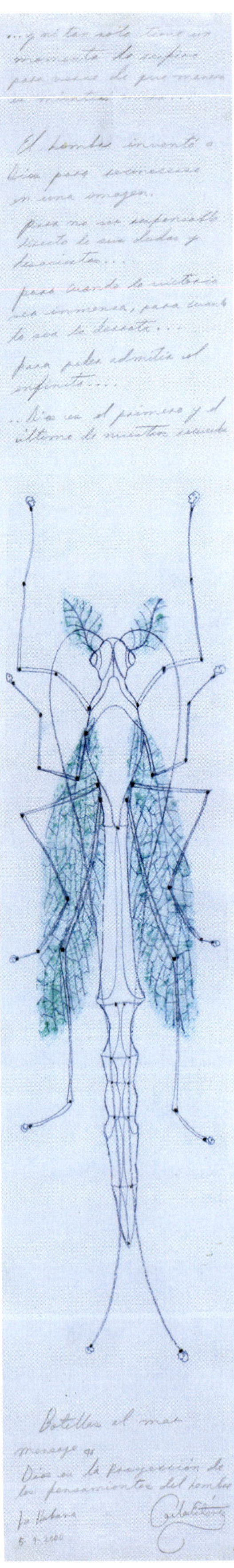

Bottles to the Sea
Message 48 "God is the Projection of Man's Thoughts"
Havana 9-5-2000

. . . and he does not even have a moment of respite to see how he is while he looks . . .

Man invented God in order to recognize himself in an image.

In order not to be directly responsible for his doubts and errors . . .

To be able to admit the infinite . . .

. . . God is the first and the last of our memories.

Botellas al mar
Mensaje 48 "Dios es la proyección de los pensamientos del hombre"
La Habana 5-9-2000

. . . y ni tan solo tiene un momento de respiro para verse de que manera es mientras mira . . .

El hombre inventó a Dios para reconocerse en una imagen.

Para no ser responsable directo de sus dudas y desaciertos . . .

Para poder admitir el infinito . . .

. . . Dios es el primero y el último de nuestros recuerdos.

Bottles to the Sea
Message 49 "*Argumentum ontologicum*"
Havana 9-6-2000

Life is 90% ordinary and 10% divine, therefore we should not abuse too much its magic, we should let it flow freely in each one of our acts.

We waste time trying to discover the sense of the order or the disorder of human creations and of nature. Knowledge is as infinite as the infinite itself and moreover it is mutable . . .

Before storms and calms we should always have an expression of invulnerability, remembering at every moment that by nature we are the exact opposite . . .

Botellas al mar
Mensaje 49 "Argumentum ontologicum"
La Habana 6-9-2000

La vida es un 90% ordinaria y un 10% divina, por tanto no debemos abusar demasiado de su magia, dejemos que fluya libremente en cada uno de nuestros actos.

Perdemos el tiempo tratando de descubrir el sentido del orden o del desorden de las creaciones humanas y de la naturaleza. El conocimiento es tan infinito como el infinito mismo y además es mutable . . .

Tengamos siempre ante las tormentas y las calmas una expresión de invulnerables, recordando en todo momento que por naturaleza somos todo lo contrario . . .

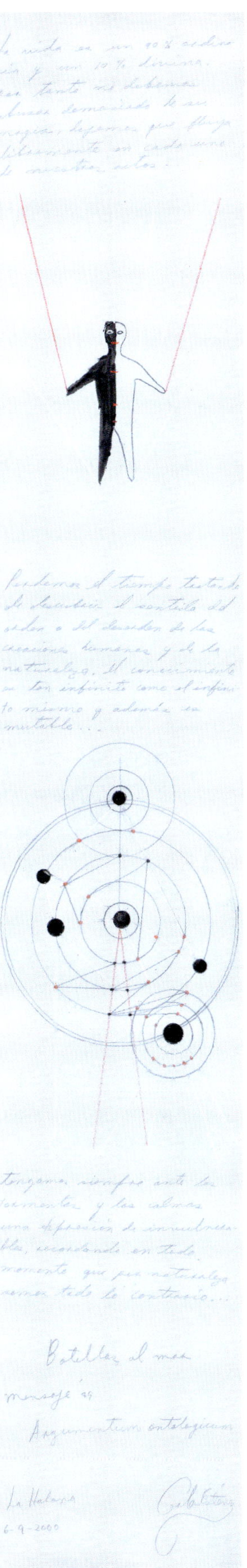

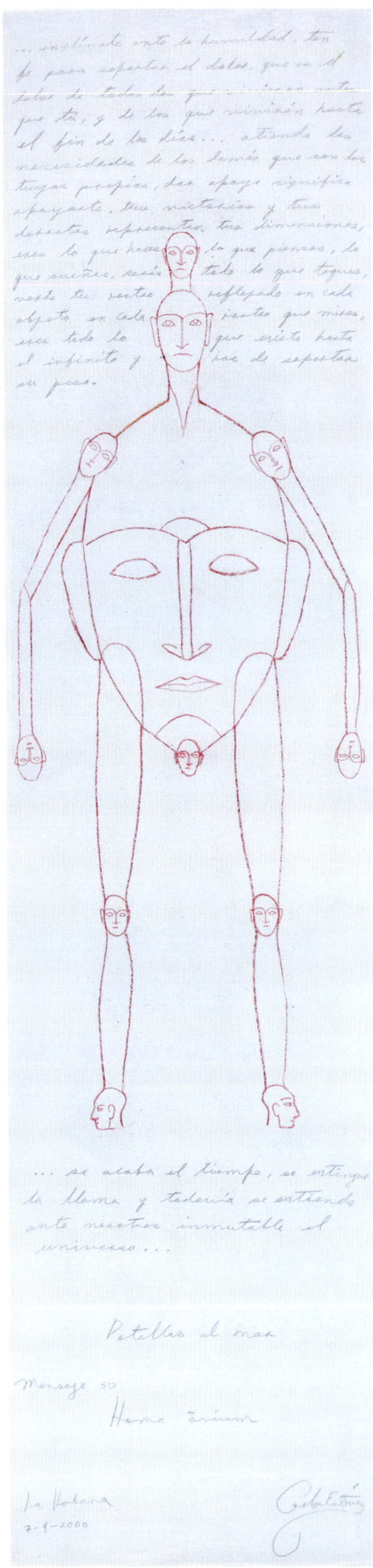

Bottles to the Sea
Message 50 "*Homo ãvium*"
Havana 9-7-2000

. . . bow before humanity, have faith to endure the pain, which is the pain of all those who lived before you, and all those who will live until the end of days . . . Take care of the needs of the others which are your own, to give support means to support yourself, your victories and your defeats represent your dimensions. You are what you do, what you think, what you dream, you will be everything you touch, you will see your face reflected in each object, in each face that you see, you are everything that exists until the infinite and you must support its weight.

. . . time is running out, the flame is going out, and the immutable universe still extends before us . . .

Botellas al mar
Mensaje 50 "Homo ãvium"
La Habana 7-9-2000

. . . inclínate ante la humanidad, ten fe para soportar el dolor, que es el dolor de todos los que vivieron antes que tú, y de todos los que vivirán hasta el fin de los días . . . Atiende las necesidades de los demás que son las tuyas propias, dar apoyo significa apoyarte, tus victorias y tus derrotas representan tus dimensiones. Eres lo que haces, lo que piensas, lo que sueñas, serás todo lo que toques, verás tu rostro reflejado en cada objeto, en cada rostro que mires, eres todo lo que existe hasta el infinito y haz de soportar su peso.

. . . se acaba el tiempo, se extingue la llama y todavía se extiende ante nosotros inmutable el universo . . .

Bottles to the Sea
Message 51 "Seeing Hand"
Havana 9-7-2000

. . . some hands have the faculty of prophecy, thus in only a handshake, a hug or a light touch of persons or objects, they can gather a voluminous and complete information that covers everything from the molecular structure to the smallest subtleties of the spirit, that encompasses said persons or objects.

Botellas al mar
Mensaje 51 "Mano vidente"
La Habana 7-9-2000

. . . algunas manos tienen la facultad de la videncia, así en sólo un estrechón, un abrazo o un leve toque a personas u objetos, pueden recoger una voluminosa y completa información que abarca desde la estructura molecular hasta las más pequeñas sutilezas del espíritu, que rodea a dichas personas u objetos.

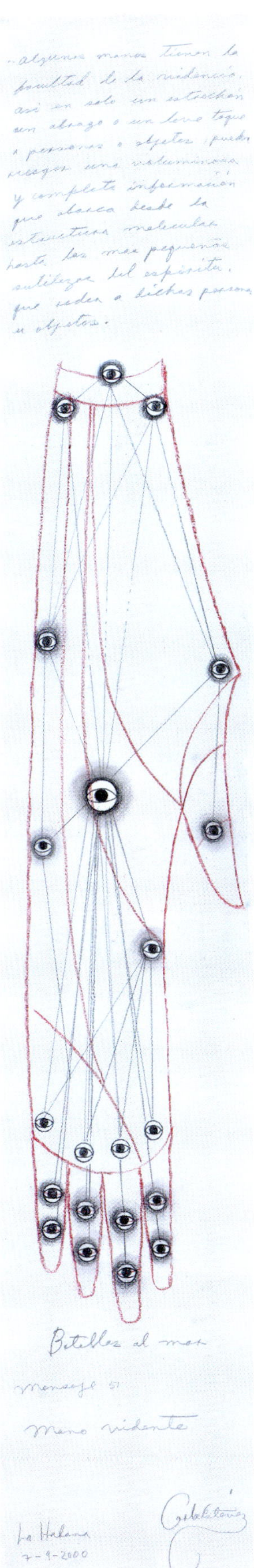

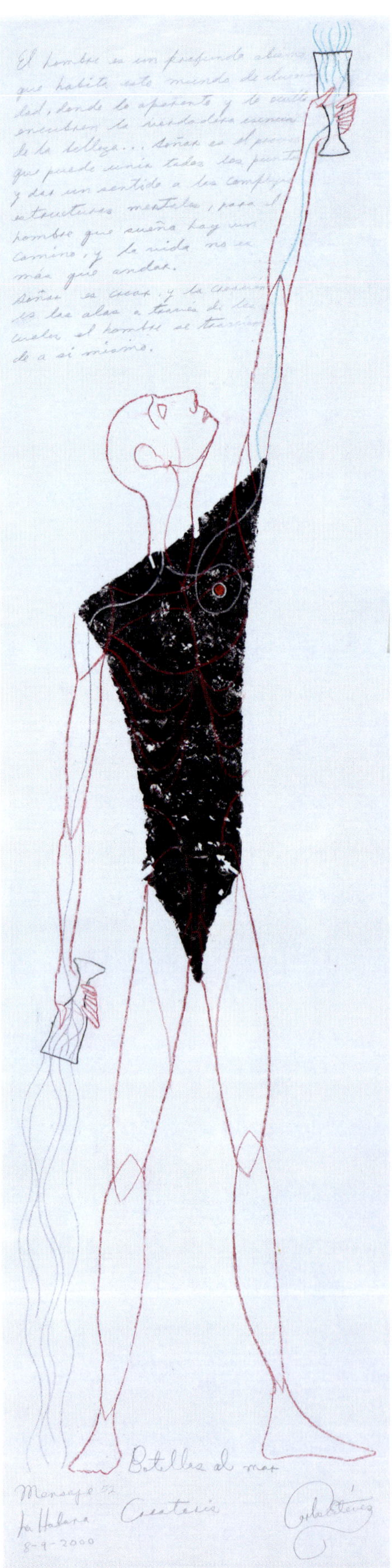

Bottles to the Sea
Message 52 "*Creatoris*"
Havana 9-8-2000

Man is a profound abyss that lives in this world of illusion, where the apparent and the occult hide the true essence of beauty . . .

Dreaming is the process that can unite all the points and give a meaning to complex mental structures. For the man who dreams there is a path, and life is nothing more than moving.

To dream is to create, and creation is the wings by which man transcends himself.

Botellas al mar
Mensaje 52 "Creatoris"
La Habana 8-9-2000

El hombre es un profundo abismo que habita este mundo de ilusoriedad, donde lo aparente y lo oculto encubren la verdadera esencia de la belleza . . .

Soñar es el proceso que puede unir todos los puntos y dar un sentido a las complejas estructuras mentales. Para el hombre que sueña hay un camino, y la vida no es más que andar.

Soñar es crear, y la creación es las alas a través de las cuales el hombre se trasciende a sí mismo.

Bottles to the Sea
Message 53 "*Ecquis hic est?*"
Havana 9-9-2000
Launched at Mississippi River,
New Orleans, Louisiana, United States.
4-27-2007

Our world is full of worlds, in turn we are the worlds of other worlds and so on to infinity.

Botellas al mar
Mensaje 53 "Ecquis hic est?"
La Habana 9-9-2000
Lanzado en el río Mississippi,
Nueva Orleans, Luisiana, Estados Unidos.
27-4-2007

Nuestro mundo está lleno de mundos, a su vez somos los mundos de otros mundos y así hasta el infinito.

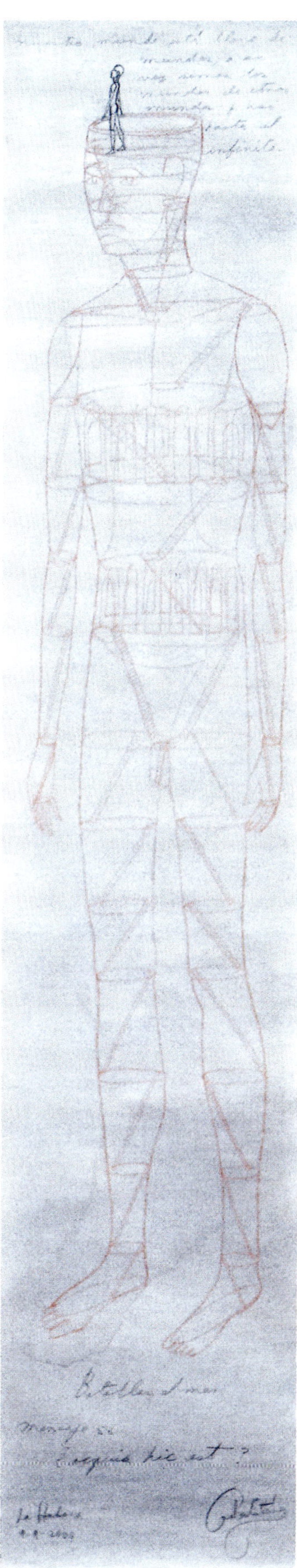

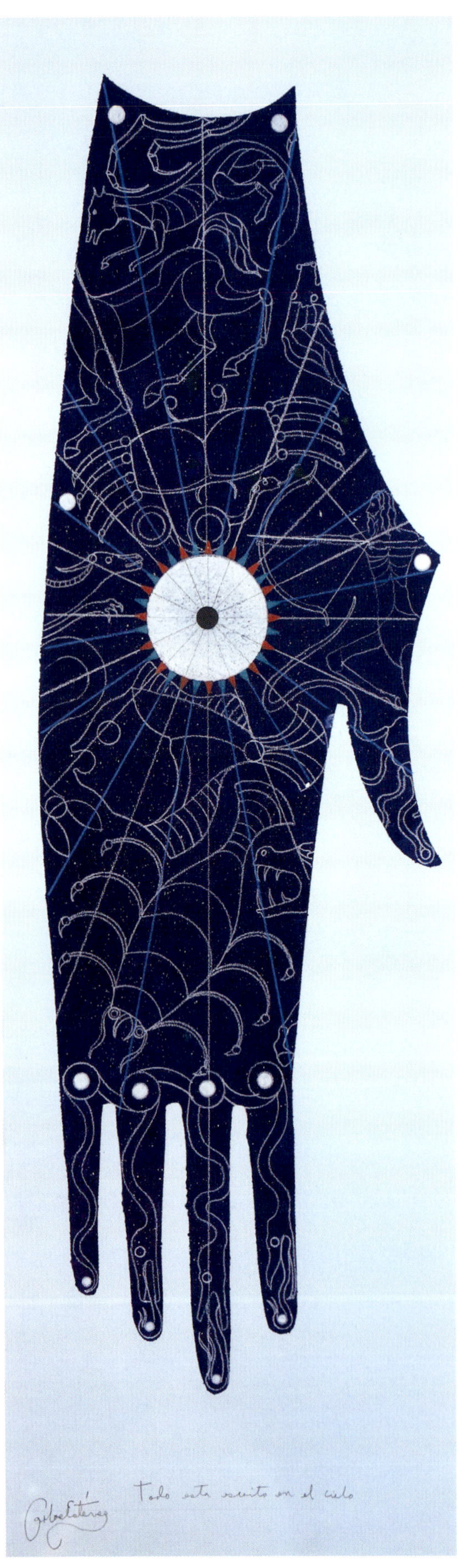

Bottles to the Sea
Message 54 "Everything is Written in Heaven"
Launched at Havana Malecon, Havana, Cuba. 12-16-2001
Version of the original
Miami 8-15-2013

Botellas al mar
Mensaje 54 "Todo está escrito en el cielo"
Lanzado en el Malecón de La Habana, Cuba. 16-12-2001
Versión del original
Miami 15-8-2013

Bottles to the Sea
Message 55 "Not Going Anywhere"
Havana 9-12-2000
Launched at Mont Saint-Michel,
Normandy, France. 5-22-2004

Given the extension of our spiritual universe, not to go anywhere is the answer that frees us from the conflict of eternity . . . that suffocating path towards nothing following the threads that sustain us, which we are traversing without the least suspicion that they return to us.

Green book 1990

Botellas al mar
Mensaje 55 "No ir a ninguna parte"
La Habana 12-9-2000
Lanzado en el Monte San Michel,
Normandía, Francia. 22-5-2004

Debido a la extensión de nuestro universo espiritual no ir a ninguna parte es la respuesta que nos libera del conflicto de la eternidad . . . ese sofocante camino hacia la nada siguiendo los hilos que nos sostienen, los cuales vamos recorriendo sin la menor sospecha de que vuelven a nosotros mismos.

Libro verde 1990

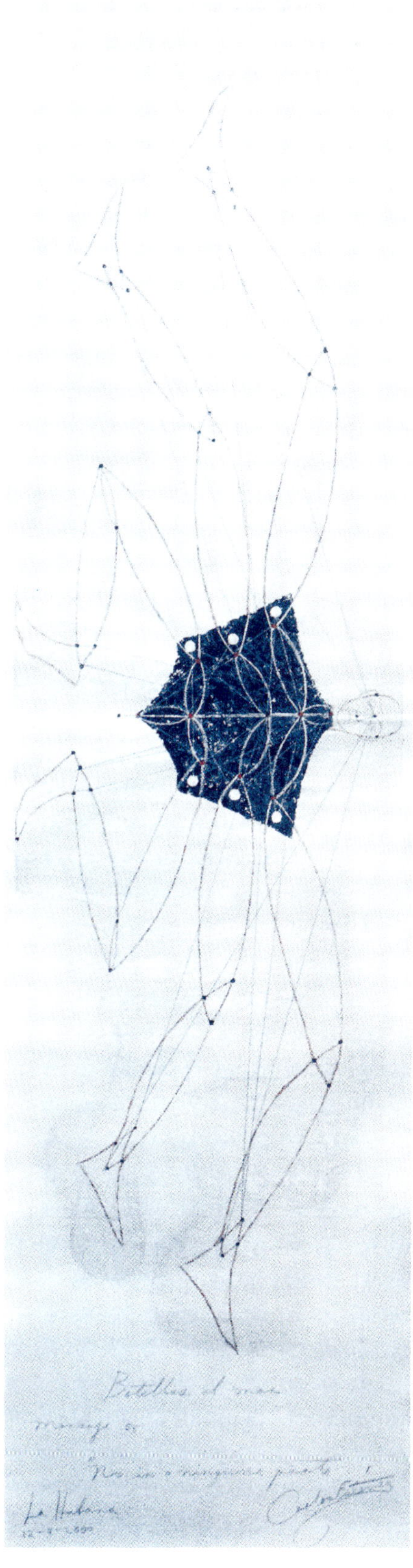

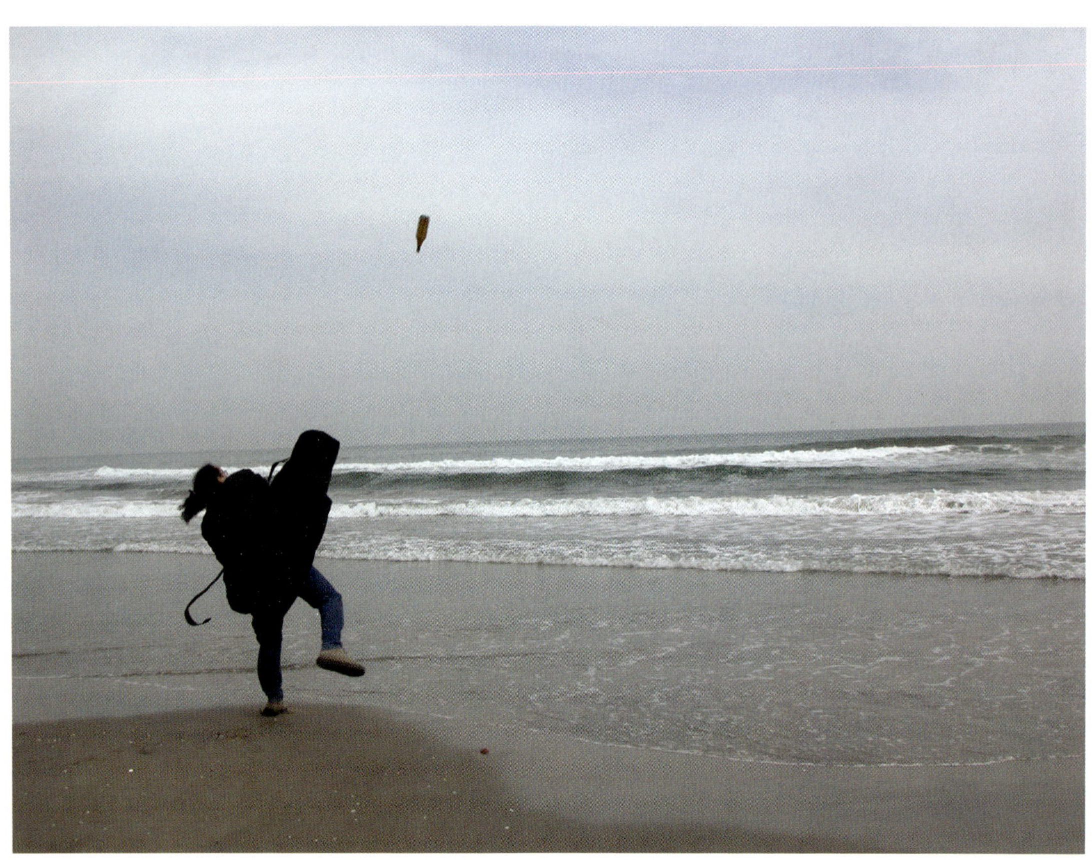

Bottles to the Sea
Message 56 "My True Face"
Havana 9-13-2000

No one suspects how many demons or how many angels live within us, and much less which of them we can become at any moment . . .

For an infinity of time I find myself alone in this desert that is the earth, I have constructed and deconstructed many cities in different ages and in different styles, I have drawn many times the map of the universe and not one has coincided in the smallest detail with another, of all my inventions only the idea of the infinite endures and not even in the clear mirrors of my waters have I been able to perceive my true face.

Botellas al mar
Mensaje 56 "Mi verdadero rostro"
La Habana 13-9-2000

Nadie sospecha cuántos demonios ni cuántos ángeles habitan dentro de nosotros, y mucho menos en cuál de ellos nos podemos convertir en cualquier momento . . .

Me encuentro solo hace una infinidad de tiempo en este desierto que es la tierra, he construido y deconstruido muchas ciudades en diferentes épocas y en diferentes estilos, he dibujado muchas veces el mapa del universo y ninguno ha coincidido en el más mínimo detalle con el otro, de todas mis invenciones solo perdura la idea del infinito y ni siquiera ante los claros espejos de mis aguas he podido percibir mi verdadero rostro.

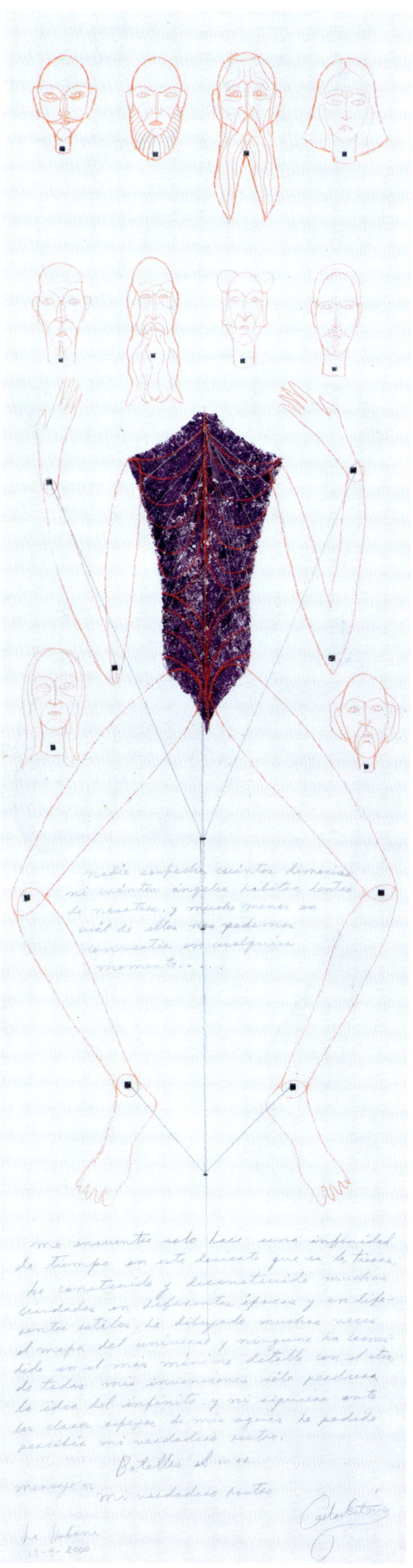

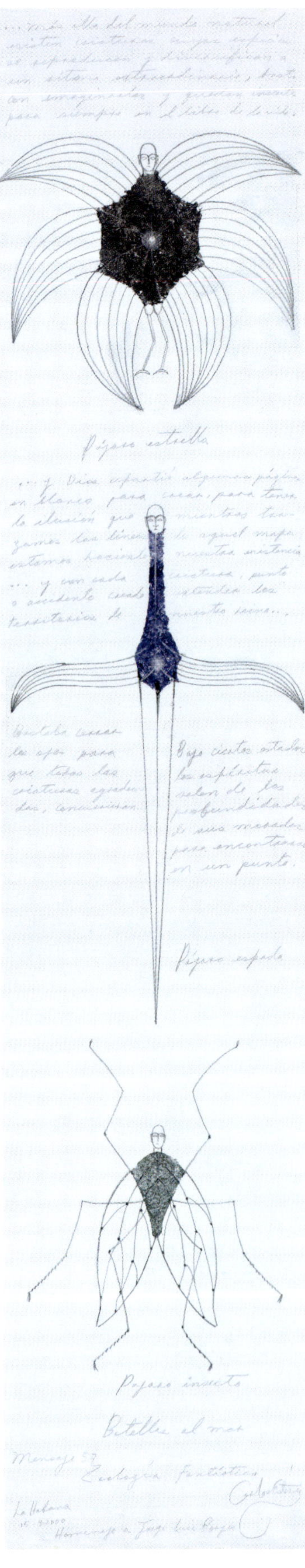

Bottles to the Sea
Message 57 "Fantastic Zoology"
Havana 9-15-2000

Homage to Jorge Luis Borges

. . . beyond the natural world exist creatures whose species reproduce and diversify at an extraordinary pace, it is enough to imagine them and they remain inscribed forever in the book of life.

Star bird

. . . and God apportioned some blank pages in order to create, in order to have the illusion that while we trace the lines of that map we are making our existence.

. . . and with each creature, point or accident created, we are extending the territories of our realm . . .

It was enough to close the eyes to make all the thankful creatures assemble . . .

Under certain conditions spirits leave the depths, of their dwellings, to find themselves in a point.

Sword bird

Insect bird

Botellas al Mar
Mensaje 57 "Zoología fantástica"
La Habana 15-9-2000

Homenaje a Jorge Luis Borges

. . . más allá del mundo natural existen criaturas cuyas especies se reproducen y diversifican a un ritmo extraordinario, basta con imaginarlos y quedan inscritas para siempre en el libro de la vida.

Pájaro estrella

. . . y Dios repartió algunas páginas en blanco para crear, para tener la ilusión que mientras trazamos las líneas de aquel mapa estamos haciendo nuestra existencia.

. . . y con cada criatura, punto o accidente creado extender los territorios de nuestro reino . . .

Bastaba cerrar los ojos para que todas las criaturas agradecidas concurrieran . . .

Bajo ciertos estados los espíritus salen de las profundidades, de sus moradas, para encontrarse en un punto.

Pájaro espada

Pájaro insecto

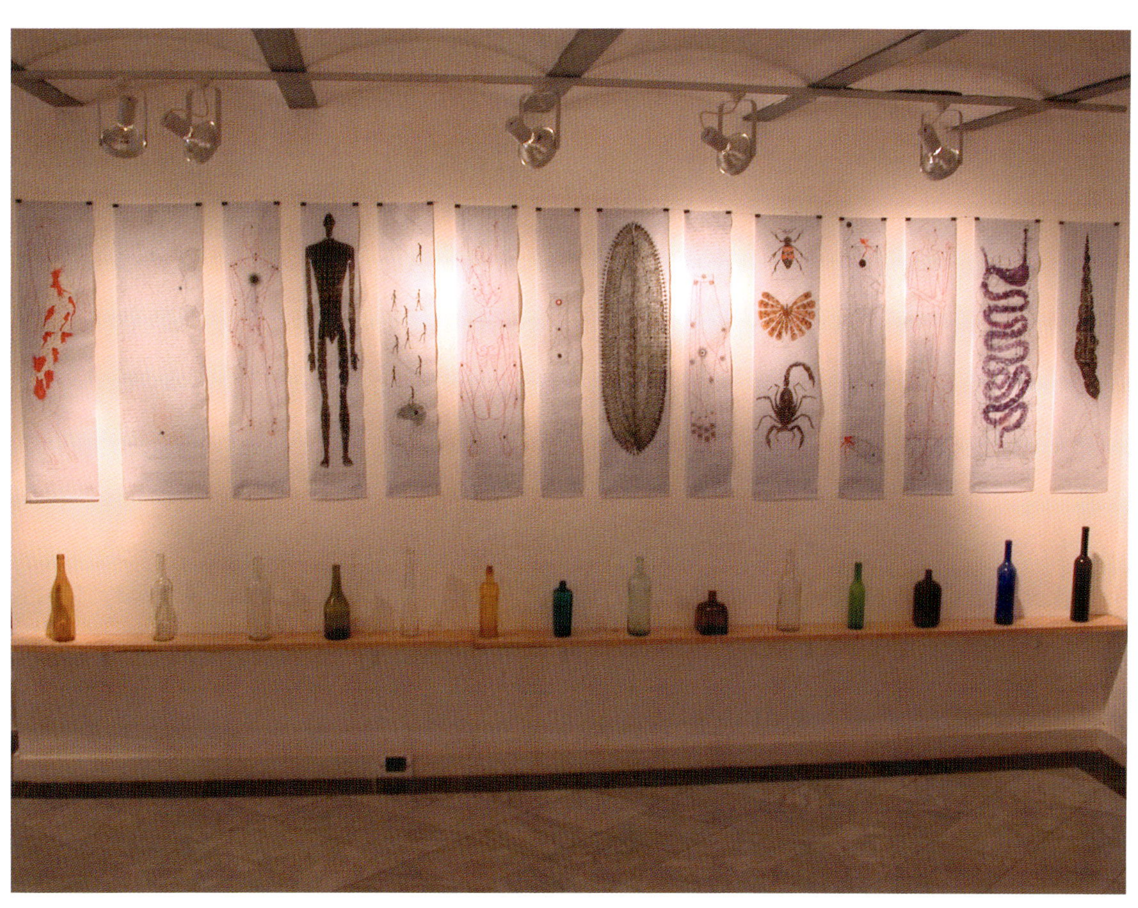

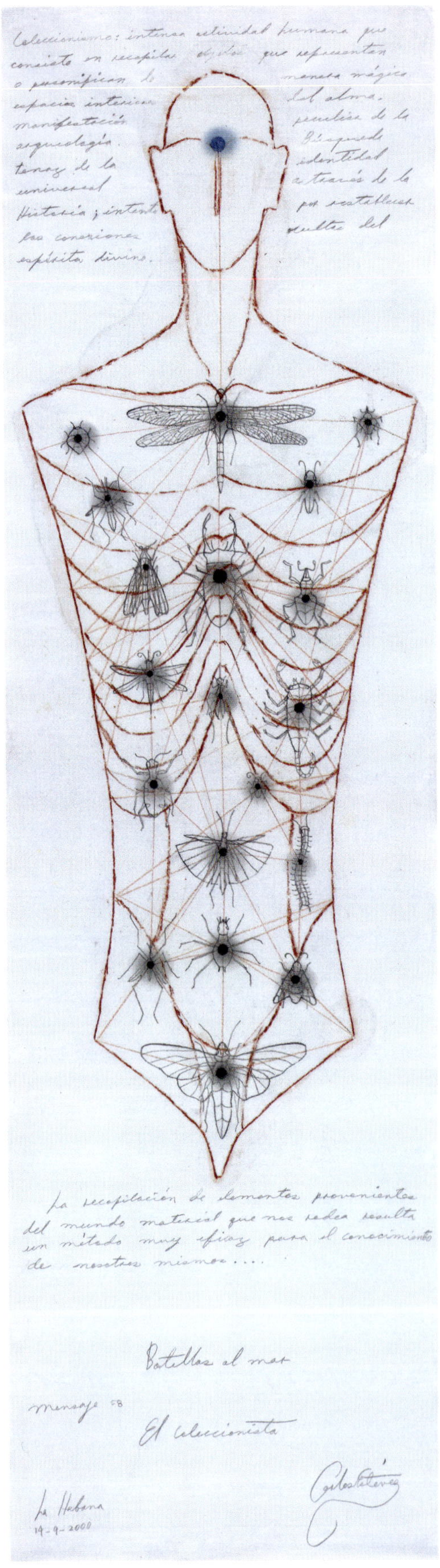

Bottles to the Sea
Message 58 "The Collector"
Havana 9-14-2000

Collecting: intense human activity that consists in gathering objects that represent or personify in a magical way interior spaces of the soul. Peculiar manifestation of archeology.

Tenacious search for universal identity through history; attempt to establish hidden connections of the divine spirit.

The gathering of elements issuing from the natural world that surrounds us is a very efficacious method for knowledge of ourselves . . .

Botellas al mar
Mensaje 58 "El coleccionista"
La Habana 14-9-2000

Coleccionismo: intensa actividad humana que consiste en recopilar objetos que representan o personifican de manera mágica espacios interiores del alma. Manifestación peculiar de la arqueología.

Búsqueda tenaz de la identidad universal a través de la historia; intento por establecer las conexiones ocultas del espíritu divino.

La recopilación de elementos provenientes del mundo material que nos rodea resulta un método muy eficaz para el conocimiento de nosotros mismos . . .

Bottles to the Sea
Message 59 "The Great Secret of Alchemy"
Havana 9-15-2000

After climbing many summits, he discovered that the summits are the end of dreams, and that life only vibrates on the climb. . . . He also discovered that the great secrets of the universe are inscribed in the maps of his soul . . .

Botellas al mar
Mensaje 59 "El gran secreto de la alquimia"
La Habana 15-9-2000

Después de escalar muchas cimas, descubrió que las cimas son el fin de los sueños, y que la vida solo vibra en la subida. . . . Descubrió también que los grandes secretos del universo estaban inscritos en los mapas de su alma . . .

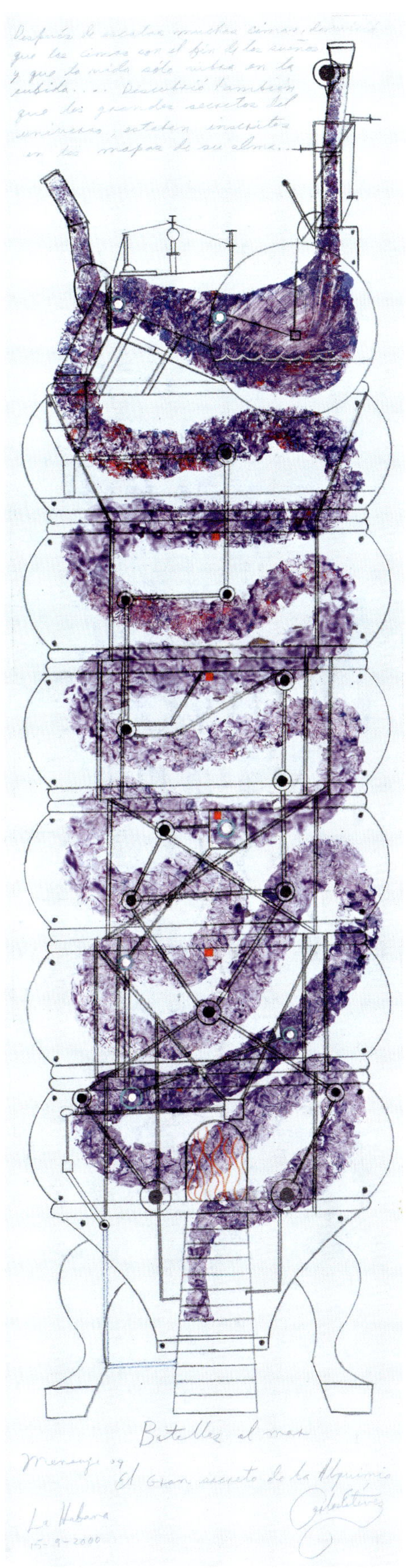

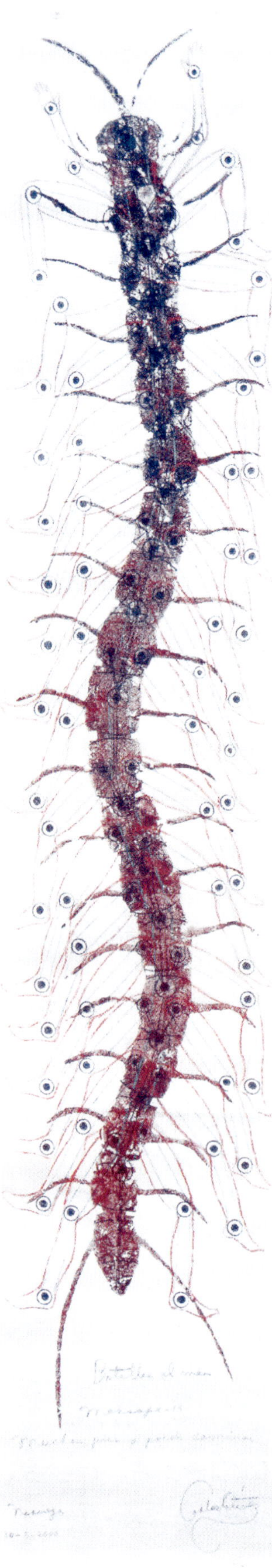

Bottles to the Sea
Message 60 "Many Feet and Few Paths"
Norway 5-10-2000
Launched at Valencia, Spain. 2-18-2004

Botellas al mar
Mensaje 60 "Muchos pies y pocos caminos"
Noruega 10-5-2000
Lanzado en Valencia, España. 18-2-2004

Bottles to the Sea
Message 61 "I Carry Everything with Me"
Havana 9-16-2000

Botellas al mar
Mensaje 61 "Todo lo llevo conmigo"
La Habana 16-9-2000

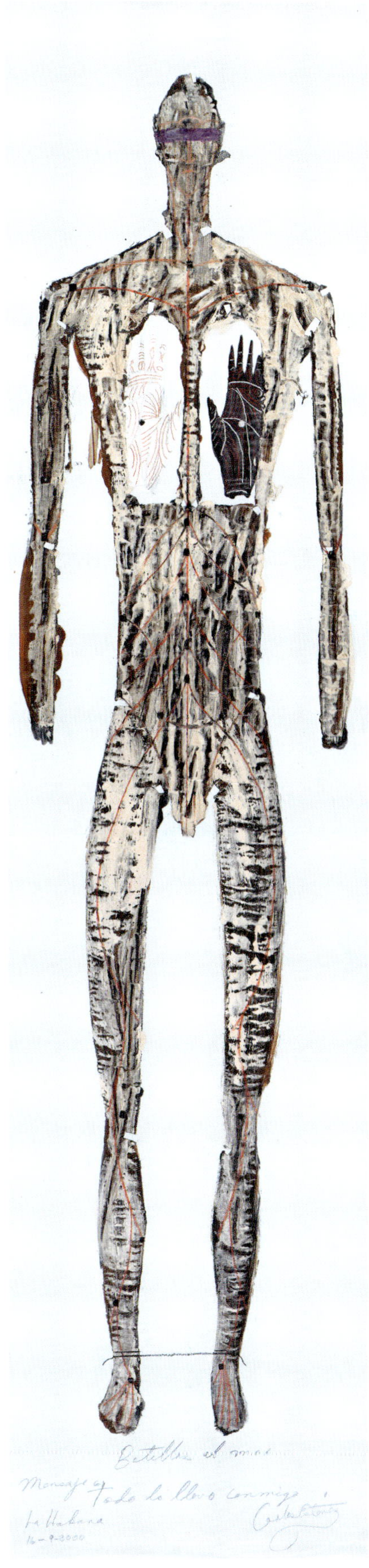

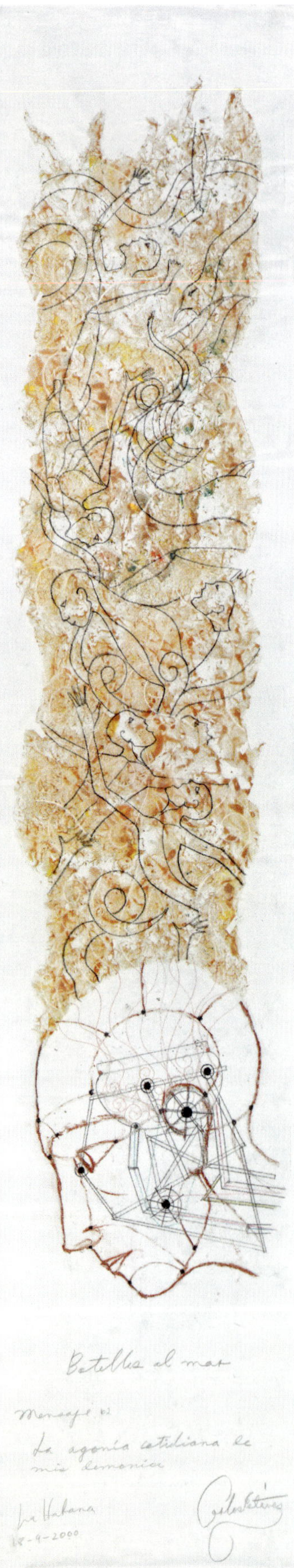

Bottles to the Sea
Message 62 "The Daily Agony of My Demons"
Havana 9-18-2000

Botellas al mar
Mensaje 62 "La agonía cotidiana de mis demonios"
La Habana 18-9-2000

Bottles to the Sea
Message 63 "The Spirit of Creation Feeds on Bodies"
Havana 9-19-2000
Launched at New London, Connecticut, United States. 1-20-2007

To create is a process of combustion that slowly consumes us and the more intense the fruits of this process, the more drastic its erosion will be . . .

. . . in each word, each instant, each dream, each sigh, life flees from us . . .

. . . and in the invisible beauty of the universe that renews itself in each birth and in each death . . .

Botellas al mar
Mensaje 63 "El espíritu de la creación se alimenta de cuerpos"
La Habana 19-9-2000
Lanzado en New London, Connecticut, Estados Unidos. 20-1-2007

Crear es un proceso de combustión que lentamente nos va consumiendo y mientras más intenso son los frutos resultado de dicho proceso, más drástico será el desgaste . . .

. . . en cada palabra, cada instante, cada sueño, cada suspiro, se nos va la vida . . .

. . . y en la belleza invisible del universo que se renueva en cada nacimiento y en cada muerte . . .

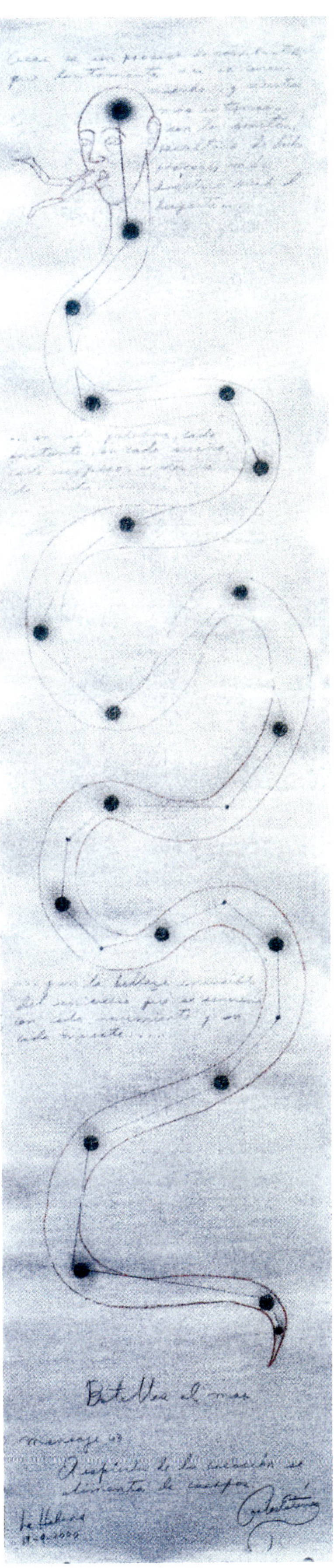

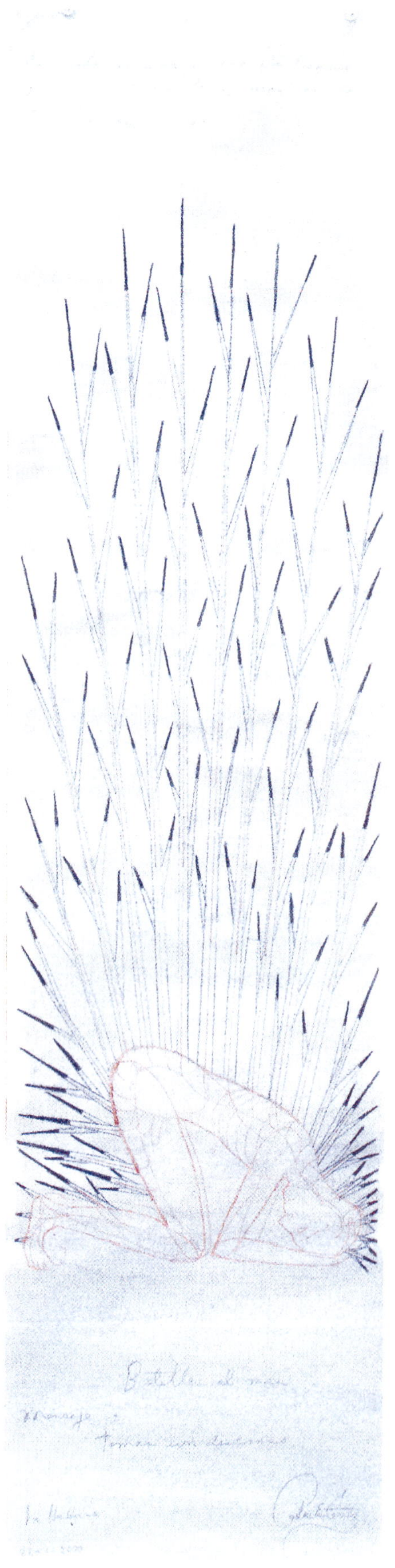

Bottles to the Sea
Message 64 "Take a Break"
Havana 4-22-2000
Launched at Punta Cacha Pregos,
Itaparica, Bahia, Brazil. 1-12-2003

Life is a war without truce and it dies with arms in hand.

Schopenhauer

Botellas al mar
Mensaje 64 "Tomar un descanso"
La Habana 22-4-2000
Lanzado en Punta Cacha Pregos, Isla
Itaparica, Salvador de Bahía, Brasil.
12-1-2003

La vida es una guerra sin tregua y se muere con las armas en la mano.

Schopenhauer

Bottles to the Sea
Message 65 "*Paucorum hominum esse*"
Havana 9-2-2000

God exists, but sometimes he sleeps: his nightmares are our existence.

Ernesto Sábato

Botellas al mar
Mensaje 65 "Paucorum hominum esse"
La Habana 2-9-2000

Dios existe, pero a veces duerme: sus pesadillas son nuestra existencia.

Ernesto Sábato

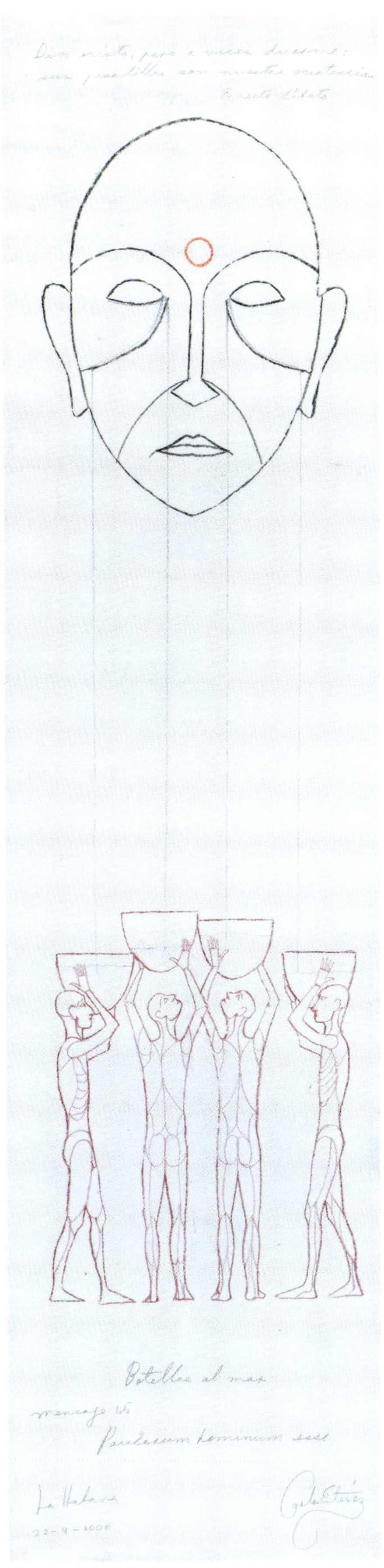

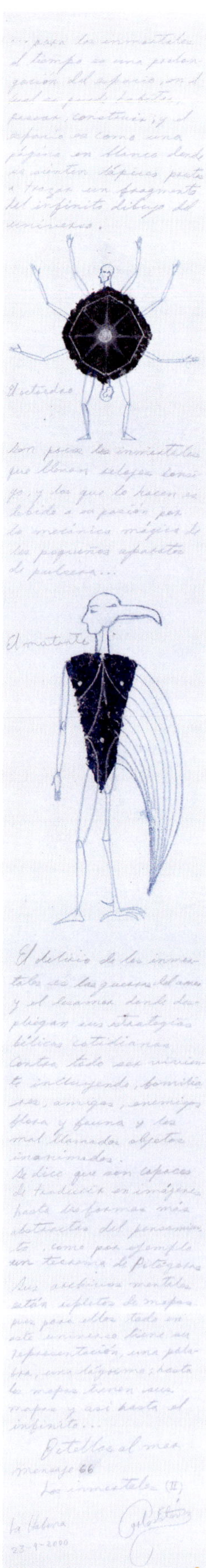

Bottles to the Sea
Message 66 "The Immortals (II)"
Havana 9-23-2000

. . . for the immortals time is a prolongation of space, in which one can live, walk, build; and the space is like a blank page where one feels pencils ready to trace a fragment of the infinite drawing of the universe.

The octahedron

Only a few immortals wear watches, and those who do it is because of their passion for the magical mechanism of the small wrist apparatuses . . .

The mutant

The delirium of the immortals is the wars of love and indifference in which they unfold their daily bellicose strategies against all living beings including relatives, friends, enemies, flora and fauna, and badly named inanimate objects.

It is said that they are able to translate into images even the most abstract forms of thought, like, for example, a Pythagorean Theorem.

Their mental archives are filled with maps, because for them everything in this universe has its representation, a word, a tear; even the maps have their maps and so on to infinity . . .

Botellas al mar
Mensaje 66 "Los inmortales (II)"
La Habana 23-9-2000

. . . para los inmortales el tiempo es una prolongación del espacio, en el cual se puede habitar, pasear, construir; y el espacio es como una página en blanco donde se sienten lápices prestos a trazar un fragmento del infinito dibujo del universo.

El octaedro

Son pocos los inmortales que llevan relojes consigo, y los que lo hacen es debido a su pasión por la mecánica mágica de los pequeños aparatos de pulsera . . .

El mutante

El delirio de los inmortales es las guerras del amor y el desamor donde despliegan sus estrategias bélicas cotidianas contra todo ser viviente incluyendo familiares, amigos, enemigos, flora y fauna, y los mal llamados objetos inanimados.

Se dice que son capaces de traducir en imágenes hasta las formas más abstractas del pensamiento, como por ejemplo, un teorema de Pitágoras.

Sus archivos mentales están repletos de mapas pues por ellos todo en este universo tiene su representación, una palabra, una lágrima; hasta los mapas tienen sus mapas y así hasta el infinito . . .

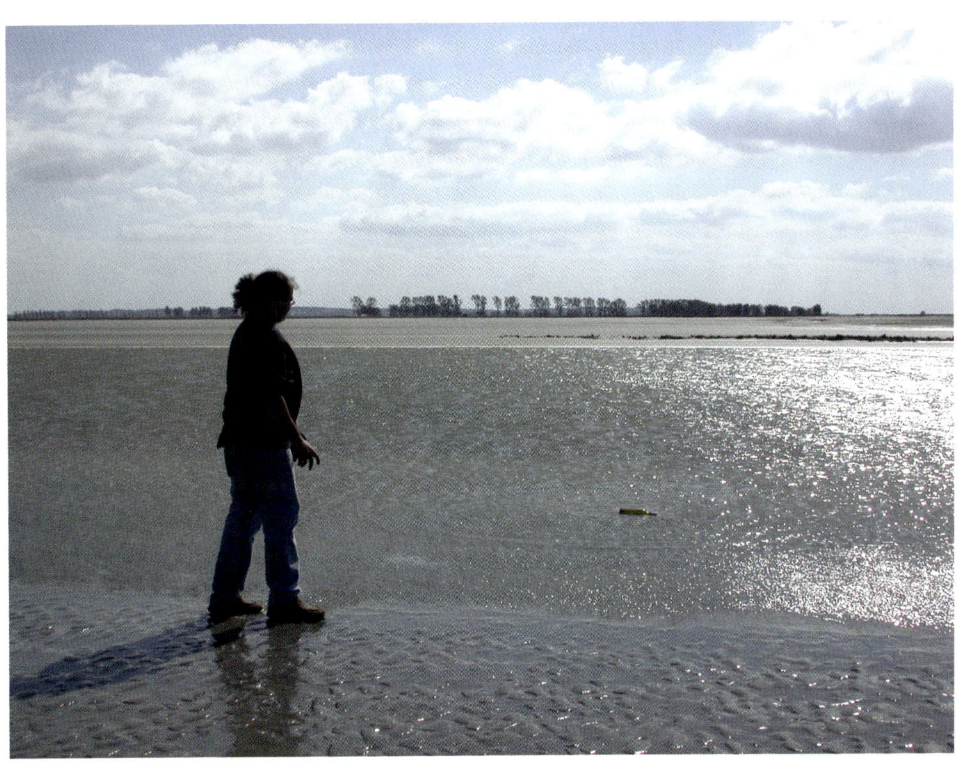

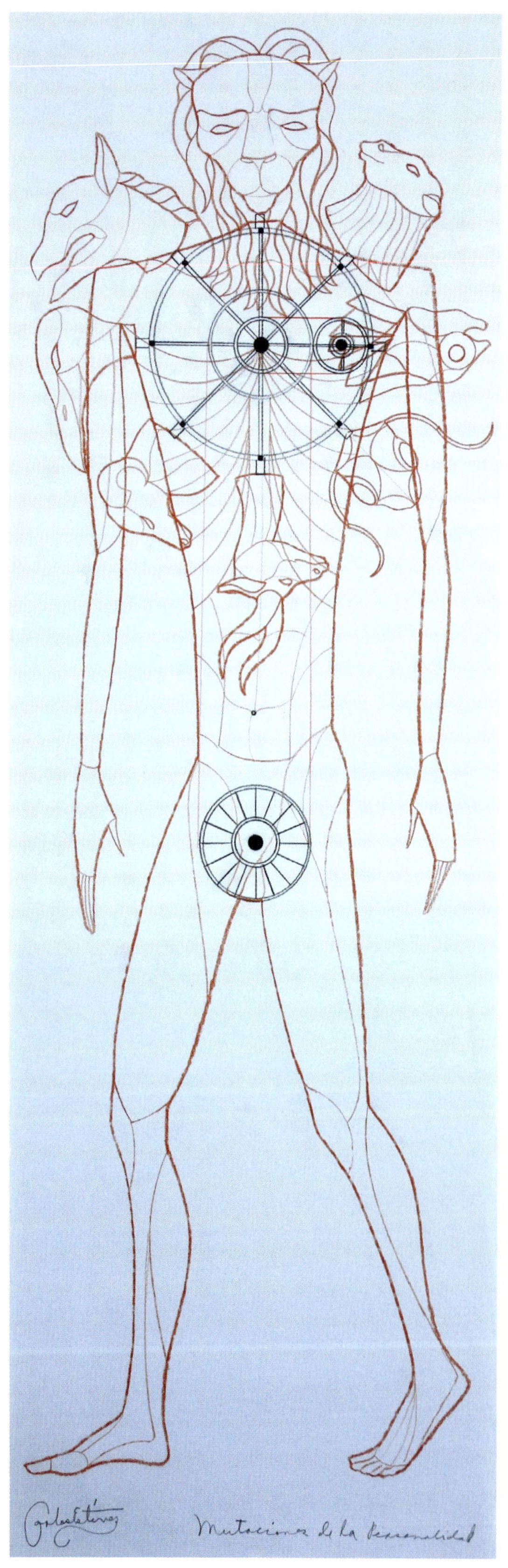

Bottles to the Sea
Message 67 "Mutations of Personality"
Launched at Ellis Island, New York,
United States. 2-3-2002
Version of the original
Miami 8-16-2013

. . . all the creatures and all the material forms live within us and in any moment can manifest themselves . . .

Botellas al mar
Mensaje 67 "Mutaciones de la personalidad"
Lanzado en Ellis Island, New York, Estados Unidos. 3-2-2002
Versión del original
Miami 16-8-2013

. . . todas las criaturas y todas las formas de la materia habitan dentro de nosotros y en cualquier momento pueden manifestarse . . .

Bottles to the Sea
Message 68 "Mutations of the Soul"
Havana 9-25-2000

. . . just like the cosmos the human being is subject to the laws of the universe, and he is sensible to the changes of time.

From the annual seasonal cycles to the most imperceptible things like a tenuous rain or sudden change in the color of the sky.

Within each being exist seasons, climates, forests, bridges, cities, unknown worlds, seas, galaxies, skies and comets . . .

There is no body part that does not have a corresponding celestial sign, a star, an intelligence, a divine name in the divine archetype . . .

Agrippa of Nettlesheim

(De occulta philosophia)

Botellas al mar
Mensaje 68 "Las mutaciones del alma’
La Habana 25-9-2000

. . . al igual que el cosmos el ser humano está sujeto a las leyes del universo, y es sensible a los cambios del tiempo.

Desde los ciclos de las estaciones del año hasta los más imperceptibles como una tenue lluvia o un repentino cambio de color del cielo.

Dentro de cada ser, existen estaciones, climas, bosques, puentes, ciudades, tierras desconocidas, mares, galaxias, cielos y cometas . . .

No hay miembro del cuerpo que no tenga correspondencia con un signo celeste, una estrella, una inteligencia, un nombre divino en el arquetipo divino . . .

Agrippa de Nettlesheim

(De occulta philosophia)

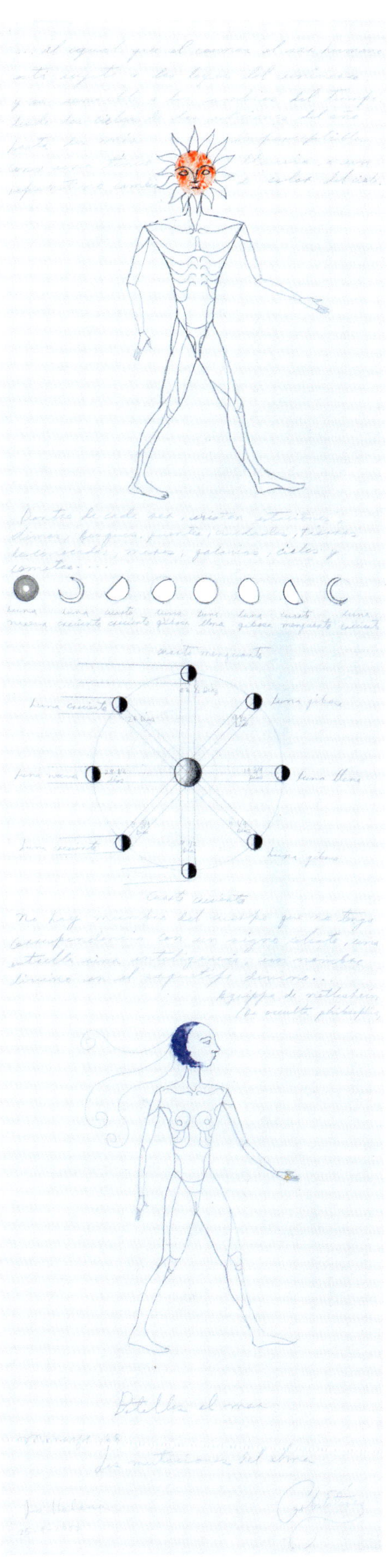

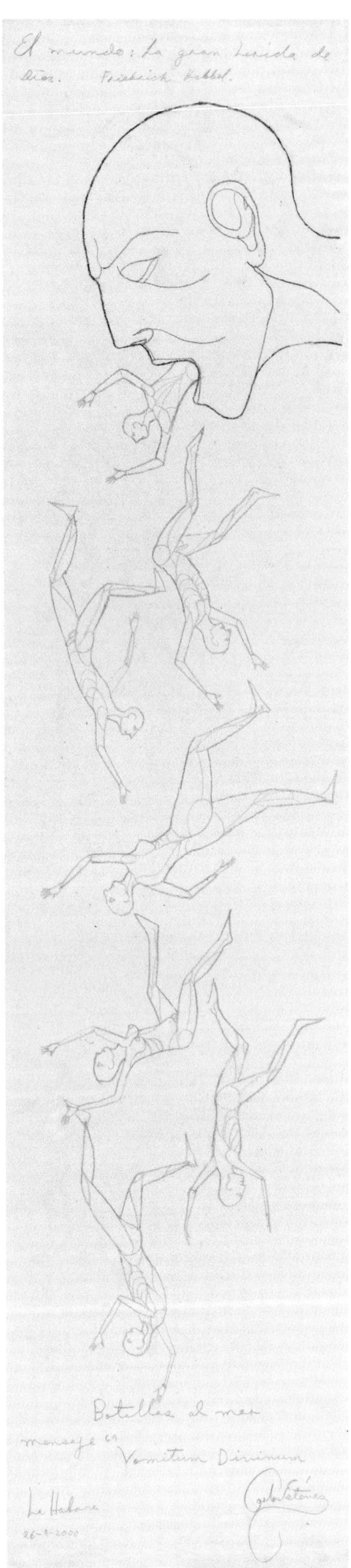

Bottles to the Sea
Message 69 "*Vomitum divinum*"
Havana 9-26-2000

The world: God's great wound

Friedrich Hebbel

Botellas al mar
***Mensaje 69* "Vomitum divinum"**
La Habana 26-9-2000

El mundo: La gran herida de Dios

Friedrich Hebbel

Bottles to the Sea
Message 70 "The Transient and the Deserted City"
Havana 9-27-2000

Botellas al mar
Mensaje 70 "El transeúnte y la ciudad desierta"
La Habana 27-9-2000

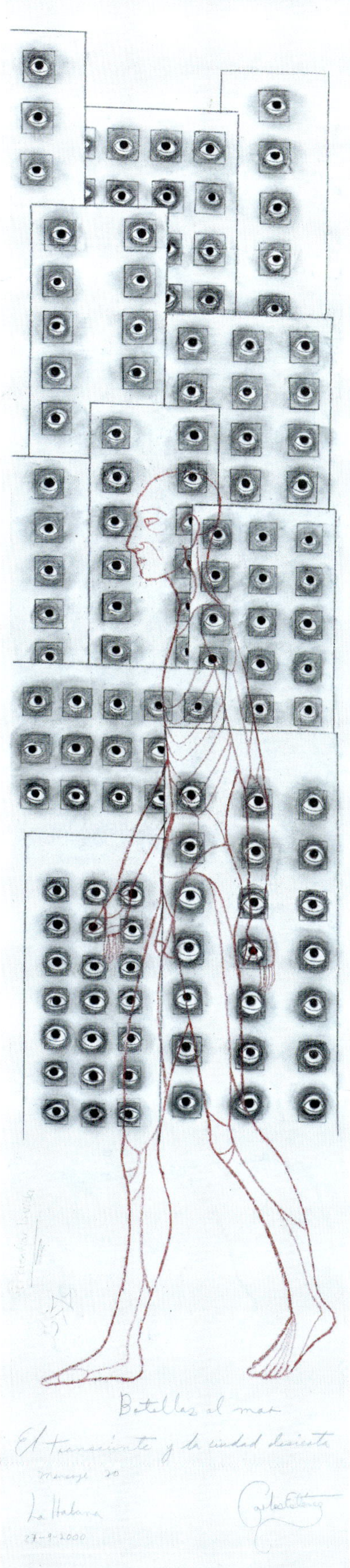

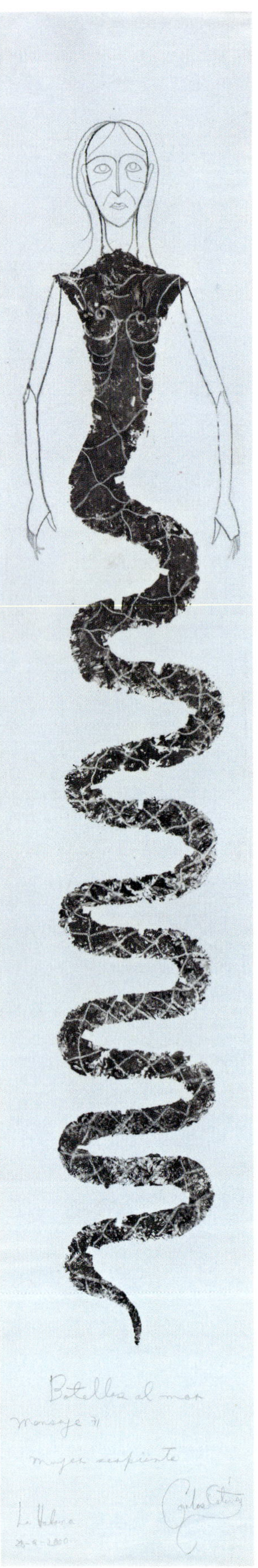

Bottles to the Sea
Message 71 “Serpent Woman”
Havana 9-28-2000

Botellas al mar
Mensaje 71 “Mujer serpiente”
La Habana 28-9-2000

Bottles to the Sea
Message 72 "Come and Go"
Havana 8-23-2000
Launched at Malibu, California, United States. 9-8-2005

And some come in the form of stories, new questions and new answers. Others leave with useless memories, irreconcilable sadnesses, finished histories, beautiful dreams that never came to happen . . . and in this coming and going we are changing . . .

Botellas al mar
Mensaje 72 "Ir y venir"
La Habana 23-8-2000
Lanzado en Malibú, California, Estados Unidos. 8-9-2005

Y unos vienen en formas de historias, nuevas interrogantes y nuevas respuestas. Otros se marchan con recuerdos inútiles, tristezas irreconciliables, historias terminadas, hermosos sueños que nunca llegaron a suceder . . . y en este ir y venir vamos cambiando . . .

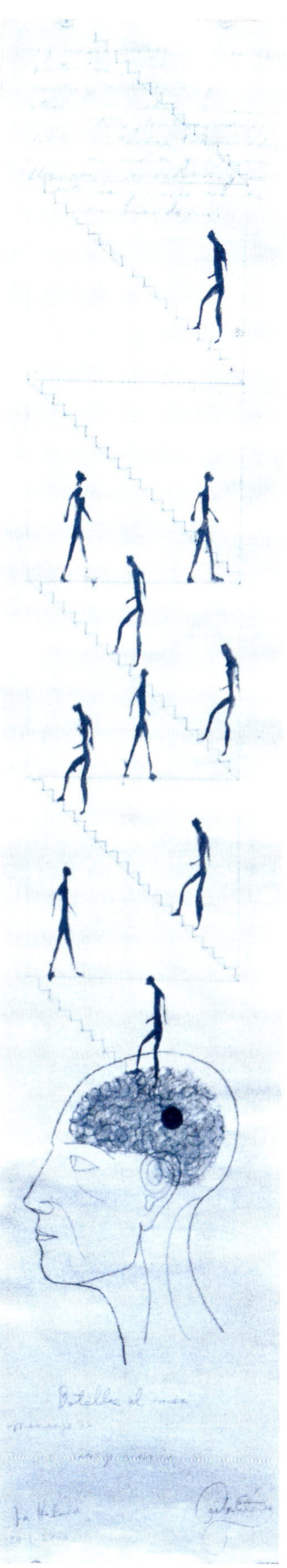

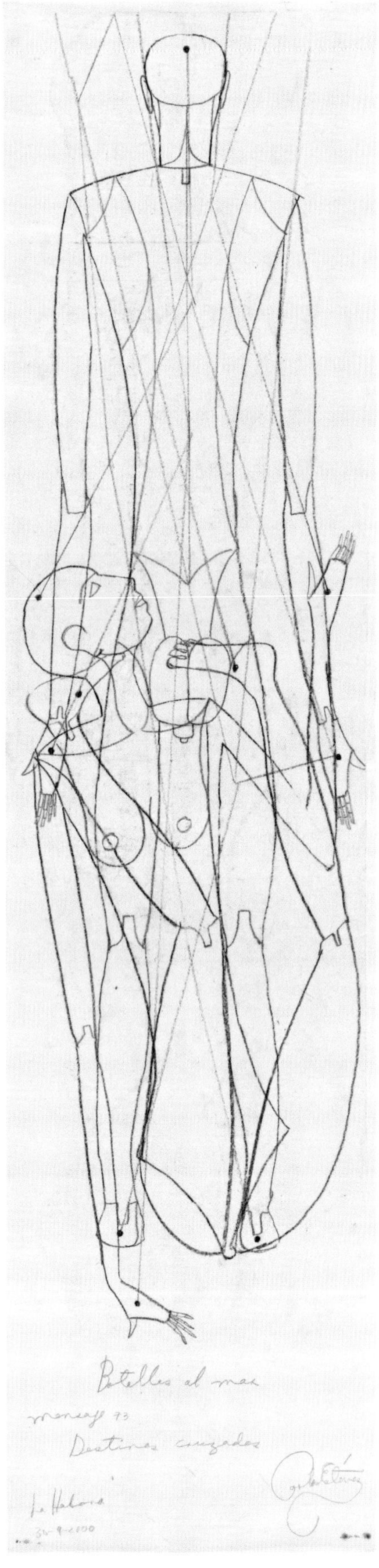

Bottles to the Sea
Message 73 "Crossed Destinies"
Norway 9-30-2000

Botellas al mar
Mensaje 73 "Destinos cruzados"
Noruega 30-9-2000

Bottles to the Sea
Message 74 “No One Can See Through My Eyes”
Havana 10-1-2000

Botellas al mar
Mensaje 74 “Nadie puede ver por mis ojos”
La Habana 1-10-2000

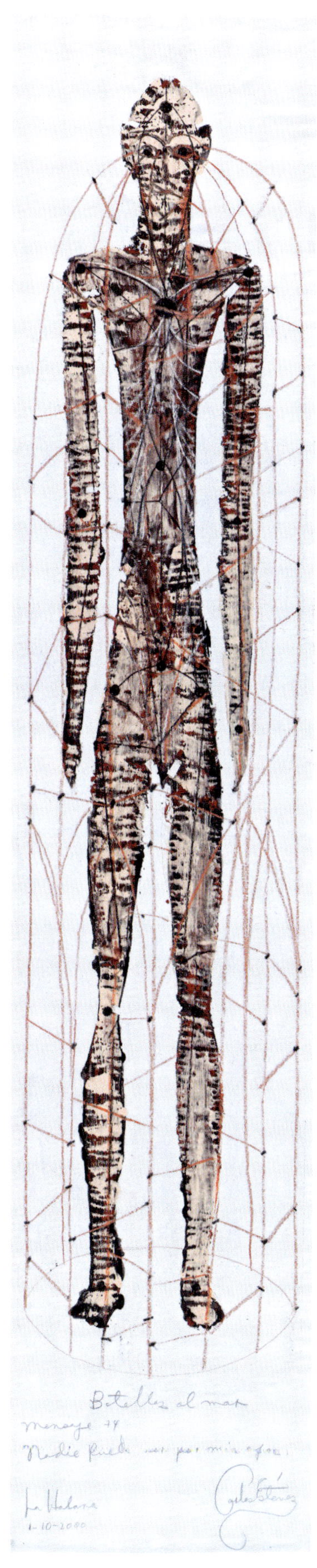

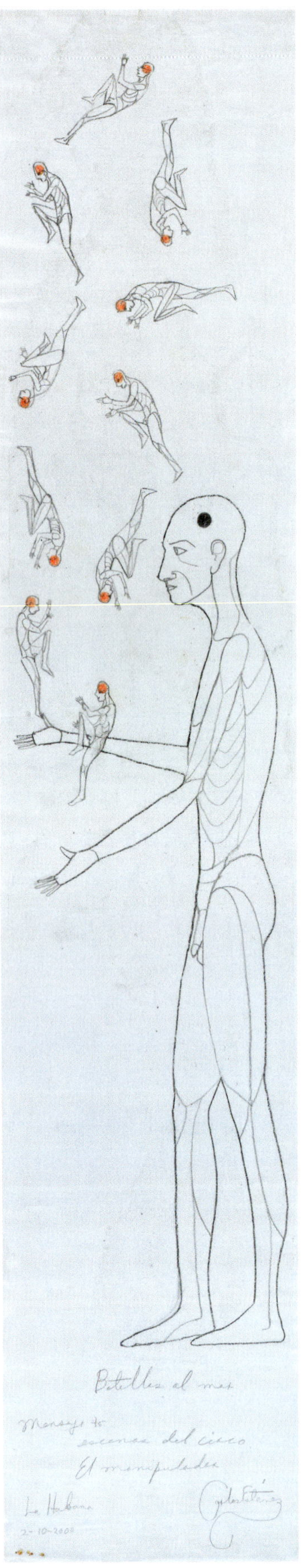

Bottles to the Sea
Message 75 "Circus Scenes. The Handler"
Havana 10-2-2000

Botellas al mar
Mensaje 75 "Escenas del circo. El manipulador"
La Habana 2-10-2000

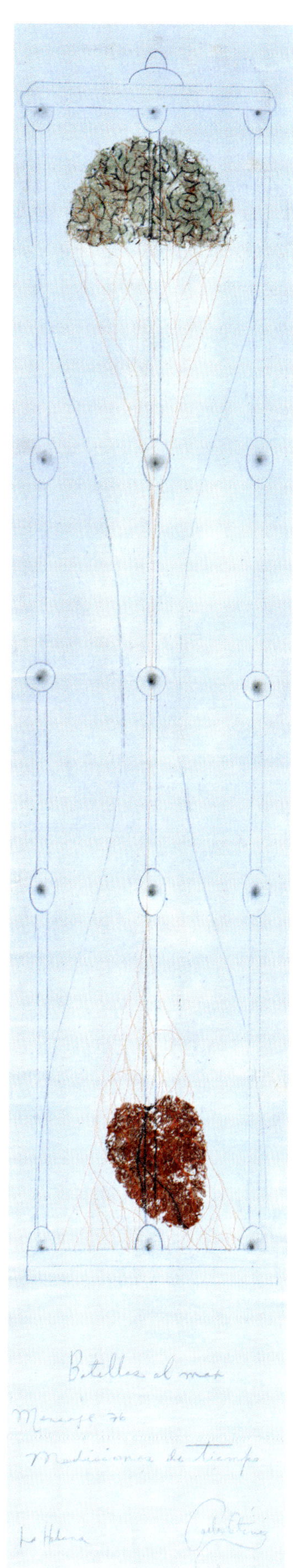

Bottles to the Sea
Message 76 "Measurements of Time"
Havana 10-3-2000

Botellas al mar
Mensaje 76 "Mediciones del tiempo"
La Habana 3-10-2000

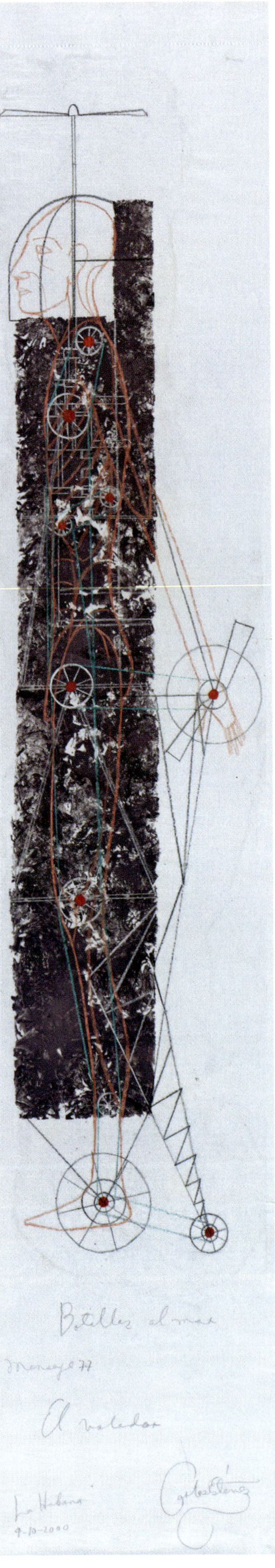

Bottles to the Sea
Message 77 “The Flyer”
Havana 10-4-2000

Botellas al mar
Mensaje 77 “El volador”
La Habana 4-10-2000

Bottles to the Sea
Message 78 "Circus Scenes. The Hooker"
Havana 4-10-2000
Launched at Barcelona, Spain. 2-15-2004

This message was found by a German tourist at Alcudia Beach, Balearic Islands, Spain. 2004

Botellas al mar
Mensaje 78 "Escenas de circo. La jinetera"
La Habana 10-4-2000
Lanzado en Barcelona, España. 15-2-2004

Este mensaje fue encontrado por una turista alemana en la playa Alcúdia, Mallorca, Islas Baleares, España. 2004

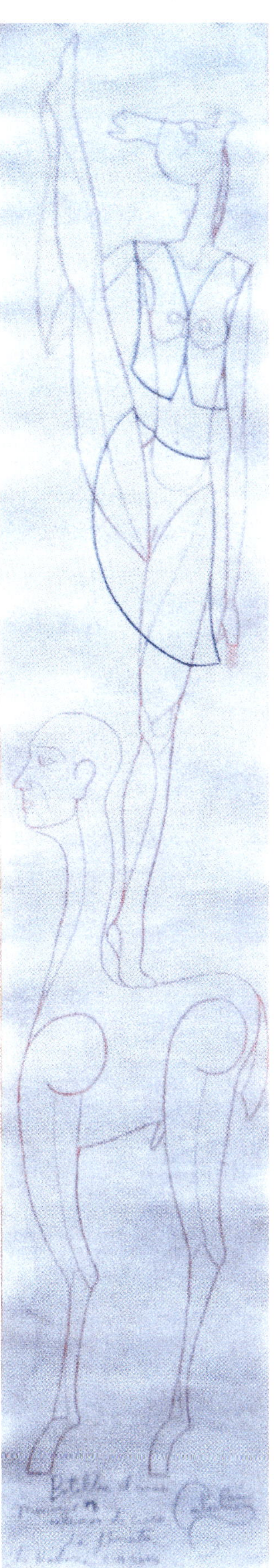

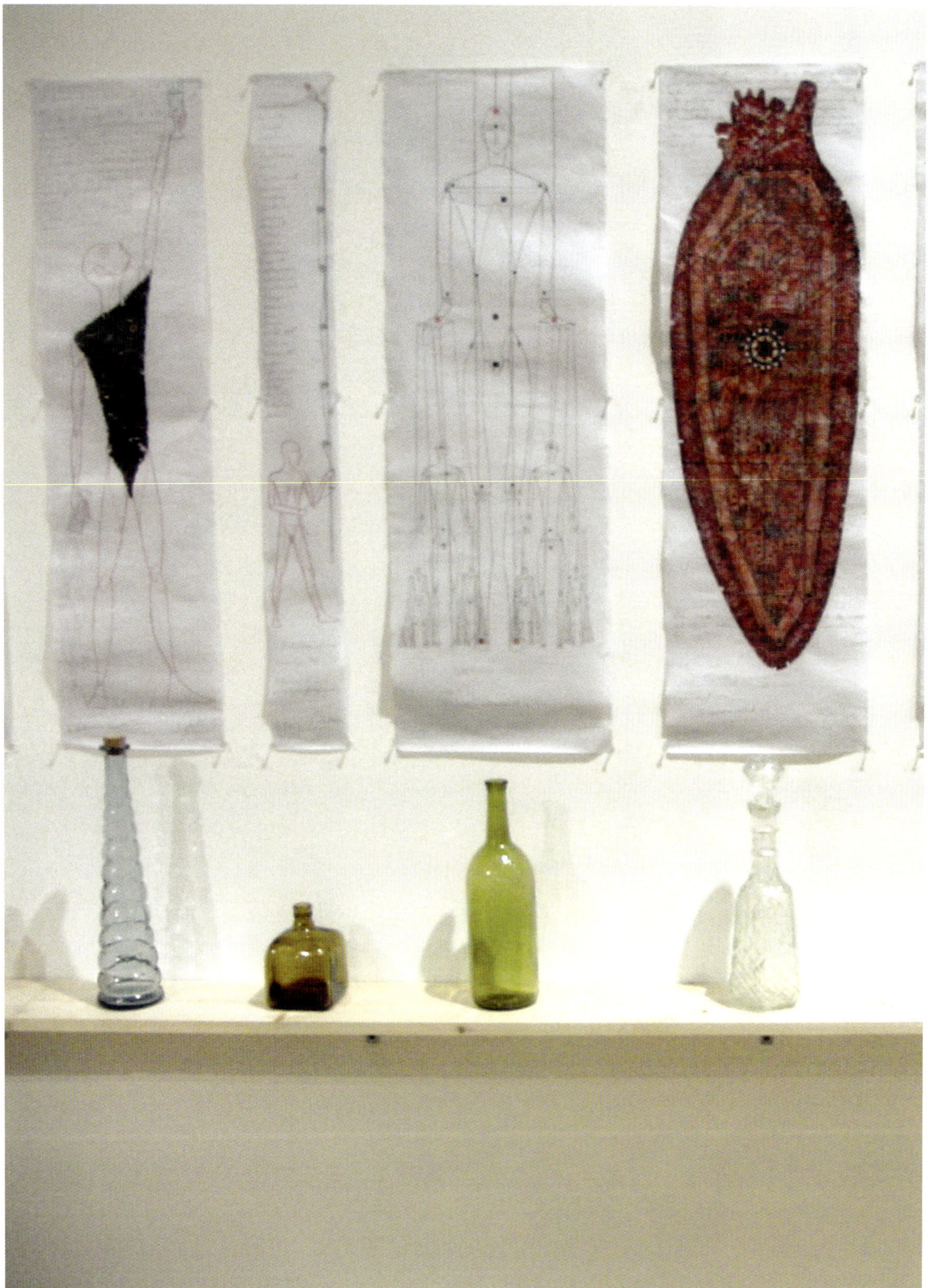

Bottles to the Sea
Message 79 "Circus Scenes. The Indoctrinator"
Havana 10-6-2000

Botellas al mar
Mensaje 79 "Escenas de circo. El adoctrinador"
La Habana 6-10-2000

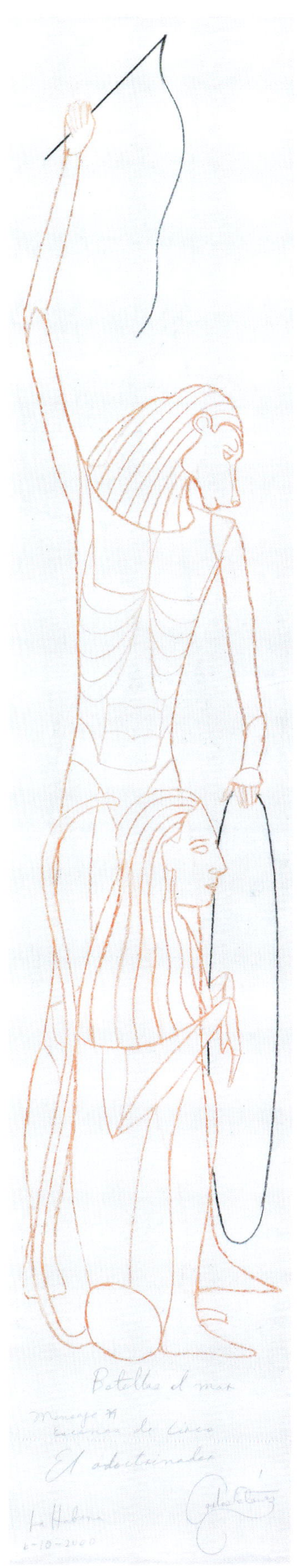

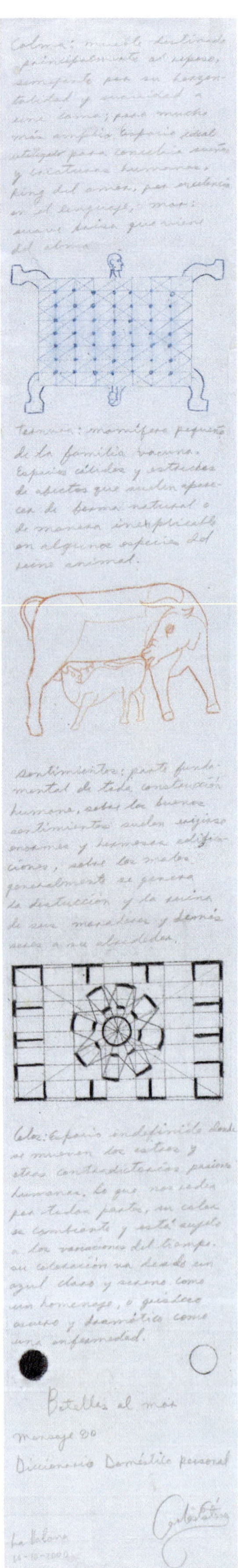

Bottles to the Sea
Message 80 "Personal Domestic Dictionary"
Havana 10-10-2000

Calm: piece of furniture principally destined for relaxation, similar in its horizontality and softness to a bed; but much larger. Ideal space used to conceive dreams and human creatures. Ring of love, par excellence in language, sea: soft breeze that comes from the soul.

Tenderness: small mammal from the bovine family. Warm and narrow spaces of feeling that typically appear naturally or inexplicably in some species of the animal kingdom.

Feelings: fundamental part of all human construction, on good sentiments large and beautiful edifications are usually established, on bad ones generally arises destruction and the ruin of their dwellings and other beings around them.

Jealousy: undefined space in which stars and other contradictory human passions move. That which surrounds us on all sides; its color is changeable and it is subject to the variations of time. Its color goes from a light and serene blue like a homage, to a dark and dramatic gray like a sickness.

Botellas al mar
Mensaje 80 "Diccionario doméstico personal"
La Habana 10-10-2000

Calma: mueble destinado principalmente al reposo, semejante por su horizontalidad y suavidad a una cama; pero mucho más amplio. Espacio ideal utilizado para concebir sueños y criaturas humanas. Ring del amor, por excelencia en el lenguaje, mar: suave brisa que viene del alma.

Ternura: mamífero pequeño de la familia vacuna. Espacios cálidos y estrechos de afectos que suelen aparecer de forma natural o de manera inexplicable en algunas especies del reino animal.

Sentimientos: parte fundamental de toda construcción humana, sobre los buenos sentimientos suelen erigirse enormes y hermosas edificaciones, sobre los malos generalmente se genera la destrucción y la ruina de sus moradores y demás seres a su alrededor.

Celos: Espacio indefinido donde se mueven los astros y otras contradictorias pasiones humanas. Lo que nos rodea por todas partes; su color es cambiante y está sujeto a las variaciones del tiempo. Su coloración va desde un azul claro y sereno como un homenaje, a grisáceo oscuro y dramático como una enfermedad.

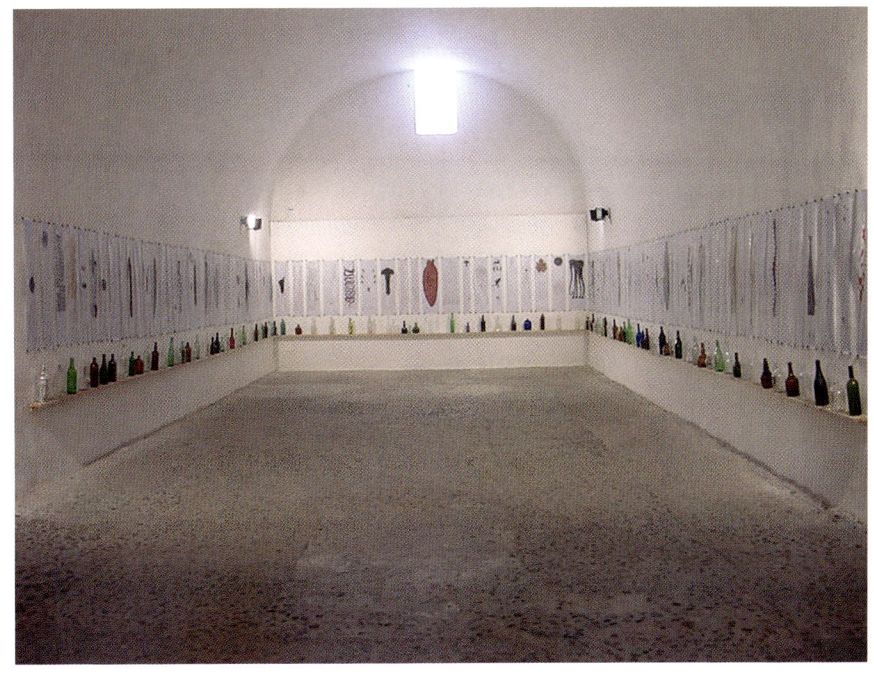

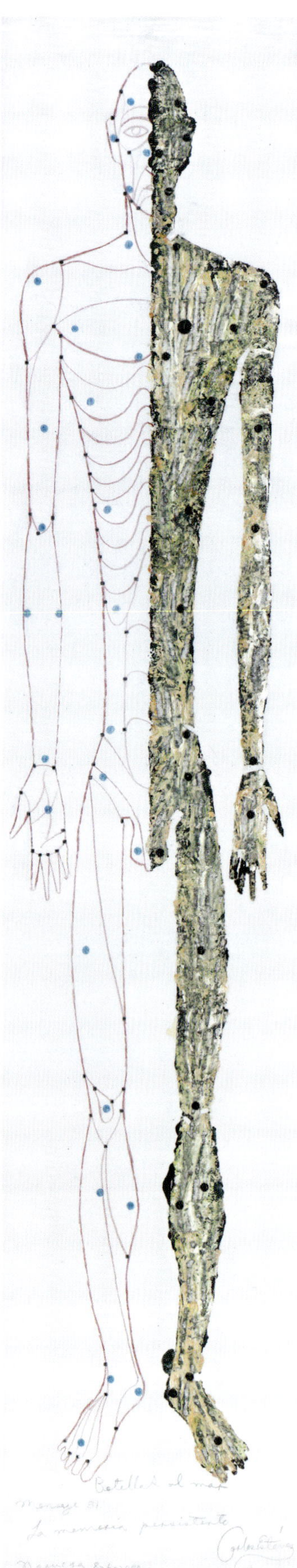

Bottles to the Sea
Message 81 "The Persistent Memory"
Norway 6-8-2000

Botellas al mar
Mensaje 81 "La memoria persistente"
Noruega 8-6-2000

Bottles to the sea
Message 82 "The Delivery of the Marionettes"
Havana 10-12-2000

Botellas al mar
Mensaje 82 "El parto de las marionetas"
La Habana 12-10-2000

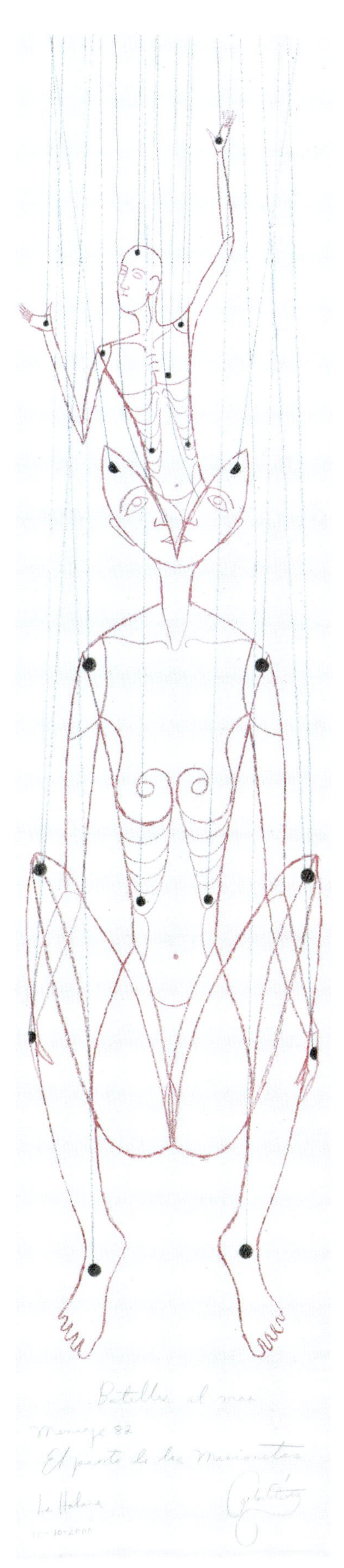

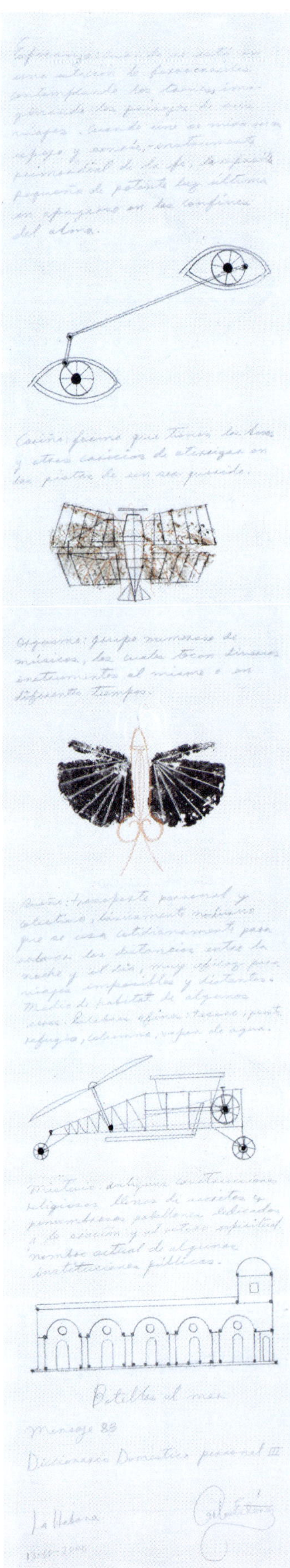

Bottles to the sea
Message 83 "Personal Domestic Dictionary III"
Havana 10-13-2000

Hope: when one is in a train station contemplating the trains, imagining the landscapes of their travels. When one looks at himself in a mirror and smiles, —-primordial instrument of faith, small lamp of powerful light, last to extinguish itself in the confines of the soul.

Endearment: form that kisses and other caresses have of landing on the runways of a loved one.

Orgasm: large group of musicians who play diverse instruments at the same or different times.

Sleep: personal and collective transport, basically nocturnal that is used daily to overcome the distance between night and day, very efficacious for impossible and distant travels. Habitat of some beings. Affinitive words: treasure, bridge, refuge, column, water vapor.

Mystery: ancient religious constructions full of secrets and penumbrous pavilions dedicated to prayer and spiritual retreat. Current name of some public institutions.

Botellas al mar
Mensaje 83 "Diccionario doméstico personal III"
La Habana 13-10-2000

Esperanza: cuando se está en una estación de ferrocarriles contemplando los trenes, imaginando los paisajes de sus viajes. Cuando uno se mira en un espejo y sonríe, -instrumento primordial de la fe, lamparilla pequeña de potente luz última en apagarse en los confines del alma.

Cariño: forma que tienen los besos y otras caricias de aterrizar en las pistas de un ser querido.

Orgasmo: grupo numeroso de músicos los cuales tocan diversos instrumentos al mismo o en diferentes tiempos.

Sueño: transporte personal y colectivo, básicamente nocturno que se usa cotidianamente para salvar las distancias entre la noche y el día, muy eficaz para viajes imposibles y distantes. Medio de hábitat de algunos seres. Palabras afines: tesoro, puente, refugio, columna, vapor de agua.

Misterio: antiguas construcciones religiosas llenas de secretos y penumbrosos pabellones dedicados a la oración y al retiro espiritual. Nombre actual de algunas instituciones públicas.

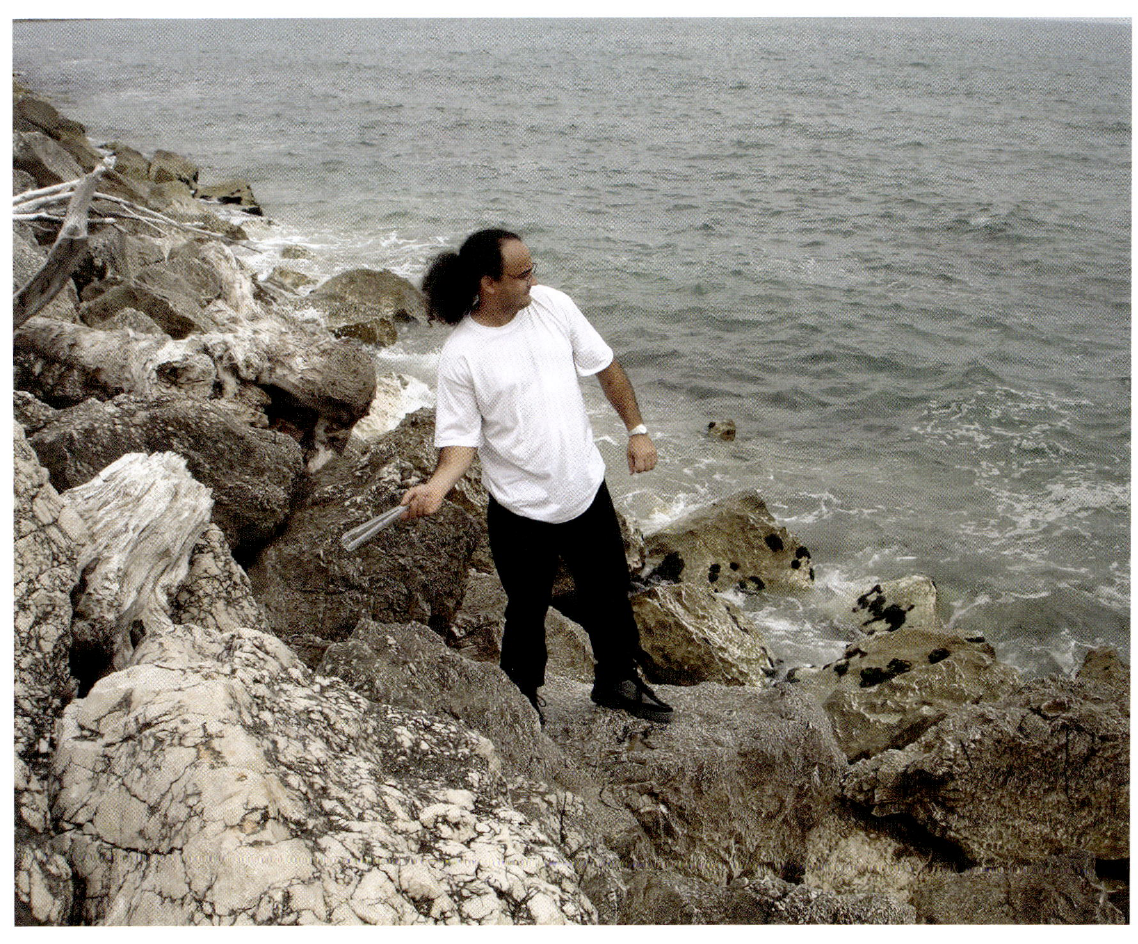

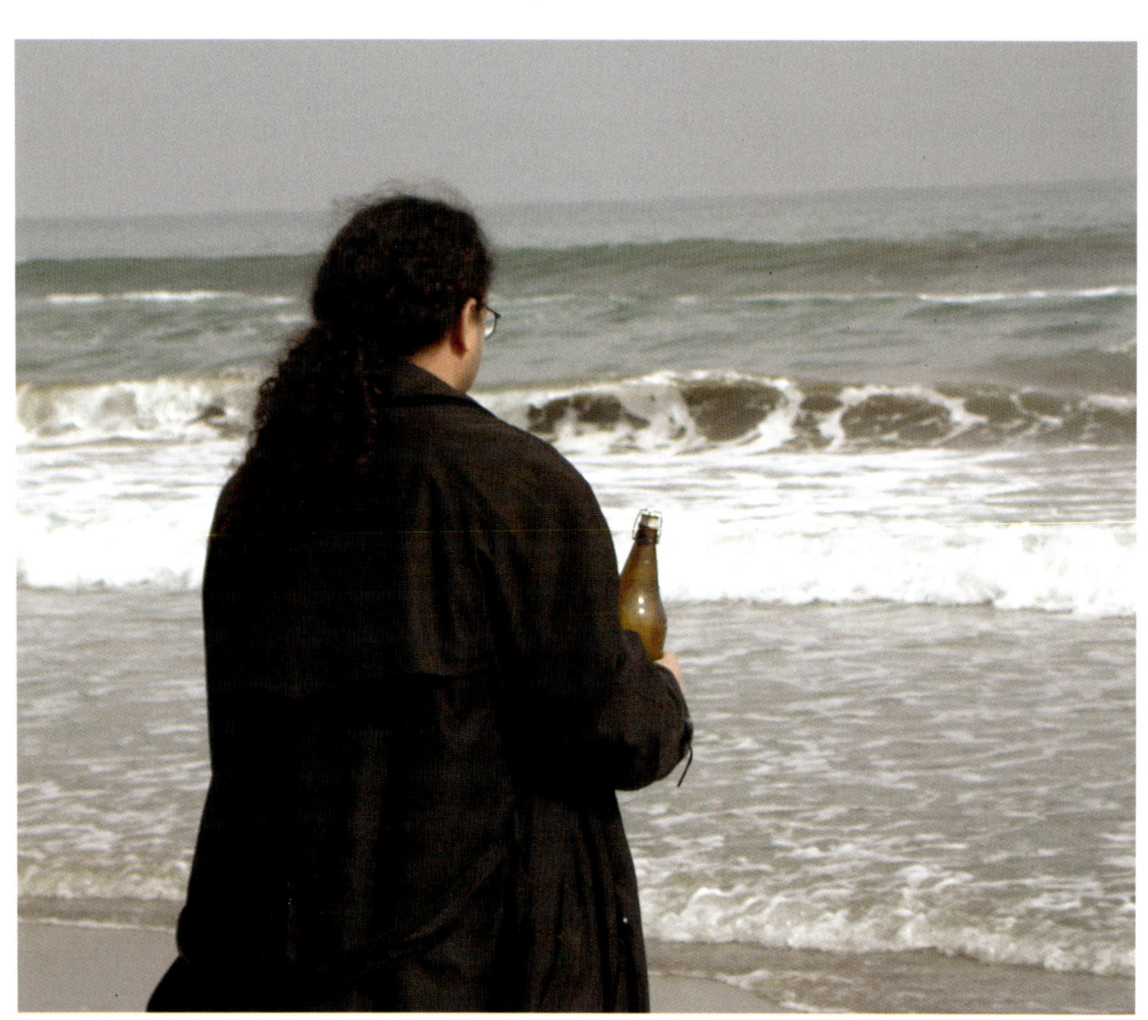

Bottles to the Sea
Message 84 "The Two Sides of the Coin"
Havana 10-14-2000

Botellas al mar
Mensaje 84 "Las dos caras de la moneda"
La Habana 14-10-2000

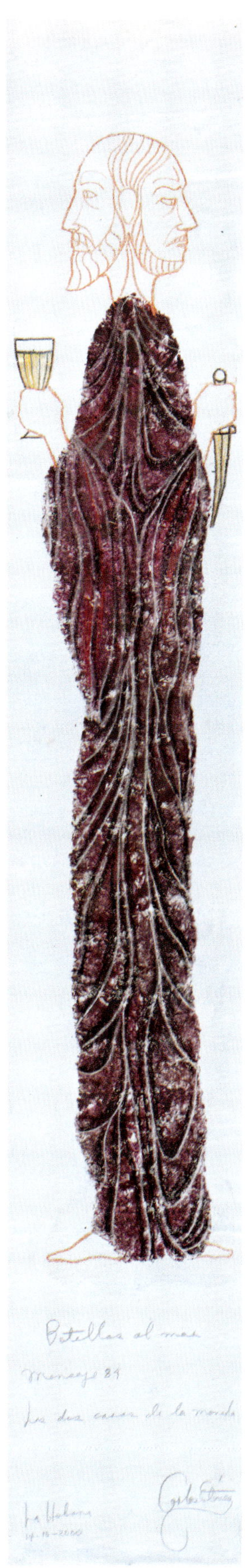

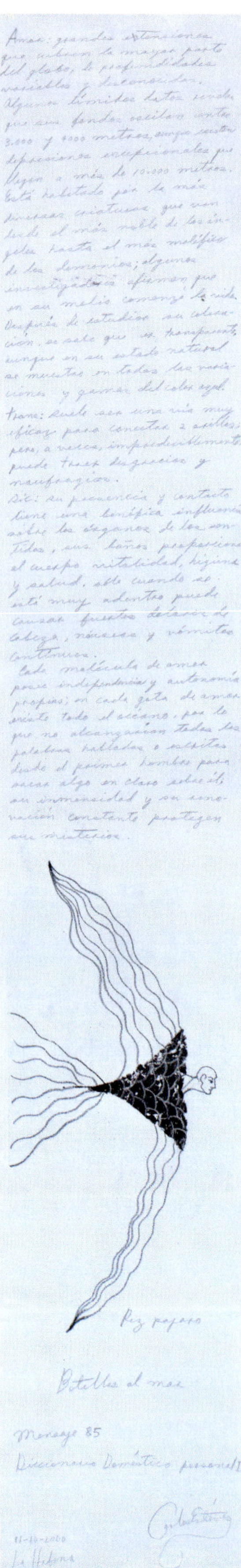

Bottles to the Sea
Message 85 "Personal Domestic Dictionary II"
Havana 10-11-2000

Love: great extensions that cover the largest part of the globe, of variable and unknown depths.

Some fearful information reveals that its bottom ranges between 3000 and 4000 meters, although there exist some exceptional depressions that reach more than 10,000 meters.

It is populated by the most diverse creatures, from the most noble of angels to the most pernicious of demons; some investigators affirm that in their habitat life began.

After studying their color it is determined that it is transparent, although in its natural state it shows itself in all the variations and range of the color blue.

Trans: it is usually a very efficacious way to connect two 2 edges; but, sometimes, unpredictably it can bring disgrace and shipwreck.

Sic: its presence and contact have a beneficial influence on the sense organs, its waters provide the body vitality, hygiene and health. But when it is very far inside it can cause intense headaches, and continuous nausea and vomiting.

Each molecule of love possesses its own independence and autonomy; in each drop of love exists the entire ocean, for which reason all the words spoken or written since the first man would not be enough to bring to light anything about it; its immensity and its constant renewal protect its mysteries.

Botellas al Mar
Mensaje 85 "Diccionario doméstico personal II"
La Habana 11-10-2000

Amor: grandes extensiones que cubren la mayor parte del globo, de profundidades variables y desconocidas.

Algunos temidos datos revelan que sus fondos oscilan entre 3,000 y 4,000 metros aunque existen depresiones excepcionales que llegan a más de 10,000 metros.

Está habitado por las más diversas criaturas que van desde el más noble de los ángeles hasta el más maléfico de los demonios; algunos investigadores afirman que en su medio comenzó la vida.

Después de estudiar su coloración se sabe que es transparente, aunque en su estado natural se muestre en todas las variaciones y gamas del color azul.

Trans: suele ser una vía muy eficaz para conectar dos 2 orillas; pero, a veces, impredeciblemente puede traer desgracias y naufragios.

Sic: su presencia y contacto tiene una benéfica influencia sobre los órganos de los sentidos, sus baños proporcionan al cuerpo vitalidad, higiene y salud. Solo cuando se está muy adentro puede causar fuertes dolores de cabeza, nauseas y vómitos continuos.

Cada molécula de amor posee independencia y autonomía propias; en cada gota de amor existe todo el océano, por lo que no alcanzarían todas las palabras habladas o escritas desde el primer hombre para sacar algo en claro sobre él; su inmensidad y su renovación constante protegen sus misterios.

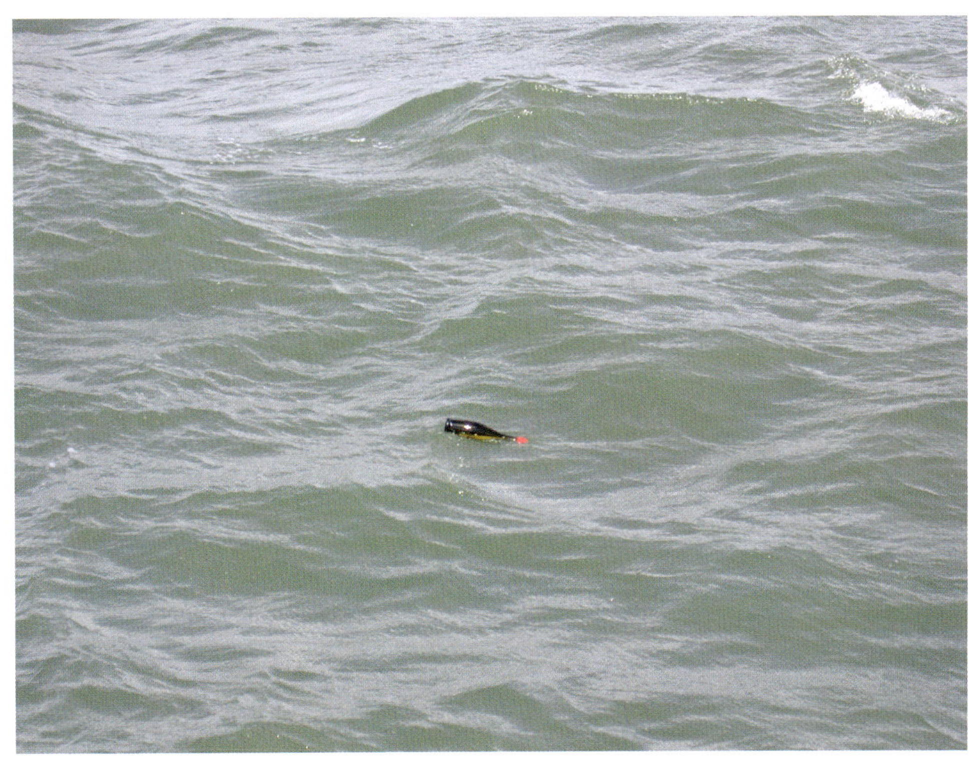

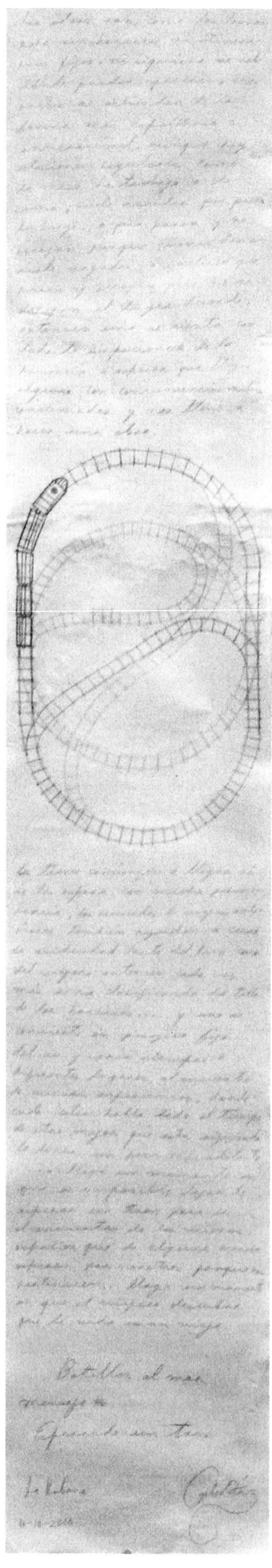

Bottles to the Sea
Message 86 "Waiting for a Train"
Havana 10-16-2000
Launched at Lisbon, Portugal. 10-2-2006

Ideas are like trains but without fixed schedules or itineraries, one never knows where they might appear, their rails extend in the most capricious and unlikely ways although there are regular stations like the work table and the bed, often it happens that they pass through, or that they stop and do not pick up because they arrive too full, or even that they pass and pick up but they do not go to the desired place, then one sits with all the impatience of patience to wait for one that arrives with mutually consummated conveniences and that takes us to make a work.

Trains begin to arrive if one awaits them with much perseverance, memories of prior journeys also help to create the assiduity as much of the train as of the travelers, then increasingly the schedule becomes clearer . . . and one becomes a regular passenger coming and going always to different places, to encounter new experiences where every place speaks all the time of another better one that is following the same line a little farther ahead.

. . . a moment arrives in which it is impossible to stop waiting for a train to go to the encounter with new spaces which in some way are waiting for us, because they belong to us . . . a moment arrives in which the traveler discovers that life is its journey.

Botellas al mar
Mensaje 86 "Esperando un tren"
La Habana 16-10-2000
Lanzado en Lisboa, Portugal. 2-10-2006

Las ideas son como los trenes pero sin horarios ni itinerarios fijos, ni siquiera se sabe donde pueden aparecer, sus raíles se extienden de la forma más caprichosa e inverosímil aunque hay estaciones regulares como la mesa de trabajo o la cama, suele suceder que pasan de largo, o que pasen y no recojan porque vienen demasiadas cargadas, o incluso que pasen y recojan pero no se dirijan al lugar deseado entonces uno se sienta con toda la impaciencia de la.paciencia a esperar que llegue alguno con conveniencias mutuas consumadas y nos lleve a hacer una obra.

Los trenes comienzan a llegar si se les espera con mucha perseverancia, los recuerdos de viajes anteriores también ayudan a crear la asiduidad tanto del tren como de los viajeros, entonces cada vez más se va clarificando la tabla de los horarios . . . y uno se convierte en pasajero fijo del ir y venir siempre a diferentes lugares, al encuentro de nuevas experiencias donde cada sitio habla todo el tiempo de otro mejor que está siguiendo la línea un poco más adelante.

. . . llega un momento en que es imposible dejar de esperar un tren para ir al encuentro de los nuevos espacios que de alguna manera esperan por nosotros, porque nos pertenecen . . . llega un momento en que el viajero descubre que la vida es su viaje.

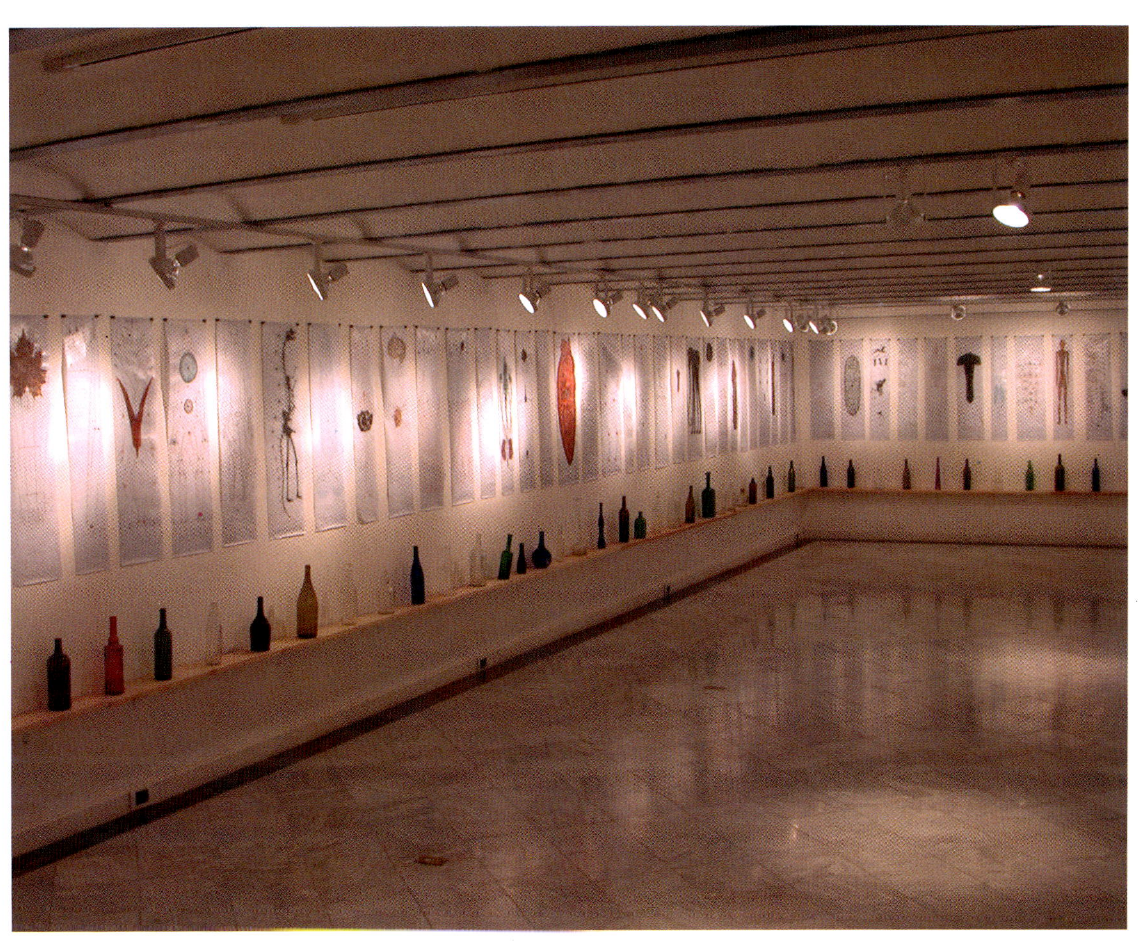

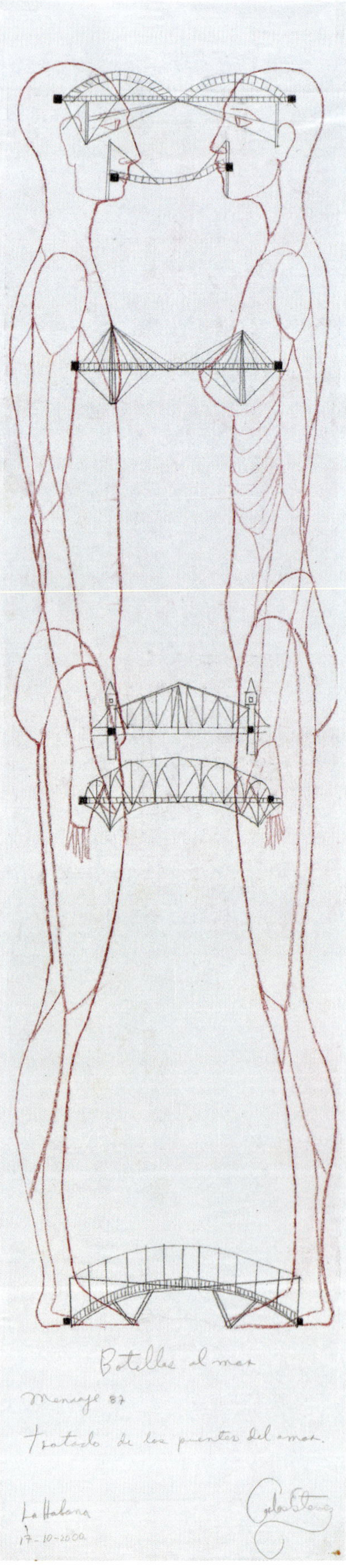

Bottles to the Sea
Message 87 "Treatise of the Bridges of Love"
Havana 10-17-2000

Botellas al mar
Mensaje 87 "Tratado de los puentes del amor"
La Habana 17-10-2000

Bottles to the Sea
Message 88 "Interaction of the Worlds"
Havana 10-18-2000
Launched at Key West, Florida, United States. 10-20-2002

Botellas al mar
Mensaje 88 "Interacción de los mundos"
La Habana 18-10-2000
Lanzado en Key West, Florida, Estados Unidos. 20-10-2002

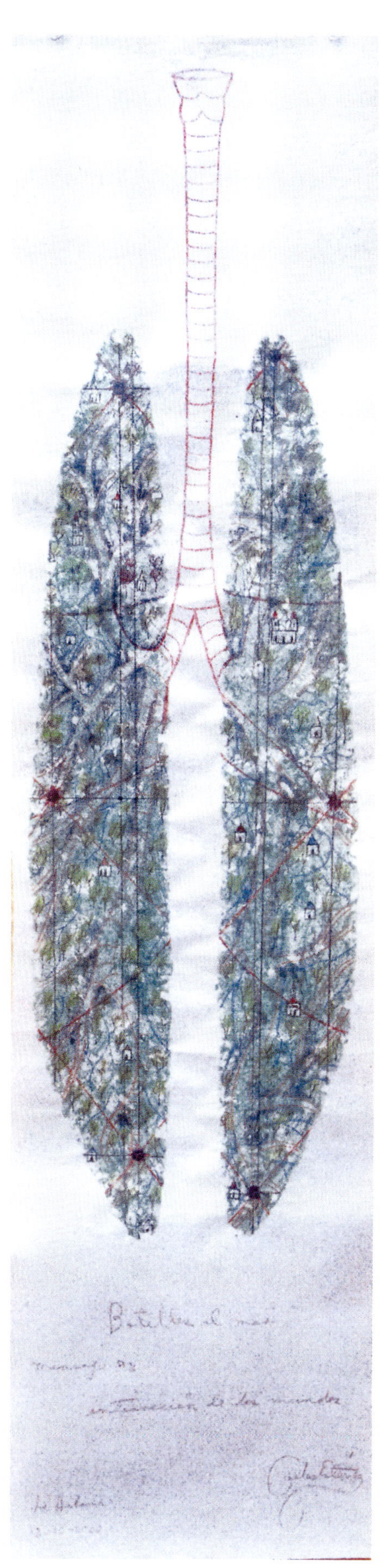

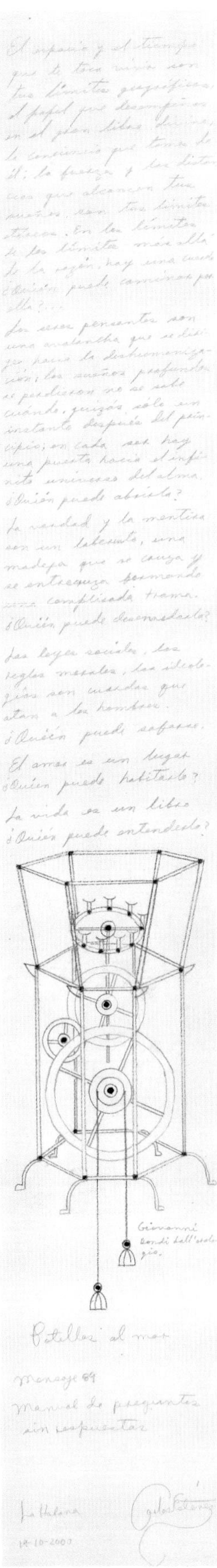

Bottles to the Sea
Message 89 "Manual of Questions without Answers"
Havana 10-19-2000

The space and time that you are given to live are your geographical limits, the role that you play in the great divine book, the consciousness that you have of it; the force and the distances that your dreams reach, are your ethereal limits. At the limit of limits, beyond reason, there is a wire. Who can walk across it? . . .

Thinking beings are an avalanche that directs itself toward dehumanization, profound dreams are lost one does not know when, perhaps only an instant after the beginning; in each being there is a door toward the infinite universe of the soul. Who can open it?

Truth and lie are a labyrinth, a ball of yarn that crosses over and through itself forming a complicated weave. Who can unravel it?

Social laws, moral rules, ideologies are ties that bind men. Who can escape?

Love is a place. Who can inhabit it?

Life is a book. Who can understand it?

Botellas al mar
Mensaje 89 "Manual de preguntas sin respuestas"
La Habana 19-10-2000

El espacio y el tiempo que te toca vivir son tus límites geográficos, el papel que desempeñas en el gran libro divino, la conciencia que tomas de él; la fuerza y las distancias que alcancen tus sueños, son tus límites etéreos. En los límites de los límites, más allá de la razón, hay una cuerda. ¿Quién puede caminar por ella?...

Los seres pensantes son una avalancha que se dirige hacia la deshumanización, los sueños profundos se perdieron no se sabe cuándo, quizás sólo un instante después del principio; en cada ser hay una puerta hacia el infinito universo del alma. ¿Quién puede abrirla?

La verdad y la mentira son un laberinto, una madeja que se cruza y se entrecruza formando una complicada trama. ¿Quién puede desenredarla?

Las leyes sociales, las reglas morales, las ideologías son cuerdas que atan a los hombres. ¿Quién puede zafarse?

El amor es un lugar ¿Quién puede habitarlo?

La vida es un libro ¿Quién puede entenderlo?

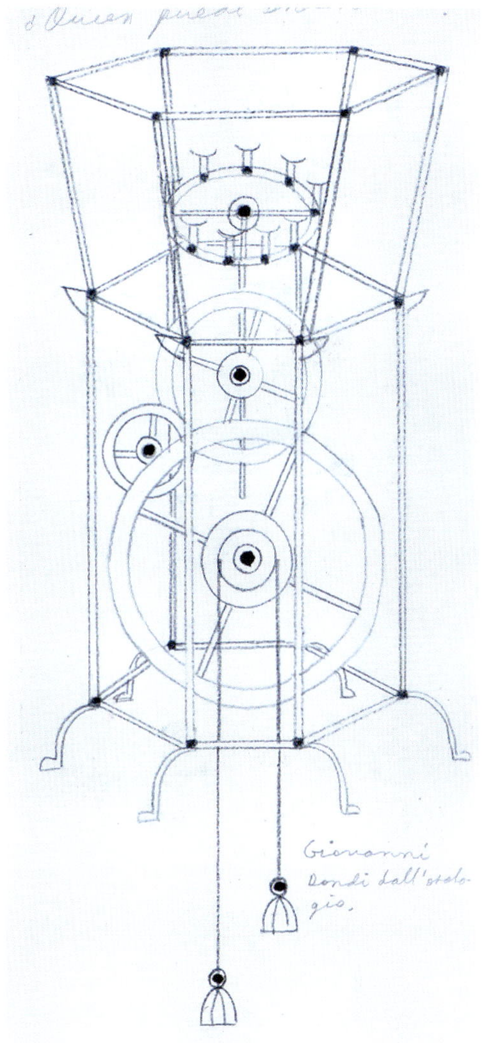

detail, Message 89

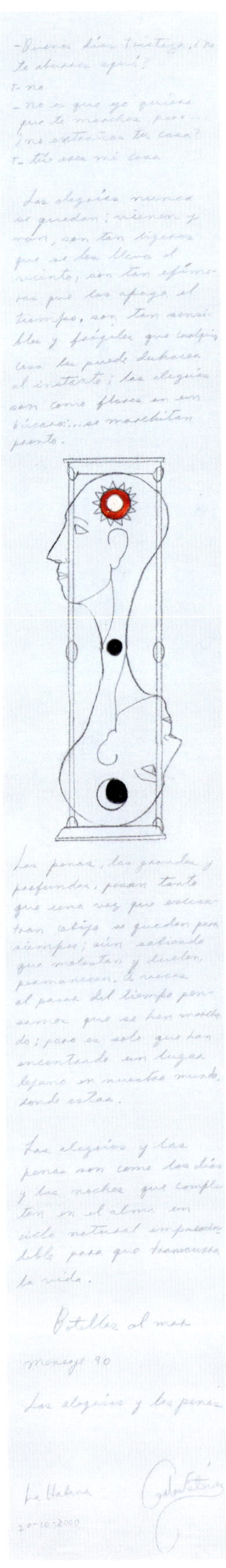

Bottles to the Sea
Message 90 "Joys and Sorrows"
Havana 10-20-2000

—Good morning sorrow! You're not bored here?

S—No

—It isn't that I want you to go but . . .

S—You are my home.

Joys never stay. They come and go, they are so light that the wind carries them off, they are so ephemeral that time extinguishes them, they are so sensitive and fragile that anything can destroy them in an instant; joys are like flowers in a vase . . . they wither quickly.

Sorrows, great and profound, weigh so much that once they find shelter they remain forever; even knowing that they upset and hurt, they remain. Sometimes with the passing of time, we think they have left; but it is only that they have found a distant place in our world in which to be.

Joys and sorrows are like days and nights, which complete in the soul a natural cycle indispensable for life to pass.

Botellas al mar
Mensaje 90 "Las alegrías y las penas"
La Habana 20-10-2000

—¡Buenos días tristeza! ¿No te aburres aquí?

T—No

—No es que yo quiera que te marches pero . . .

T—Tú eres mi casa.

Las alegrías nunca se quedan: vienen y van, son tan ligeras que se las lleva el viento, son tan efímeras que las apaga el tiempo, son tan sensibles y frágiles que cualquier cosa las puede deshacer al instante; las alegrías son como flores en un búcaro: . . . se marchitan pronto.

Las penas, las grandes y profundas, pesan tanto que una vez que encuentran cobijo se quedan para siempre; aun sabiendo que molestan y duelen, permanecen. A veces al pasar del tiempo pensamos que se han marchado; pero es sólo que han encontrado un lugar lejano en nuestro mundo donde estar.

Las alegrías y las penas son como los días y las noches, que completan en el alma un ciclo natural imprescindible para que transcurra la vida.

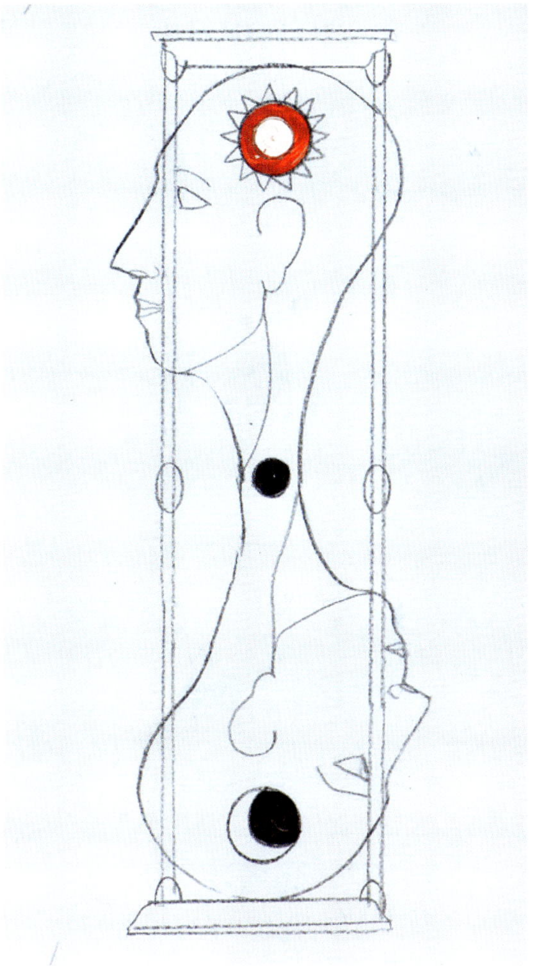

detail, Message 90

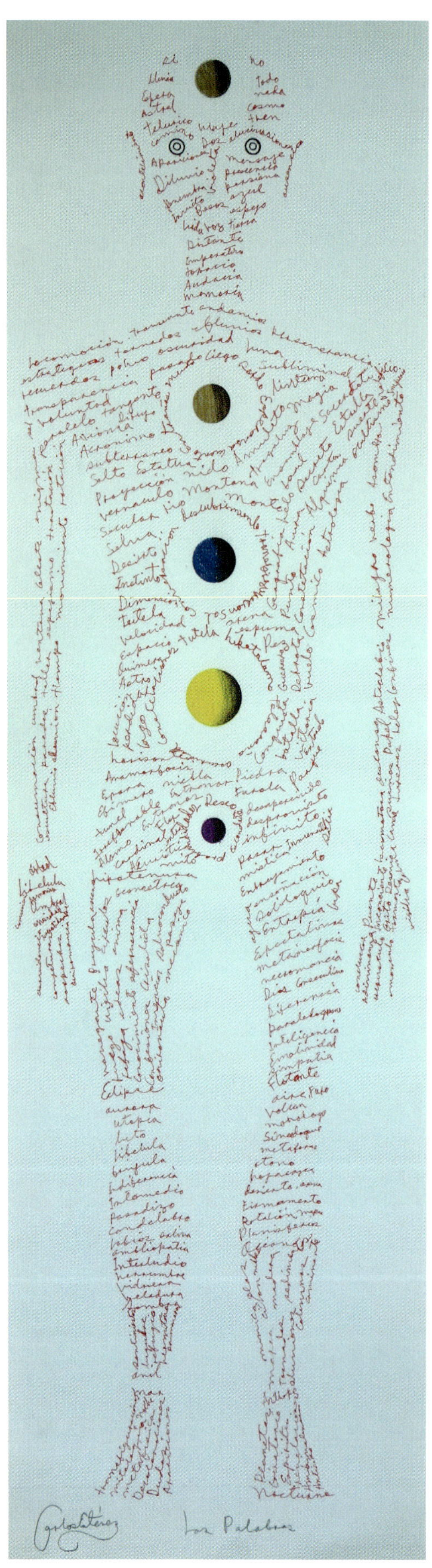

Bottles to the Sea
Message 91 "Words"
Version of the original
Miami 8-17-2013
Launched at Fortress San Juan de Ulua,
Veracruz, Mexico. 11-9-2003

Botellas al mar
Mensaje 91 "Las palabras"
Versión del original
Miami 17-8-2013
Lanzado en la Fortaleza San Juan de Ulúa,
Veracruz, México. 09-11-2003

Bottles to the Sea
Message 92 "The Message, or the Juggling of History"
Havana 10-21-2000

Botellas al mar
Mensaje 92 "El mensaje, o los malabares de la historia"
La Habana 21-10-2000

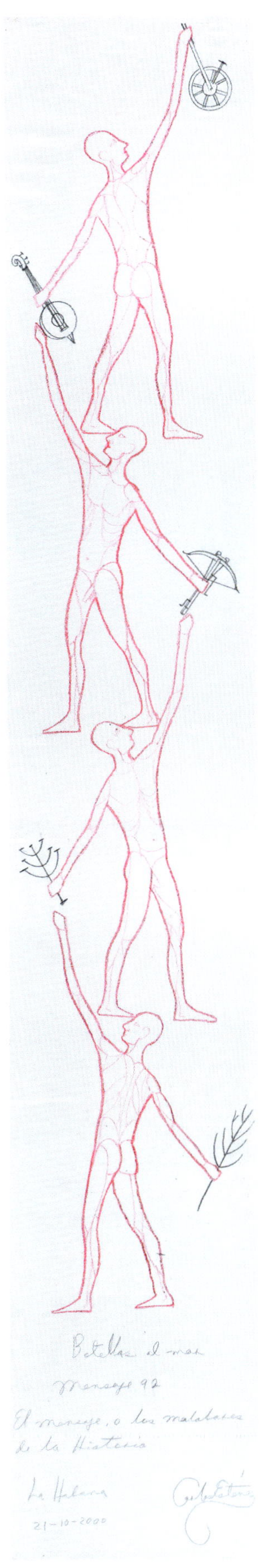

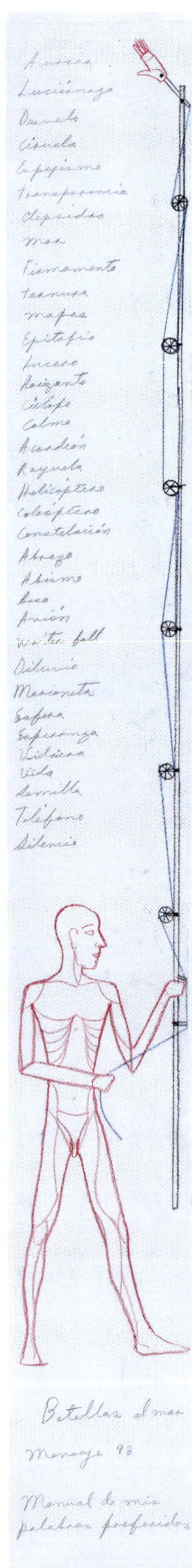

Bottles to the Sea
Message 93 "Manual of my Preferred Words"
Havana 10-23-2000

Aurora
Firefly
Sleepless
Plum
Mirage
Transparency
Clepsydra
Sea
Firmament
Tenderness
Maps
Epitaph
Star
Horizon
Cyclops
Calm
Accordion
Hopscotch
Helicopter
Coleopterous
Constellation
Embrace
Abyss
Kiss
Airplane
Water Fall
Deluge
Marionette
Sphere
Hope
Window
Life
Seed
Telephone
Silence

Botellas al mar
Mensaje 93 "Manual de mis palabras preferidas"
La Habana 23-10-2000

Aurora
Luciérnaga
Desvelo
Ciruela
Espejismo
Transparencia
Clepsidra
Mar
Firmamento
Ternura
Mapas
Epitafio
Lucero
Horizonte
Cíclope
Calma
Acordeón
Rayuela
Helicóptero
Coleóptero
Constelación
Abrazo
Abismo
Beso
Avión
Water Fall
Diluvio
Marioneta
Esfera
Esperanza
Vidriera
Vida
Semilla
Teléfono
Silencio

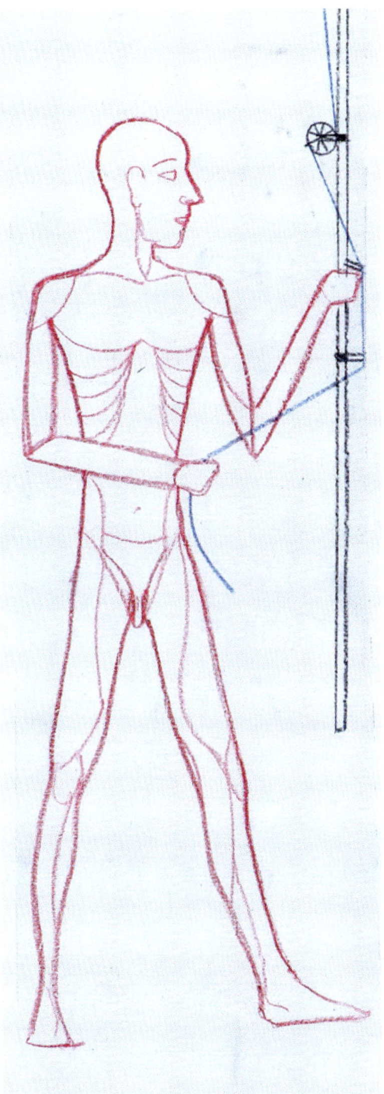

detail, Message 93

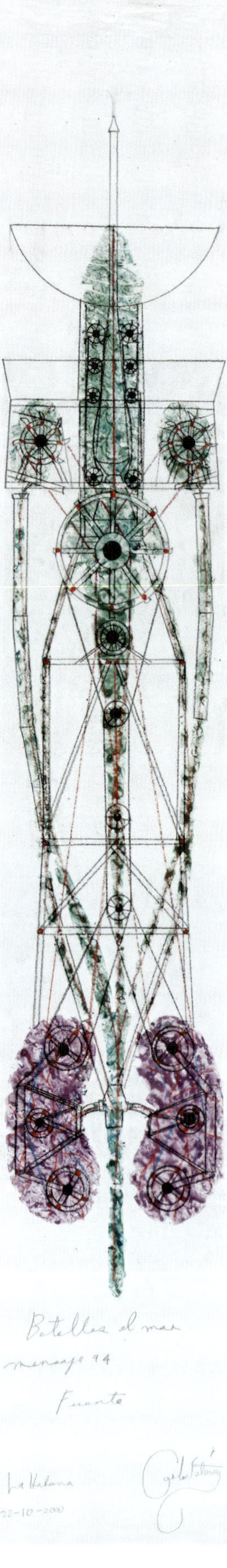

Bottles to the Sea
Message 94 "Fountain"
Havana 10-22-2000

Botellas al mar
Mensaje 94 "Fuente"
La Habana 22-10-2000

Bottles to the Sea
Message 95 "Elementary Treatise on Optometry"
Havana 10-24-2000

For humans, cognitive and affective spaces have oriented in a definitive way their vision of life . . .

In technical terms it can be said that each knowing, each feeling, each element of the material world and of consciousness constitutes a complex variety of lenses with diverse focal graduations.

. . . each fragment of the cosmic universe and the universe of thought is in constant movement and change, from their positional relations are formed new optical combinations ad infinitum . . .

Nothing is the same; any distance, relation, presence or absence, dream or sleeplessness; any gesture or gaze, temporal state or color of the sea, any delay or haste, a kiss, an embrace, a drawing, any ecstasy or emptiness, definitively confuses the form of seeing life.

Botellas al Mar
Mensaje 95 "Tratado elemental de optometría"
La Habana 24-10-2000

Para los humanos los espacios cognoscitivos y afectivos han orientado de forma definitiva su visión de la vida . . .

En términos técnicos puede decirse que cada saber, cada sentir, cada elemento del mundo material y de la conciencia constituye una compleja variedad de vidrios con diversas graduaciones focales.

. . . cada fragmento del universo cósmico y el universo del pensamiento están en constante movimiento y cambio, se forman nuevas combinaciones ópticas hasta el infinito a partir de sus relaciones posicionales . . .

Nada da igual; cualquier distancia, relación, presencia o ausencia, sueño o desvelo; cualquier gesto o mirada, estado del tiempo o coloración del mar, cualquier demora o premura, un beso, un abrazo, un dibujo, cualquier éxtasis o vacío, marean definitivamente la forma de ver la vida.

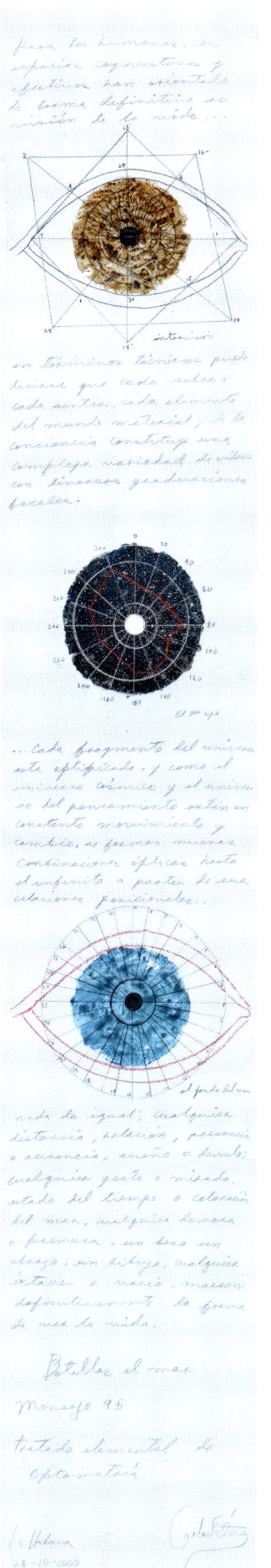

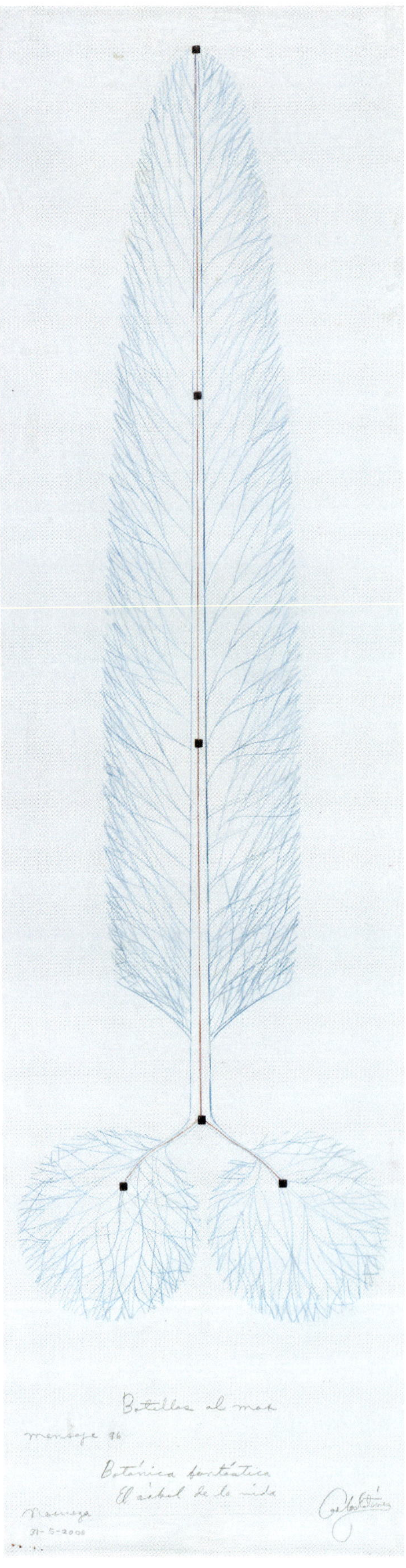

Bottles to the Sea
Message 96 “Imaginary Garden” “The Tree of Life”
Norway 5-31-2000

Botellas al mar
Mensaje 96 “Botánica fantástica” “El árbol de la vida”
Noruega 31-5-2000

Bottles to the Sea
Message 97 "Some Notes on Natural History"
Norway 5-30-2000

Nicrophorous vespillo

Hexadactyla

Buthus occitanus

Botellas al mar
Mensaje 97 "Algunas notas sobre historia natural"
Noruega 30-5-2000

Nicrophorous vespillo

Hexadactyla

Buthus occitanus

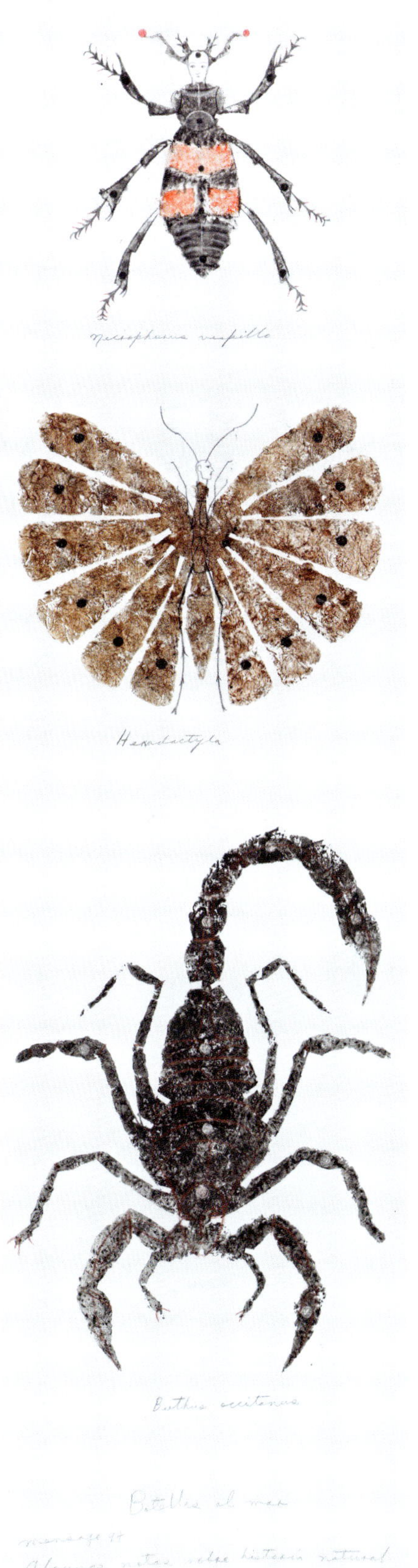

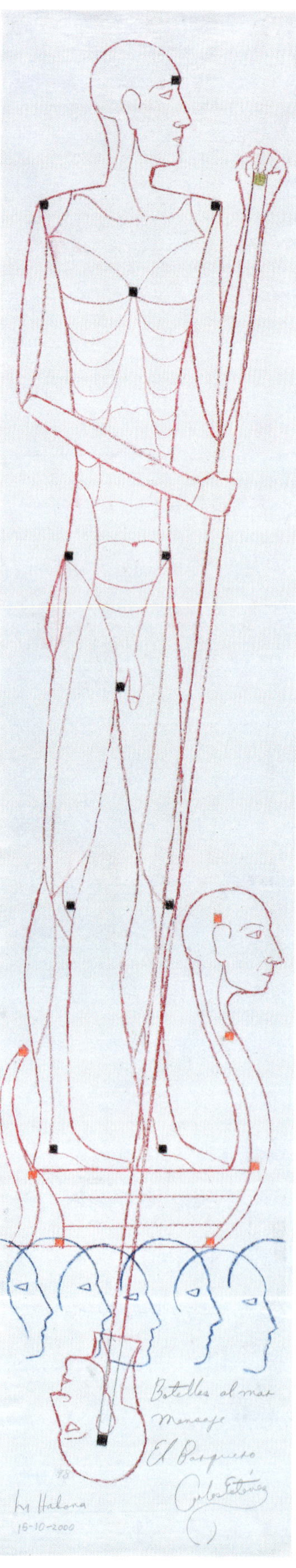

Bottles to the Sea
Message 98 "The Ferryman"
Havana 10-15-2000

Botellas al mar
Mensaje 98 "El barquero"
La Habana 15-10-2000

Bottles to the Sea
Message 99 "Our Father Who Art in Our Hearts"
Havana 9-14-2000

Our father who art in our hearts: I imagine you are satisfied with the vitality of us your characters, sure that we are not the only ones, but we feel as if we were; in sum, is not the final truth of the cosmos that the universe revolves around each being? . . . I like your book, it fascinates me how you can change the course of events, how you can put anything in any place and at any moment, making us believe that we do not possess any other home than our body and only during our stay in the world; you are very wise not to confide to anyone whence emanate love and the divine, thus we have to look for things everywhere, because everything deserves to be seen, touched, reviewed, at least once; you neglected nothing, only we mortals know of forgetting and neglect.

You ought to feel very secure in your reign since you have disposed of it so that no one trespasses your limits; no one can exit the stage no matter how easy it seems. Those of the plains, you did not blindfold them, but they cannot see beyond their stature; moreover, those of the mountains: those yes, so that they only feel the height, but they do not believe it; you already know that we do not understand very well the illusoriness of the world, that all the images are nothing more than drawings of your secret maps of the universe, and that reality only happens in our thoughts and dreams, no one even imagines that perfection is born of chaos and instability.

You already know, that like some others, I dream of being like you, not only for vanity, but also for your fecund imagination—Who has been able to decipher a single one of your paradoxes?—sometimes, hidden, I pretend to be you, I provoke things, I decide others, I make prognostications and I calculate results, I tempt destiny, I repress my impatience and I follow instructions to the letter in order to be happy or sad, I orient my will, but finally love reminds me that I am mortal, that is to say, vulnerable, that my weapons are my impatience and imperfection, that my goals are unattainable, that I win over weakness and that in

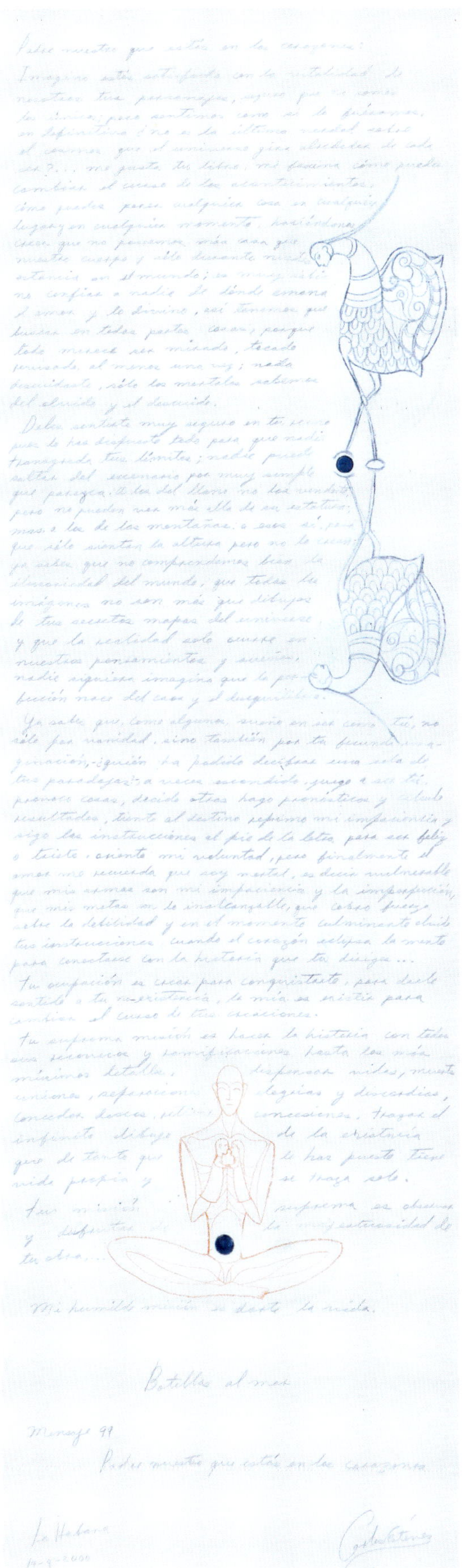

the culminating moment I forget your instructions when the heart eclipses the mind in order to connect with that history that you direct . . .

Your occupation is to create to conquer yourself, to give meaning to your non-existence, mine is to exist in order to change the course of your creations.

Your supreme mission is to make history with all its turns and ramifications even the most minimal details, to dispense life, deaths, unions, separations, joys and discords, concede desires, withdraw concessions, trace the infinite drawing of the existence that, from all you have put into it, has its own life and traces itself alone.

Your supreme mission is to observe and enjoy the majesty of your work . . .

My humble mission is to give you life.

Botellas al mar Mensaje 99 "Padre nuestro que estás en nuestros corazones" La Habana 14-9-2000

Padre nuestro que estás en los corazones: Imagino estás satisfecho con la vitalidad de nosotros tus personajes, seguro que no somos los únicos, pero sentimos como si lo fuéramos; en definitiva ¿no es la última verdad sobre el cosmos que el universo gira alrededor de cada ser? . . . me gusta tu libro, me fascina como puedes cambiar el curso de los acontecimientos, como puedes poner cualquier cosa en cualquier lugar y en cualquier momento, haciéndonos creer que no poseemos mas casa que nuestro cuerpo y solo durante nuestra estancia en el mundo; es muy sabio no confiar a nadie de donde emana el amor y lo divino, así tenemos que buscar en todas partes cosas, porque todo merece ser mirado, tocado, revisado, al menos una vez; nada descuidaste, solo los mortales sabemos del olvido y el descuido.

Debes sentirte muy seguro en tu reino pues lo has dispuesto todo para que nadie transgreda tus límites; nadie puede saltar del escenario por muy simple que parezca. A los del llano no los vendaste, pero no pueden ver más allá de su estatura; más, a los de las montañas: a esos sí, para que sólo sientan la altura pero no lo crean; ya sabes que no comprendemos bien la ilusoriedad del mundo, que todas las imágenes no son más que dibujos de tus secretos mapas del universo, y que la realidad sólo ocurre en nuestros pensamientos y sueños, nadie siquiera imagina que la perfección nace del caos y el desequilibrio.

Ya sabes, que como algunos, sueño en ser como tú, no sólo por vanidad, sino también por tu fecunda imaginación -¿Quién ha podido descifrar una sola de tus paradojas?- a veces, escondido, juego a ser tú, provoco cosas, decido otras, hago pronósticos y calculo resultados, tiento al destino, reprimo mi impaciencia y sigo las instrucciones al pie de la letra para ser feliz o triste, oriento mi voluntad, pero finalmente el amor me recuerda que soy un mortal, es decir, vulnerable, que mis armas son mi impaciencia y la imperfección, que mis metas son lo inalcanzable, que cobro fuerza sobre la debilidad y en el momento culminante olvido tus instrucciones cuando el corazón eclipsa la mente para conectarse con la historia que tu diriges . . .

Tu ocupación es crear para conquistarte, para darle sentido a tu no-existencia, la mía es existir para cambiar el curso de tus creaciones.

Tu suprema misión es hacer la historia con todos sus recovecos y ramificaciones hasta los más mínimos detalles, dispensar vida, muertes, uniones, separaciones, alegrías y discordias, conceder deseos, retirar concesiones, trazar el infinito dibujo de la existencia que de tanto que le has puesto tiene vida propia y se traza solo.

Tu misión suprema es observar y disfrutar de la majestuosidad de tu obra . . .

Mi humilde misión es darte vida.

Bottles to the Sea
Message 100 "Each End is a New Beginning"
Havana 10-25-2000

. . . because dreams have the capacity to extend and renew themselves like the tides . . .

Botellas al mar
Mensaje 100 "Cada final es un nuevo comienzo"
La Habana 25-10-2000

. . . porque los sueños tienen esa capacidad de extenderse y renovarse como las mareas . . .

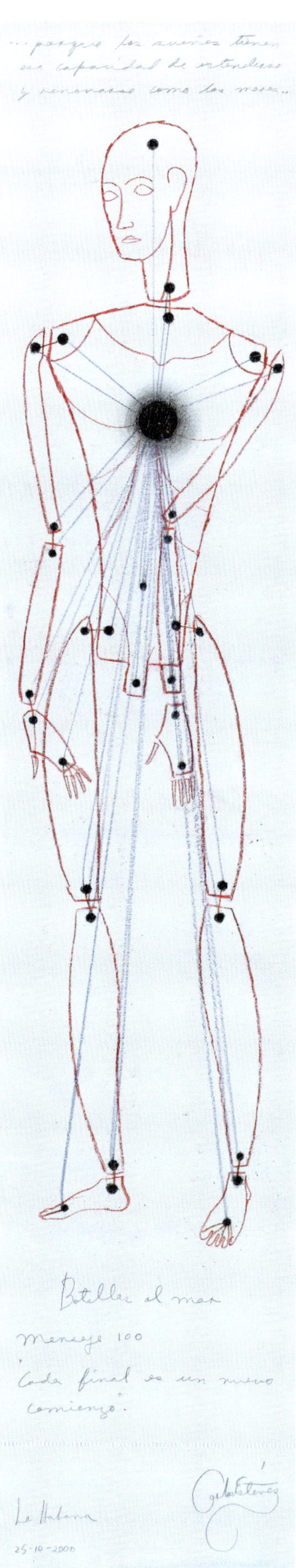

BIBLIOGRAPHY

http://www.carlosestevez.net

Albertini, Rosanna. (2001). "Carlos Estévez: The Theater of Life." In *Carlos Estévez: The Theater of Life*. Exhibition catalogue. Los Angeles, CA: Couturier Gallery.

"Art from Cuba. The Ludwig Collection." (2002). *Ludwig Forum for International Art*. Peter and Irene Ludwig Foundation. Ludwig Museum in the Russian Museum, pp. 76–79.

Block, Holly, ed. (2001). *Art Cuba: The New Generation*. New York, NY: Abrams.

Bosch, Lynette F. M. (2004). *Cuban-American Art in Miami: Exile, Identity and the Neo-Baroque*. London: Lund Humphreys Press.

Brattetveit, Ørjan. (1998). "Cubansk Kunst inntar Drammen," *Tirsdag* 2.

Camnitzer, Luis. (1994). "La V Bienal de La Habana," *Art Nexus* 14:55.

Carvalho, John. (2010). "What Is Interpretation? Images and Thoughts about Philosophy and Art," *American Philosophical Association Newsletter on Hispanic/Latino Issues* 1, 2.

Castellanos, Lázara. (1995). "El viajero y su sombra (en el estilo de Octavio Paz)." In *El destino es tuyo, exhibition catalogue*. Havana: Galería Latinoamericana, Casa de Las Américas.

Crow, Kelly. (2008). "The Cuban Art Revolution," *The Wall Street Journal*, March 22–23, W1, W6.

Cuba. Contemporary Art from Cuba. Arte Contemporáneo de Cuba. (1999). Exhibition catalogue. Tempe, AZ: Arizona State University Art Museum, pp. 94–96.

Damian, Carol. (2008). "A Cosmic Viewpoint," *Idoménée* 3:172–9.

———. (2009). "Carlos Estévez: Un punto de vista existencial," *Artes* 32, 8:28–33.

Evora, José Antonio. (2006). "Carlos Estévez. El collage en su tinta." *El Nuevo Herald*, Miami, FL, April 9.

García Gutiérrez, Enrique. (2006). "Le voyage inmobile." In *Carlos Estévez*. Exhibition catalogue. San Juan, Puerto Rico: Gómez Fine Art Galería.

Gracia, Jorge J. E. (2006–). *Cuban Art Outside Cuba: Identity, Philosophy, and Art*. http://www.philosophy.buffalo.edu/capenchair/CAOC/index.html.

———. (2009a). *Carlos Estévez's Images of Thought*. Exhibition brochure. UB Art Gallery. Albany, NY: State University of New York.

———. (2009b). *Images of Thought: Philosophical Interpretations of Carlos Estevez's Art*. Albany, NY: State University of New York Press.

———. (2010). "The Philosophical Interpretation of Visual Art: Response to Mariana Ortega and John Carvalho," *American Philosophical Association Newsletter on Hispanic/Latino Issues* 1, 2.

———. (2012). *Painting Borges: Philosophy Interpreting Art Interpreting Literature*. Albany, NY: State University of New York Press, pp. 14–15, 74–78, 114–7, 278–9.

———, Lynette F. M. Bosch and Isabel Alvarez Borland, eds. (2008). *Identity, Memory, and Diaspora: Voices of Cuban-American Artists, Writers, and Philosophers*. Albany, NY: State University of New York Press.

Grant, Annette. (2000). "Ebullient Cubans Make a Lot Out of a Little," *New York Times*, June 11.

Hernández, Erena. (2002). "Carlos Estévez. Centro de Arte Wifredo Lam," *Art Nexus* 4, 46:133–4.

Herrera, Adriana. (2004). "Carlos Estévez y la alquimia de su pintura," *El Nuevo Herald*, Miami, FL, September 19.

Keough, Jeffrey, and Lisa Tung. (2002). "Foreword." In *Carlos Estévez: Dreamcomber*. Exhibition catalogue. Boston, MA: Huntington Gallery, Massachusetts College of Art.

Leyva, Irina. (2006). "Carlos Estevez. Alonso Art," *Art Nexus* 5, 61:135–6.

———. (2008). "Carlos' Treatises," *Wynwood. The Art Magazine* 2, 1:38–43.

Luis, Carlos M. (2002). "El teatro metafísico de Carlos Estévez," *El Nuevo Herald*, Miami, FL, November 10.

———. (2003). "The Transparent Being." In *Carlos Estévez: The Transparent Being*. Exhibition catalogue. Los Angeles, CA: Couturier Gallery.

Mena Chicuri, Abelardo G., et al. (2007). *Cuba AvantGarde: Contemporary Cuban Art from the Farber Collection/Arte contempóraneo cubano de la colección Farber*. Gainesville, FL: Samuel P. Harn Museum of Art.

Mosquera, Gerardo. (1994). "Sobre religión y nuevo arte cubano." In *Catálogo de la exposición Iluminación*. Havana: Centro de Desarrollo de las Artes Visuales.

———. (1995). "Cuerpo y cosmos," *Atlántica* 10:153–6.

Pinos-Santos, Carina. (1995). "Viaje al centro del hombre, una travesía de Carlos Estévez," *Revolución y Cultura* 5:33–4.

Ollman, Leah. (2008). "Elusive Themes in Metaphors," *Los Angeles Times*, April 4, E25.

Ortega, Mariana. (2010). "A Philosophical Hermeneutics of Visual Art: On Gracia's Images of Thought, Philosophical Interpretations of Carlos Estévez's Art," *American Philosophical Association Newsletter on Hispanic/Latino Issues* 1, 2.

Ottesen, Stein-Arne. (1998). "Same tema, forskjellige uttrykk," *Tysdag* 9.

Quirós, Luis Fernando and Moya, Nelson. (1996). "Un constructor de cauces. Carlos Estévez," *FANAL* 2, 13:14–18.

Sánchez, Osvaldo. (1997). *Visionario II*. Exhibition catalogue. Mexico City: Galería Nina Menocal.

Schneider Enríques, Mary. (2002). "Behind the Malecón: The Unexpected Visions of Carlos Estévez." In *Carlos Estévez: Dreamcomber*. Exhibition Catalogue. Boston, MA: Huntington Gallery, Massachusetts College of Art.

Stafne, Anne Lise. (1998). "Skapende liv mellom fjord og fjell," *Aftenpoften*, April 26, 53.

Suárez de Jesús, Carlos. (1995). "Carta de La Habana," *Art Nexus* 18:50–51.

———. (2006). "Cut It Out," *Miami New Times*, April 13–19.

Sullivan, Edward J. (1999). "The Bestiarium of Carlos Estévez." In *Carlos Estévez: Bestiarium*. Exhibition Catalogue. Los Angeles, CA: Couturier Gallery.

Temin, Christine. (2002). "A Message in the Bottles," *The Boston Globe*, March 8.

Valdés, Zoe. (2009). "Peintres Cubains," *Art absolument* 31:72–82.

Valencia, Luis Fernando. (1997). "El individuo y su memoria," *6ta. Bienal de La Habana. El Mundo*, May 24, 9–11.

Veigas, José, et al. (2003). *Memoria: Cuban Art of the 20th Century*. Los Angeles, CA: California International Arts Foundation.

Weinstein, Joel. (2005). "Knowingness." *In Existir en el tiempo/Existing in Time*. Exhibition catalogue. Miami, FL: The Olga M. & Carlos Saladrigas Gallery, The Ignatian Center for the Arts.

Weiss, Rachel. (1997). "La Sexta Bienal de La Habana," *Art Nexus* 26:70–77.

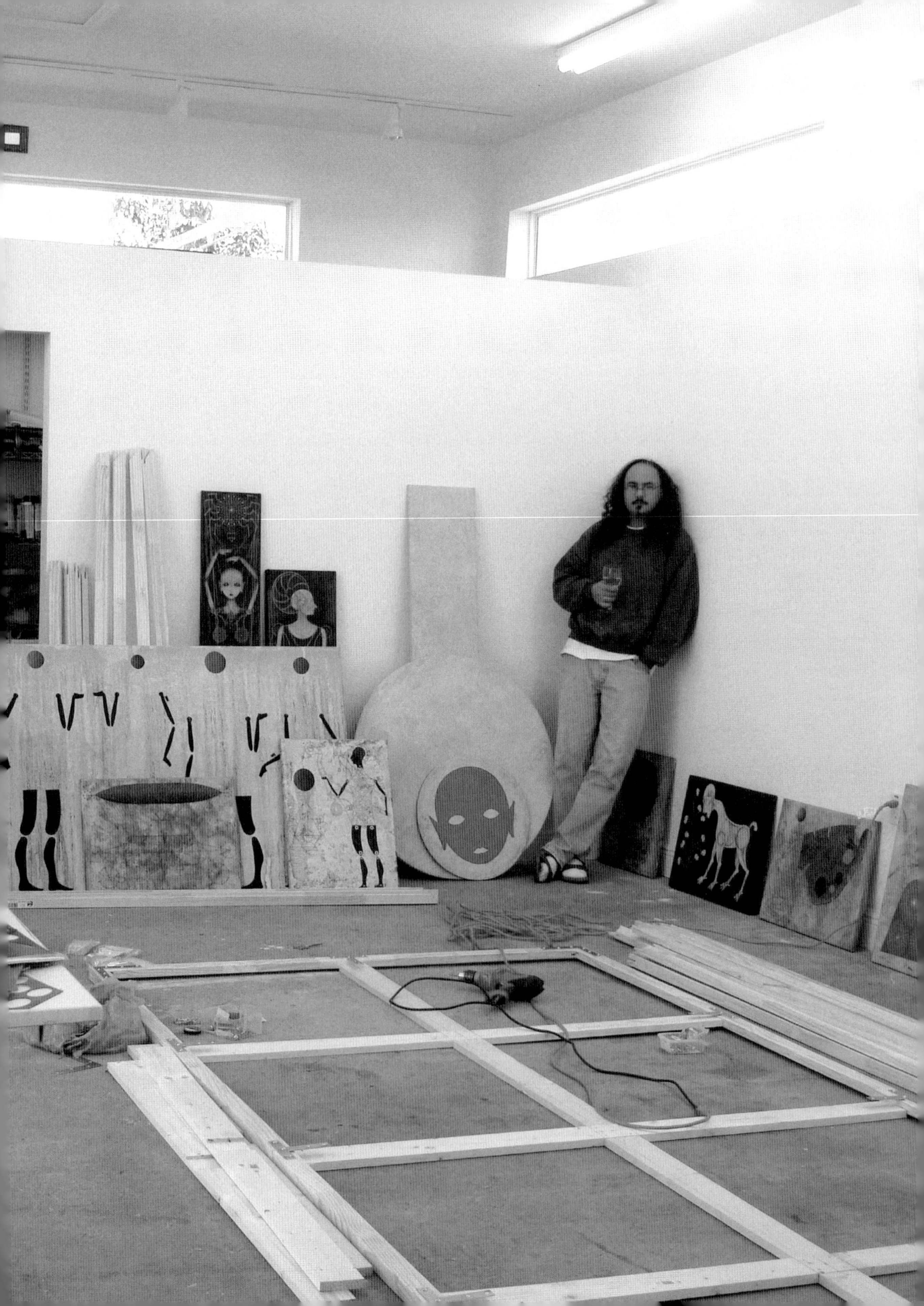

ARTIST BIOGRAPHY

CARLOS ESTÉVEZ was born in Havana, Cuba in 1969. He currently resides and works in Miami, Florida. Estévez graduated from the Instituto Superior de Arte, Havana, Cuba in 1992 and received the Grand Prize in the First Salon of Contemporary Cuban Art in 1995. Residencies include Academia de San Carlos, UNAM, Mexico (1997); Gasworks Studios, London, England (1997); The UNESCO-Aschberg in Nordic Artists' Centre, Dale, Norway (1998); OMI International Arts Center, New York (1998); Massachusetts College of Art and Design, Boston (2002); Cité Internationale des Arts, Paris, France (2003-2004); and Montclair State University, New Jersey. Solo exhibitions have been held at the Fine Art Museum, Havana, Cuba; Couturier Gallery, Los Angeles; Contemporary Art Center, New Orleans; Pan American Art Projects, Miami; Gómez Fine Art Gallery, San Juan, Puerto Rico; Allegro Gallery, Panama; Havana Galerie, Zurich, Switzerland; JM' Arts Galerie, Paris, France; Alva Gallery, New London, Connecticut; Clark Gallery, Lincoln, Massachusetts; Promo-arte Gallery, Tokyo, Japan; Lyle O. Reitzel Gallery, Santo Domingo, Dominican Republic; Taylor Bercier Gallery, New Orleans; Raymaluz Art Gallery, Madrid, Spain; and Evan Lurie Gallery, Carmel, Indiana. In 2009, he had his first midcareer retrospective at UB Art Galleries, at the University at Buffalo, in New York. Group exhibitions include VI and VII Havana Biennale, Cuba; the traveling exhibition Contemporary Art from Cuba: Irony and Survival on the Utopian Island at Arizona State University Art Museum, Tempe; and Cuba Avant-Garde: Contemporary Cuban Art from the Farber Collection. Public and private collections include the National Museum of Fine Arts, Havana, Cuba; The Ludwig Forum for International Art, Aachen, Germany; the Bronx Museum of the Arts, New York; Museum of Fine Arts, Boston; Miami Art Museum, Miami;

Drammens Museum for Kunst og Kulturhistorie, Drammens, Norway; Arizona State University Art Museum, Tempe; Museum of Art, Fort Lauderdale; Patricia and Phillip Frost Art Museum at Florida International University, Miami; Lynda and Stewart Resnick Collection, Los Angeles; Lowe Art Museum, University of Miami; and the Farber Collection. Talks and lectures given include the Celeste Bartos Theater, Museum of Modern Art, New York; the Patricia and Phillip Frost Art Museum at Florida International University, Miami; Massachusetts College of Art and Design, Boston; Boston Art Academy, Boston; Fleming Museum, University of Vermont, Burlington; and Wake Forest University, Winston-Salem.

BIOGRAPHIES

editor and translators

JORGE J. E. GRACIA holds the Samuel P. Capen Chair in Philosophy and is State University of New York Distinguished Professor. He was educated in Cuba, the United States, Canada, and Spain. His PhD is from the University of Toronto and he holds United States and Canadian citizenship. He was born in 1942, in Cuba. Gracia is the author of twenty books and the editor of twenty-six. He has published more than 250 articles in journals in the Americas, Europe, and Asia. He has organized more than a dozen international conferences and has curated five art exhibitions. He works primarily in metaphysics, hermeneutics, medieval and Latin American philosophy, ethnic and racial issues, philosophy of religion, and more recently in art. He has been president of the Metaphysical Society of America, Society for Medieval and Renaissance Philosophy, Society for Iberian and Latin American Thought, International Federation of Latin American and Caribbean Studies, and American Catholic Philosophical Association (ACPA). Among several distinctions he was awarded the ACPA Aquinas medal and his book *Individuality* (1988) received the Findlay Prize. Among his art books are (with Ilan Stavans) *Thirteen Ways of Looking at Latino Art* (2014), *Painting Borges: Philosophy Interpreting Art Interpreting Literature* (2012), *Images of Thought: Philosophical Interpretations of Carlos Estévez's Art* (2009), and (edited with Lynette Bosch and Isabel Alvarez Borland) *Identity, Memory, and Diaspora: Voices of Cuban-American Artists, Writers, and Philosophers* 2008). He was the first chair of the American Philosophical Association's (APA) Committee for Hispanics in Philosophy and has been a member of the executive committee of the Eastern Division of the APA and chair of the program committee. He chaired the Department of Philosophy at the University at Buffalo from 1980 to 1986. He sits on the boards of more than a dozen philosophy journals and half a dozen book series in Europe and the United States, and edits an interdisciplinary book series on Iberian and Latin American culture and thought for State University of New York Press. He has received several fellowships, including a National Endowment for the Humanities (NEH) research fellowship, and has directed an NEH summer institute and an NEH summer seminar. Two volumes have been devoted to the discussion of his work, one to his metaphysical views and another to his work on race and ethnicity.

DAVID E. JOHNSON is professor of comparative literature at the State University of New York at Buffalo. He is the author of *Kant's Dog: On Borges, Philosophy, and the Time of Translation* (SUNY 2012); and co-author of *Anthropology's Wake: Attending to the End of Culture* (Fordham 2008). He has co-edited two volumes, *Border Theory: The Limits of Cultural Politics* (Minnesota 1997) and *Thinking with Borges* (Davies 2009). Since 2000, he is co-editor of *CR: The New Centennial Review*.

PAULA CUCURELLA is a PhD candidate in comparative literature at the State University of New York at Buffalo, currently completing a dissertation on Chilean poetry, dictatorship, and deconstruction.

INDEX OF MESSAGES

43 Message 17, "*Cucullus non facit monachum*"
Norway 5-6-2000
Launched at Hull Gut Beach, Boston, Massachusetts, USA. 10-2-2002
Version of the original
Miami 8-14-2013
Measurements of original not available

44 Message 18, "Navigation Chart"
Norway 5-8-2000
39-1/4 x 9-1/8 inches

46 Message 19, "The Seer"
Norway 5-8-2000
39-1/4 x 9-3/4 inches

47 Message 20, "To Sail"
Norway 5-15-2000
39-1/4 x 10-1/4 inches

48 Message 21, "Gulliver in Love"
Norway 9-16-2000
Measurements not available

50 Message 22, "The Female Cyclops"
Norway 5-26-2000
39-1/4 x 7-1/4 inches

52 Message 23, "The Secret City of the Soul"
Norway 5-27-2000
39-1/4 x 12 inches

53 Message 24, "The World is a Description of the Soul"
Norway 5-28-2000
39-1/4 x 9-7/8 inches

54 Message 25, "At the Bottom of the Sea"
Norway 5-29-2000
39-1/4 x 7-5/8 inches

55 Message 26, "*Novem cephalus*"
Norway 5-31-2000
39-1/4 x 7-1/8 inches

56 Message 27, "Planetarium"
Havana 9-6-2000, Launched at the Rhine, Basel, Switzerland. 8-27-2003
39-1/4 x 7-7/8 inches

57 Message 28, "Some Notes on the World of Insects"
Norway 6-1-2000
39-1/4 x 10-1/4 inches

58 Message 29, "Vow of Silence"
Norway 6-6-2000
39-1/4 x 9-7/8 inches

59 Message 30, "*Sero sevi satum*"
Norway 6-6-2000
39-1/4 x 9-5/8 inches

60 Message 31, "What Cannot Be Left Behind"
Norway 6-7-2000
39-1/4 x 8-3/8 inches

61 Message 32, "The Spirit of the Night"
Norway 6-7-2000
39-1/4 x 10-7/8 inches

62 Message 33, "I Am My House"
Norway 6-10-2000
Launched at Lido, Venice, Italy. 6-19-2006
Measurements not available

63 Message 34, "The Election"
Norway 6-12-2000
Launched at Le Havre, Normandy, France. 6-19-2004
Measurements not available

64 Message 35, "The Chosen One"
Norway 6-12-2000
39-1/4 x 10 inches

65 Message 36, "The Invention of Destiny"
Norway 6-12-2000
39-1/4 x 9-7/8 inches

66 Message 37, "If I Don't Die, I Will Grow"
Norway 6-13-2000
39-1/4 x 10 inches

67 Message 38, "The Rain of the Soul"
Norway 6-13-2000
39-1/4 x 8-3/8 inches

69 Message 39, "Autumn Leaves"
Norway 6-14-2000
39-1/4 x 10 inches

70 Message 40, "The Indescribable of Maps"
Norway 6-15-2000
39-1/4 x 8 inches

71 Message 41, "Calculating Distances"
Norway 6-16-2000
39-1/4 x 11-3/8 inches

72 Message 42, "RAM Memory"
Norway 6-18-2000
Launched at Salvador de Bahia, Brazil. 2-2-2003
Measurements not available

73 Message 43, "The Invention of the Constellations"
Havana 9-1-2000
39-1/4 x 13 inches

75 Message 44, "*Vestigium sacrum*"
Havana 9-2-2000
39-1/4 x 12-1/2 inches

76 Message 45, "Notes on the Anatomy of Spirit"
Havana 9-2-2000
39-1/4 x 10-3/8 inches

78 Message 46, "Some Notes on the Lost Diary of Creation"
Havana 9-3-2000
39-1/4 x 8 inches

79 Message 47, "Plant Man"*
*Notes on the lost diary of creation, Havana 9-4-2000
39-1/4 x 10 inches

80 Message 48, "God is the Projection of Man's Thoughts"
Havana 9-5-2000
39-1/4 x 6-3/8 inches

81 Message 49, "*Argumentum ontologicum*"
Havana 9-6-2000
39-1/4 x 6-7/8 inches

82 Message 50, "*Homo ăvium*"
Havana 9-7-2000
39-1/4 x 9-7/8 inches

83 Message 51, "Seeing Hand"
Havana 9-7-2000
39-1/4 x 6-3/4 inches

84 Message 52, "*Creatoris*"
Havana 9-8-2000
39-1/4 x 10-1/4 inches

85 Message 53, "*Ecquis hic est?*"
Havana 9-9-2000
Launched at New Orleans, Mississippi River, Louisiana, USA. 4-27-2007
Measurements not available

86 Message 54, "Everything is Written in Heaven"
Version of the original
Miami 8-15-2013
Launched at Havana Malecon, Havana, Cuba. 12-16-2001
Measurements of original not available

87 Message 55, "Not Going Anywhere"
Havana 9-12-2000
Launched at Mont Saint-Michel, Normandy, France. 5-22-2004
Measurements not available

89 Message 56, "My True Face"
Havana 9-13-2000
39-1/4 x 10-5/8 inches

90 Message 57, "Fantastic Zoology"
Havana 9-15-2000
39-1/4 x 8-1/4 inches

92 Message 58, "The Collector"
Havana 9-14-2000
39-1/4 x 11-3/8 inches

93 Message 59, "The Great Secret of Alchemy"
Havana 9-15-2000
39-1/4 x 10-3/4 inches

94 Message 60, "Many Feet and Few Paths"
Norway 5-10-2000
Launched at Valencia, Spain. 2-18-2004
Measurements not available

95 Message 61, "I Carry Everything with Me"
Havana 9-16-2000
39-1/4 x 9-1/2 inches

96 Message 62, "The Daily Agony of My Demons"
Havana 9-18-2000
39-1/4 x 8 inches

97 Message 63, "The Spirit of Creation Feeds on Bodies"
Havana 9-19-2000
Launched at New London, Connecticut, USA. 1-20-2007
Measurements not available

98 Message 64, "Take a Break"
Havana 4-22-2000
Launched at Punta Cacha Pregos, Itaparica, Bahia, Brazil. 1-12-2003
Measurements not available

99 Message 65, "*Paucorum hominum esse*"
Havana 9-2-2000
39-1/4 x 10 inches

100 Message 66, "The Immortals (II)"
Havana 9-23-2000
39-1/4 x 5-5/8 inches

102 Message 67, "Mutations of Personality"
Launched at Ellis Island, New York, USA. 2-3-2002
Version of the original
Miami 8-16-2013
39-1/4 x 10-3/8 inches

103 Message 68, "Mutations of the Soul"
Havana 9-25-2000
39-1/4 x 10-3/8 inches

104 Message 69, "*Vomitum divinum*"
Havana 9-26-2000
39-1/4 x 9 inches

105 Message 70, "The Transient and the Deserted City"
Havana 9-27-2000
39-1/4 x 9-1/8 inches

106 Message 71, "Serpent Woman"
Havana 9-28-2000
39-1/4 x 6-3/4 inches

107 Message 72, "Come and Go"
Havana 8-23-2000
Launched at Malibu, California, USA.
9-8-2005
Measurements not available

108 Message 73, "Crossed Destinies"
Norway 9-30-2000
39-1/4 x 9-7/8 inches

109 Message 74, "No One Can See Through My Eyes"
Havana 10-1-2000
39-1/4 x 8 inches

110 Message 75, "Circus Scenes. The Juggler"
Havana 10-2-2000
39-1/4 x 8 inches

111 Message 76, "Measurements of Time"
Havana 10-3-2000
39-1/4 x 7-1/8 inches

112 Message 77, "The Flyer"
Havana 10-4-2000
39-1/4 x 7-1/2 inches

113 Message 78, "Circus Scenes. The Hooker"
Havana 4-10-2000
Launched at Barcelona, Spain. 2-15-2004
Measurements not available

115 Message 79, "Circus Scenes. The Indoctrinator"
Havana 10-6-2000
39-1/4 x 7-1/2 inches

116 Message 80, "Personal Domestic Dictionary"
Havana 10-10-2000
39-1/4 x 6-1/4 inches

118 Message 81, "The Persistent Memory"
Norway 6-8-2000
39-1/4 x 8 inches

119 Message 82, "The Delivery of the Marionettes"
Havana 10-12-2000
39-1/4 x 8-3/8 inches

120 Message 83, "Personal Domestic Dictionary III"
Havana 10-13-2000
39-1/4 x 7-5/8 inches

123 Message 84, "The Two Sides of the Coin"
Havana 10-14-2000
39-1/4 x 6-3/8 inches

124 Message 85, "Personal Domestic Dictionary II"
Havana 10-11-2000
39-1/4 x 6-3/8 inches

126 Message 86, "Waiting for a Train"
Havana 10-16-2000
Launched at Lisbon, Portugal. 10-2-2006
Measurements not available

128 Message 87, "Treatise of the Bridges of Love"
Havana 10-17-2000
39-1/4 x 9-1/4 inches

129 Message 88, "Interaction of the Worlds"
Havana 10-18-2000
Launched at Key West, Florida, USA.
10-20-2002
Measurements not available

130 Message 89, "Manual of Questions without Answers"
Havana 10-19-2000
39-1/4 x 6 inches

132 Message 90, "Joys and Sorrows"
Havana 10-20-2000
39-1/4 x 6 inches

134 Message 91, "Words"
Launched at Fortress San Juan de Ulua, Veracruz, Mexico. 11-9-2003
Version of the original
Miami 8-17-2013
Measurements of original not available

135 Message 92, "The Message, or the Juggling of History"
Havana 10-21-2000
39-1/4 x 6-3/4 inches

136 Message 93, "Manual of my Preferred Words"
Havana 10-23-2000
39-1/4 x 4-3/4 inches

138 Message 94, "Fountain"
Havana 10-22-2000
39-1/4 x 6-1/4 inches

139 Message 95, "Elementary Treatise on Optometry"
Havana 10-24-2000
39-1/4 x 6-3/4 inches

140 Message 96, "Imaginary Garden" "The Tree of Life"
Norway 5-31-2000
39-1/4 x 10-3/4 inches

141 Message 97, "Some Notes on Natural History"
Norway 5-30-2000
39-1/4 x 10 inches

142 Message 98, "The Ferryman"
Havana 10-15-2000
39-1/4 x 8 inches

143 Message 99, "Our Father Who Art in Our Hearts"
Havana 9-14-2000
39-1/4 x 11-7/8 inches

145 Message 100, "Each End is a New Beginning"
Havana 10-25-2000
39-1/4 x 7-7/8 inches

Book design, Eleven Suns Media
Photography, Carlos Estévez and Gary Mercer